Toward Artificial Sapience

Rene V. Mayorga · Leonid I. Perlovsky
Editors

Toward Artificial Sapience

Principles and Methods for Wise Systems

 Springer

Editors

Rene V. Mayorga
Fac. Engineering
University of Regina,
Saskatchewan, Canada
3737 Wascana Parkway
Regina S4S 0A2
Rene.mayorga@uregina.ca

Leonid I. Perlovsky
Air Force Research Laboratory,
Hanscom,
USA
80 Scott Road
Hanscom AFB 01731
Leonid.Perlovsky@hanscom.af.mil

ISBN: 978-1-84996-698-6   e-ISBN: 978-1-84628-999-6

Printed on acid-free paper

9 8 7 6 5 4 3 2 1

Springer Science+Business Media
springer.com

To our families and friends

Preface

Although for many years much effort has been devoted to advancing artificial/computational intelligence and soft computing, no formal studies have ever been conducted to properly address the concept of sapience (wisdom) in the context of artificial techniques. We believe that the attempt to attain human sapience (wisdom) by artificial means and its formalization is a step in the right direction beyond the artificial/computational intelligence and soft computing disciplines. Is it warranted? Have we achieved a level of modeling smart systems that justifies talking about sapience (wisdom)? This book presents computational paradigms describing lower- and higher-level cognitive functions, including mechanisms of concepts, instincts, emotions, situated behavior, language communication, and social functioning. Hierarchical organization of the mind is considered, leading to explanations of the highest human abilities for the beautiful and the sublime. The opening chapters discuss philosophical, historical, and semiotic ideas about what properties are expected from sapient (wise) systems. Subsequent chapters describe mathematical and engineering views on sapience, relating these to philosophical, semiotic, cognitive, and neuro biological perspectives.

Chapter 1, "Can Creativity Be Formalized? Peircean Reflections on the Role of Abduction in Human Intelligence," by Darin McNabb Costa, discusses fundamental ideas of Peircean semiotics. According to C. S. Peirce abduction is the main mechanism of hypothesis formation. The chapter situates abduction in the architectonic structure of Peirce philosophy, its relation to his categorial scheme, and the metaphysical consequences that it implies. Categories are abstract conceptions whose function is to divide up reality into its basic constituents and to unify experience so as to make reality knowable. With a complete set of categories, there is a way to account for anything that we might experience. Aristotle delineated a list of ten categories (substance, quantity, time, relation, position, etc.), and Kant had twelve. Peirce defined only three: firstness, secondness, and thirdness, designating them in terms of numbers because they are relational concepts, referring to the basic ways in which things can relate to one another. Simplifying Peircean definitions, firstness can be understood as a complete unity; secondness is an unconscious unique unrepeatable existences-interactions in space and time; and thirdness encompasses relationships and consciousness. Sapient systems should exhibit all three types of abilities in order to form fruitful hypotheses for advancing their knowledge of the world around them.

Chapter 2, "On Plasticity, Complexity, and Sapient Systems," by Carlos Rubén de la Mora-Basáñez, Alejandro Guerra-Hernández, V. Angélica García-Vega, and Luc Steels, emphasizes that sapient agents should be capable of "insight" and "sound judgment." Understanding cognitive functionality of such systems requires biological referents. New mathematical methods required to achieve sapience include so-called complex networks, characterized by small-world and scale-free networks, which relate to anatomical and functional properties of cognitive processes. Human sapience includes innate biological motivations for abstracting knowledge and adapting its behavior to drive further knowledge acquisition and improve social interactions (mainly through language).

Chapter 3, "Sapience, Consciousness, and the Knowledge Instinct (Prolegomena to a Physical Theory)," by Leonid Perlovsky, presents a mathematical theory of sapience and consciousness. It includes higher mental abilities for concepts, emotions, instincts, understanding, imagination, intuition, creativity, beautiful, and sublime. The knowledge instinct drives our understanding of the world. Aesthetic emotions, our needs for beautiful and sublime, are related to the knowledge instinct. Perlovsky considers neurobiological grounds as well as difficulties encountered since the 1950s by previous attempts at mathematical modeling of the mind. Dynamic logic, the mathematics of the knowledge instinct, is related to cognitive and philosophical discussions about the mind and sapience. It describes how firstness evolves into secondness and thirdness in processes of differentiation and synthesis, leading to the creation of a multitude of forms—models in the mind corresponding to life experience. Evolution of consciousness and the role of the unconscious is related to the hierarchy of the mind's organization. The chapter gives a mathematical description of symbol processes, which, according to Jung, connect the conscious and the unconscious. Mathematical discussions are related to the thoughts of Aristotle and Kant, Freud and Jung, Searle, Chalmers, and Grossberg. Consciousness is considered as a process in a state of continuing emergence. The knowledge instinct is similar to the most general physical laws in the following aspect: There is no contradiction between causality and teleology; they are mathematically equivalent at the very basic level of fundamental physics. For complex systems, described by statistical physics, entropy rules and random chance prevails. A revolutionary aspect of the knowledge instinct is that it defines a purposeful evolution for a very complex system. The human mind guided by maximization of knowledge evolves so that causal dynamics and purposeful dynamics (teleology) are equivalent.

Chapters 4 through 9 discuss various aspects of what is expected of sapient agents. "A Real-Time Agent System Perspective of Meaning and Sapience," by Ricardo Sanz, Julita Bermejo, Ignacio López, and Jaime Gómez, proposes an interpretation of sapience in terms of social interactions. Sapient agents are able to generate meanings and knowledge useful for the other, beyond the generation of meanings for the self. Wisdom is attributed to an agent by others when they can use knowledge generated by the agent. "Toward BDI Sapient Agents: Learning Intentionally," by Alejandro Guerra-Hernández, and Gustavo Ortíz-Hernández, discusses intentional and social learning necessary for the practical implementations of the BDI (belief, desire, intention) agents. These agents take a step toward introspection: they evaluate the validity of their practical reasons and modify them trying to avoid failure. Discussion of this type of agent continues in "Toward Wisdom in Procedural Reasoning: DBI, not BDI," by Kirk A. Weigand. A fundamental shift in order from BDI to DBI is proposed so that desire precedes belief and intention. DBI agents utilize procedural reasoning, an essential aspect of sapience, following the process philosophy of Alfred North Whitehead and the philosophy of embodiment of George Lakoff and Mark Johnson. DBI agents use aesthetic, affective, and emotional mechanisms. "Sapients in a Sandbox," by Pablo Noriega, approaches the notion of sapient systems from the contrarian and unlikely perspective of stupidity. It considers agents whose cognitive capabilities are limited by design, whereas sapient behavior results from the collective interaction within a regulated social environment. In "Sapient Agents—Seven Approaches," Zbigniew Skolicki and Tomasz Arciszewski suggest that sapient agents are characterized by multiple levels of knowledge representation, including domain knowledge; abilities for tactical decisions and global strategies in the context of planning; exploration of new representations; and evolutionary computation. In "A Characterization of Sapient Agents," Martijn van Otterlo, Marco Wiering, Mehdi Dastani, and John-Jules Meyer consider beliefs, desires, emotions, goals, and plans among sapient abilities. A sapient agent learns its cognitive state and capabilities through experience using relational reinforcement learning; it interacts with other agents and the social environment.

In Chapter 10, René V. Mayorga presents a paradigm, from a cybernetics point of view, which can contribute with some essential aspects toward establishing a baseline for the development of artificial / computational sapience (wisdom) as new disciplines. It is demonstrated that, under the proposed paradigm, artificial/computational sapience (wisdom) methodologies can be developed as a natural extension of some soft computing and computational intelligence approaches. It is also shown that the proposed paradigm serves as a general framework for the development of intelligent/sapient (wise) systems. In particular, some principles of learning, adaptation, and knowledge (essential for cognition) are properly addressed, and the concepts of stability, discerning, and inference (as a condition for judgment) are considered. It is postulated that under the proposed paradigm, artificial systems' inferential capabilities, their ability to determine (concurrently and/or sequentially) direct and inverse relationships, and their capability to consider global aspects and objectives, can contribute to built-up knowledge with a capacity for cognition and sound judgment, thus, leading to sapient (wise) systems. Furthermore, it is also demonstrated that under the proposed paradigm, it is possible to establish some performance criteria for the proper design and operation of intelligent and sapient (wise) systems.

Chapters 11 through 15 discuss mechanisms of various aspects of sapience. "Bisapient Structures for Intelligent Control," by Ron Cottam, Willy Ranson, and Roger Vounckx suggests that sapience emerges as an ability for autonomous control in a birational hierarchical structure. Birational hierarchy involves two sapiences interacting through mechanisms of mirror neurons. This is a useful metaphor for all of the brain's information processing, including autoempathy, responsible for theory of self, Metzinger's 'illusory self,' presence transfer, and theory of mind. José Negrete-Martínez, in "Paradigms behind a Discussion on Artificial Intelligent/Smart Systems," discusses the roles of consciousness, logic, recognition, self-organized responses, and low-level modular structures. Quantum computations are considered as mechanisms of consciousness; artificial neural networks for recognition; and chaotic behavior for symbol generation. An essential aspect of smart systems is to combine paradigms so that a system is smarter than its individual components. "Kinetics, Evolution and Sapient Systems," by V. Angélica García-Vega, Carlos Rubén De La Mora-Basáñez, and Ana María Acosta-Roa, considers anticipatory behavior as an essential aspect of a sapient system. Anticipation is related to locomotion modulated by perception. In "Emotions and Sapient Robots," V. Angélica García-Vega and Carlos Rubén de la Mora-Basáñez review the role of emotions in reasoning and behavior. They model emotions as special types of adaptive cognitive processes and propose architectures for sapient robots with an embedded emotion model. In "Scheme of an Abducing Brain-Based Robot," by José Negrete-Martínez, sapience is modeled as inverse perception. The inverse perception ability provides a representation of the real world (by abduction). Inverse perception drives local incremental motor functions, whereas planning large movements requires global inverse motor function. The robot-brain modules are tentatively mapped to the human-brain modules.

Finally, Chapter 16 describes a new robot control architecture based on self-organization of self-inhibiting modules. The architecture is modular and can generate a complex behavior repertoire by the addition of new modules. This architecture can evolve, in the hands of the designer, to a robotic version of Nilsson's habile system. Required evolutionary steps begin with improved mechatronics, continue with improved pattern recognition, and end with a symbol manipulation that adapts the previous improvements.

This book will be most useful for researchers, practitioners, and professionals in the areas of artificial and computational intelligence, soft computing, intelligent systems, decision and control, predictive systems, financial engineering, pattern recognition, biologically inspired algorithms, and modeling of the mind. It will also be of great interest to quantitative psychology scholars and for psychologists interested in mathematical models, and can be recommend as a supplemental reading for advanced undergraduates and graduate students in these areas.

René V. Mayorga
Leonid I. Perlovsky
December 2007

Acknowledgments

The editors would like to express their gratitude to Dr. Alex Meystel, for steering discussion on sapient systems within the advisory board for the IEEE International Conference on Integration of Knowledge Intensive Multi-Agent Systems (KIMAS) in 2003; and for his encouragement for the organization of the first ever Special Technical Sessions and Workshops on Sapient Systems for KIMAS-2003, and again for the KIMAS-2005.

Contents

Part III   Paradigms for Sapient Systems/Agents

Part IV   On the Development of Sapient systems

Contributors

Ana María Acosta Roa
Dept. de Inteligencia Artificial, Universidad Veracruzana, Xalapa, Veracruz,
México
anamary@hotmail.com

Tomasz Arciszewski
Department of Civil Environmental and Infrastructure Engineering, George Mason
University, Fairfax, VA, USA
tarcisze@gmu.edu

Julita Bermejo
UPM Autonomous Systems Lab, Universidad Politécnica de Madrid, Madrid,
Spain
jbermejo@etsii.upm.es

Ron Cottam
The Evolutionary Processing Group, Department of Electronics & Informatics,
Vrije Universiteit Brussel, Brussels, Belgium
evol@etro.vub.ac.be

Mehdi Dastani
Intelligent Systems Group, Department of Information and Computing Sciences,
Utrecht University, The Netherlands
mehdi@cs.uu.nl

Carlos R. de la Mora Basáñez
Artificial Intelligence Laboratory, Vrije Universiteit Brussel, Brussels, Belgium
carlos@arti.vub.ac.be

V. Angélica García Vega
Dept. de Inteligencia Artificial, Universidad Veracruzana, Xalapa, Veracruz,
México
angegarcia@uv.mx

Jaime Gómez
UPM Autonomous Systems Lab, Universidad Politécnica de Madrid, Madrid,
Spain
jagomez@etsii.upm.es

Alejandro Guerra Hernández
Dept. de Inteligencia Artificial, Universidad Veracruzana, Xalapa, Veracruz,
México
aguerra@uv.mx

Ignacio López
UPM Autonomous Systems Lab, Universidad Politécnica de Madrid, Madrid,
Spain
ilopez@etsii.upm.es

René V. Mayorga
Faculty of Engineering, University of Regina, Regina, Saskatchewan, Canada
Rene.Mayorga@uregina.ca

Darin McNabb Costa
Instituto de Filosofía, Universidad Veracruzana, Xalapa, Veracruz, México
soydarin@yahoo.com

John-Jules Meyer
Intelligent Systems Group, Department of Information and Computing Sciences,
Utrecht University, The Netherlands
jj@cs.uu.nl

José Negrete Martínez
Departamento de Biología Celular, y Fisiología, Instituto de Investigaciones
Biomédicas, Unidad Periférica Xalapa, UNAM, Xalapa, Veracruz, México
jnegrete@uv.mx

Pablo Noriega
IIIA, CSIC. Artificial Intelligence Research Institute of the Spanish Scientific
Research Council, Barcelona, Spain
pablo@iiia.csic.es

Gustavo Ortíz Hernández
Dept. de Inteligencia Artificial, Universidad Veracruzana, Xalapa, Veracruz,
México
unicornius@hotmail.com

Leonid I. Perlovsky
Harvard University, Cambridge, MA, USA
leonid@seas.harvard.edu

Air Force Research Laboratory, Sensors Directorate
leonid.perlovsky@hanscom.af.mil

Willy Ranson
The Evolutionary Processing Group, Department of Electronics & Informatics,
Vrije Universiteit Brussel, Brussels, Belgium
wranson@etro.vub.ac.be

Ricardo Sanz
UPM Autonomous Systems Lab, Universidad Politécnica de Madrid, Madrid,
Spain
Ricardo.Sanz@upm.es

Zbigniew Skolicki
Department of Computer Science, George Mason University, Fairfax, VA, USA
zskolick@gmu.edu

Luc Steels
Artificial Intelligence Laboratory, Vrije Universiteit Brussel, Brussels, Belgium
steels@arti.vub.ac.be

Martijn van Otterlo
Human Media Interaction, Department of Computer Science, University of Twente,
The Netherlands
otterlo@cs.utwente.nl

Roger Vounckx
The Evolutionary Processing Group, Department of Electronics & Informatics,
Vrije Universiteit Brusse, Brussels, Belgium
rvounckx@etro.vub.ac.be

Kirk A. Weigand
Air Force Research Laboratory, Information Directorate, Wright-Patterson AFB,
Ohio, USA
Kirk.Weigand@WPAFB.AF.MIL

Marco Wiering
Intelligent Systems Group, Department of Information and Computing Sciences,
Utrecht University, The Netherlands
marco@cs.uu.nl

Part I
Intelligence and Sapience

Can Creativity Be Formalized? Peircean Reflections on the Role of Abduction in Human Intelligence

Darin McNabb Costa

Abstract C.S. Peirce's notion of abduction, or hypothesis formation, is of great interest among researchers in diverse disciplines. In the cognitive sciences and artificial intelligence communities especially, the possibility of formalizing the abductive process has generated much discussion. However, much of what is said about abduction in these contexts betrays little understanding of Peirce's thought as a whole, an understanding that would serve to heuristically limit many claims about abduction, such as the possibility of its formalization. This chapter aims to situate abduction in the architectonic structure of Peirce's philosophy. Its relation to his categorial scheme and the metaphysical consequences it implies, as well as numerous strategies for hypothesis formation, are considered.

1 Introduction

Think of twentieth-century philosophers, and a host of polysyllabic European names, by turns guttural and sibilant, come immediately to mind. Pronounce the odd-sounding "Peirce," and many will either not know what you are talking about, think you have sneezed, or direct you to the bearded nineteenth-century logicians conference in the next building. But it is a name well worth looking into. Charles Sanders Peirce was a logician and scientist whose thought spawned pragmatism and modern semiotics. In the words of Max Fisch he was a:

> Philosopher, mathematician, astronomer, geodesist, surveyor, cartographer, metrologist, spectroscopist, engineer, inventor, psychologist, philologist, lexicographer, historian of science, mathematical economist, lifelong student of medicine, phenomenologist, semiotician, logician, and metaphysician. He was the first modern experimental psychologist in the Americas, the first metrologist to use a wave-length of light as a unit of measure, the inventor of the quincuncial projection of the globe, and the first known conceiver of the design and theory of an electric switching-circuit computer. (Fisch, 1982)

D.M. Costa
Instituto de Filosofía, Universidad Veracruzana Xalapa, Veracruz, México
e-mail: soydarin@yahoo.com

R.V. Mayorga, L.I. Perlovsky (eds.), *Toward Artificial Sapience,*
© Springer 2008

Though neglected for much of the twentieth century, his thought is enjoying a renaissance as researchers from disciplines as diverse as logic, psychology, pedagogy, cognitive science, mathematics, and artificial intelligence are discovering a veritable goldmine of ideas that allow them to obviate the positivistic clockwork conception that has so profoundly informed modern research into the natural and human worlds.

Of the myriad concepts that make up the constellation of Peirce's thought, there is one that is of special interest to many researchers in cognitive science and artificial intelligence, namely, his notion of hypothesis formation or what he called abduction. As the available literature attests, the AI community is interested in abduction in hopes that the process can be formalized and implemented in a wide array of intelligent or expert systems (Aliseda 1997; Aravindan and Dung 1994; Kakas et al. 1995; Konolige 1996). Although the idea is intriguing and merits research, I have found that most discussions of abduction in the AI context betray little or no understanding of Peirce's thought as a whole. The abductive process is considered in isolation from the general architecture of Peirce's philosophical vision, which leads to erroneous or unfounded claims about abduction that a better understanding of Peirce's thought would avoid. Thus, what I wish to do here is sketch the contours of Peirce's philosophy relevant to what he says about abduction in hopes that it may make clear its nature and limits and the possibilities of its formalization.

2 The Categories

The best way to understand Peirce's philosophy is by first understanding how its diverse components are structured and interrelated. Whether it be the vast scale of his cosmological reflections or his minute analysis of the syllogism, we find that everything in his thought is explicated in terms of his famous triad of categories: firstness, secondness, and thirdness. Before speaking of these directly let us reflect on the function of philosophical categories in general. Categories are abstract conceptions whose function is to divide reality up into its basic constituents and to unify experience so as to make reality knowable. With a complete set of categories there is a way to account for anything that we might experience. Aristotle had a list of ten categories (substance, quantity, time, relation, position, etc.), and Kant had twelve. Peirce has only three: firstness, secondness, and thirdness. He designates them in terms of numbers because they are relational concepts, referring to the basic ways in which things can relate to one another. He defines them as follows[1]:

- *Firstness* is the mode of being of that which is such as it is, positively and without reference to anything else. It is that whose being is simply in itself, not referring to anything nor lying behind anything. In the psychical realm firstness

---

[1] These definitions are amalgams of different characterizations of the categories that Peirce gives in numerous places in his writings. The musical metaphor I use to illustrate them is taken from Zeman (see Sebeok, 1977)

corresponds to pure feeling. It is consciousness that involves no analysis, comparison or any process whatsoever, but is characterized as a simple positive quality. The adjectives he uses to describe it are freshness, presentness, immediacy, newness, possibility, indeterminacy, originality, spontaneity, and freedom. "It is what the world was to Adam on the day he opened his eyes to it, before he had drawn any distinctions, or had become conscious of his own existence." As feeling, firstness is the category of the prereflexive. Sitting back and enjoying a piece of music (without reflecting on the enjoyment) is close to experiencing a first.

- *Secondness* is the mode of being of that which is such as it is with respect to a second but regardless of any third. This category refers to brute factual existence, to any interaction involving two elements. It is compulsion, effort, effect, negation, occurrence, brute shock, and resistance. To continue the metaphor, it is the knock on the door that interrupts the musical reverie. Seconds are unique unrepeatable existences in space and time. For an empiricist, secondness is exhaustive of reality, but for Peirce reality is more than a matter of discrete events occurring at given points in space-time. Reality is also a matter of the relations between events. Here is where thirdness enters in.

- *Thirdness* characterizes that which is what it is owing to things between which it mediates and which it brings into relation to each other. It is the category of law, habit, continuity, relatedness, and generality. Returning to the metaphor of a musical performance, the performance in its unreflected immediacy is firstness; in the actual space-time thereness of its individual notes it is secondness; and in the identifiable structurings relating its notes, rhythms, and harmonies, it is thirdness.

Figure 1 gives some examples of how the categories manifest themselves in Peirce's philosophy.

A final note concerns the ordinal relationship between the categories. Its not one, two, three (cardinal), but rather first, second, third (ordinal). There can be no thirdness, e.g., without firstness and secondness, no mentality or intelligence without a physical substrate and the capacity to feel, at least for human intelligence. I will leave this question for the moment and return to discuss firstness in the context of what Peirce says about abduction.

Let us take a look at the organizational structure of Peirce's philosophy to see where abduction is found and the role it plays in the whole (Fig. 2).

	Firstness	Secondness	Thirdness
Ontology	Possibility	Existence	Generality
Metaphysics	Chance	Facticity	Lawfulness
Logic	Abduction	Induction	Deduction
Semiotic	Icon	Index	Symbol
Epistemology	Qualities	Reactions	Mediation
Syllogism	Term	Proposition	Argument
Psychology	Feeling	Perception	Reasoning
Normative science	Aesthetics	Ethics	Logic

Fig. 1 Application of Peirce's Categories

Fig. 2 Architectonic
Structure of Peirce's
Philosophy

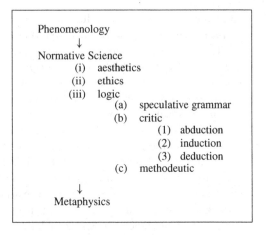

As in all things Peircean we find the structuring activity of the categories here as well. As we would expect, these three main branches of philosophy are ordinally related with metaphysics (thirdness) depending on normative science, which in turn depends on phenomenology. Abduction is to be found in the normative science of logic. Logic, as we know, is the study of valid reasoning, but it is also, for Peirce, synonymous with semiotic, the study of signs, given that all thought takes place in signs. The science of logic is divided into three branches. Speculative grammar has to do with the formal conditions of a sign being a sign; critic with the formal conditions under which a symbol can express truth, i.e., the relation between symbols and their objects; and methodeutic with the formal conditions for the attainment or communication of truth, i.e., the relation between signs and their interpretants.

In the branch of critic we find another tripartite division, that between abduction, induction, and deduction (Fig. 3). These of course are the three forms of inference. As I stated, this part of logic concerns itself with the valid conditions of passing from one sign to another, which is the very movement of thought. Peirce gives an example of these three forms of inference.

Deduction
Rule: All the beans from this bag are white.
Case: These beans are from this bag.
Result: These beans are white.

Induction
Case: These beans are from this bag.
Result: These beans are white.
Rule: All the beans from this bag are white.

Hypothesis
Rule: All the beans from this bag are white.
Result: These beans are white.
Case: These beans are from this bag.

Fig. 3 Forms of Inference

The syllogistic forms of deduction and induction are familiar to us. In the first, a general rule or law is applied to a particular case in order to infer a result (universal → particular), and in the second we take a series of particular cases in our experience and generalize them in order to infer a rule or law (particular → universal).[2] Now, since Archimedes let go his famous "Eureka," scientists have understood that the process of discovery begins with a good idea, a hypothesis, but given the mysterious nature of arriving at such an idea it had been left out of the methodical process of scientific research. Peirce was the first to insist that hypothesis, or abduction, is an essential element of scientific procedure and that it is, in fact, the only logical operation that adds anything new to knowledge. Any scientific investigation, in the pure sense, begins with the recognition of some surprising fact in our experience, surprising because our current web of beliefs, or general rules of inference, does not predict it. What is required is a revision of or addition to these beliefs so that the fact is no longer surprising. So, we are faced with some surprising fact, X. But if Y were true X would not be surprising. Thus we have reason to believe the Y is true. Y is the result of the abductive process and is the first step in scientific discovery. "That which is to be done with the hypothesis," says Peirce, "is to trace out its consequences by deduction and compare them with the results of experiment by induction."

3 Pragmatism and Abduction

One of the criteria Peirce establishes for the formation of hypotheses is that they have deducible consequences. It is in fact for this reason that he introduced his famous pragmatic maxim, as a way to make this passage from one thought to another as clear as possible, and he directly links the use of the maxim with the abductive process. Peirce states the maxim as follows: "Consider what effects, that might conceivably have practical bearings, we conceive the object of our conception to have. Then, our conception of these effects is the whole of our conception of the object" (CP 5.2).[3]

The point here is that the meaning of any idea or concept is a function of its effects. The concept of an object is equivalent to all the conceivable practical effects of that object in our experience.[4] Since a hypothesis is generated so as to remove the

---

[2] It is important to note that for Peirce induction does not *discover* laws but rather *tests* hypotheses, which, if they remain unrefuted by experience, come to assume the mantel of law.

[3] I cite two different sources for Peirce's works. The most common is the *Collected Papers of Charles Sanders Peirce*, vols. 1–6, Charles Hartshorne and Paul Weiss (eds.), vols. 7–8, Arthur W. Burks (ed.), Harvard University Press, Cambridge, MA, 1931–1935, 1958. Citations of this text take the form n.m indicating volume and paragraph number. The other source is the two volumes of *The Essential Peirce, Selected Philosophical Writings*, Nathan Houser and Christian Kloesel (eds.), Indiana University Press, Bloomington and Indianapolis, IN, 1992, 1998. References take the form n, m indicating volume and page number.

[4] This, by the way, seems to me a completely analogous restatement of the Turing test.

surprising character of some element of our experience, pragmatism amounts, for Peirce, to analyzing the effect that that hypothesis will have in modifying our expectations with regard to future experience. The application of the maxim to a given hypothesis tells us if it is capable of manifesting itself in experiential consequences. If no such consequences can be imagined, if it is incapable of experimental verification, then it is empty, and we should turn our attention to another hypothesis. Peirce says, "Every single item of scientific theory that stands established today has been due to abduction . . . Abduction is the process of forming an explanatory hypothesis, and it is the only logical operation which introduces any new idea" (CP 5.172). Given that the growth of knowledge depends on abduction, it is vitally important that we be clear about what a hypothesis entails so that its consequences may be deduced and inductively tested. This, essentially, is the doctrine of pragmatism.

4 Finding the Right Hypothesis

The maxim is certainly a necessary link in the chain of scientific discovery, but its exclusive use is hardly sufficient. What most interests the AI community is how the hypothesis is arrived at. From the possibly infinite fund of available hypotheses how is it that we arrive relatively quickly at the right one? And more concretely, can this process be formalized? Peirce says the following about the logic of abduction:

- No reason whatsoever can be given for it, as far as I can discover; and it needs no reason, since it merely offers suggestions (CP 5.171).
- Abduction is, after all, nothing but guessing (CP 7.219).
- Abduction is the spontaneous conjecture of instinctive reason (CP 6.475).
- However man may have acquired his faculty of divining the ways of Nature, it has certainly not been by a self-controlled and critical logic. Even now he cannot give an exact reason for his best guesses (EP2, 217).
- The abductive suggestion comes to us like a flash. It is an act of insight, although of extremely fallible insight (CP 5.181).

These are comments interspersed throughout Peirce's writings and reflect his general belief that the formation of hypotheses is not a rule-governed process, that it is more instinctual than rational. At this point we can return to my initial discussion of the categories to understand one of the reasons why abduction is of this nature. Abduction, as I noted, corresponds to the category of firstness (induction–secondness and deduction–thirdness). Firstness has to do with that which is as it is without reference to anything else. A first is monadic and completely undetermined by anything else. Inductions are determined by the successive dyadic force of objects of our experience and deduction by the mediating force of syllogistic reasoning, but abductions by nothing. They come to us, as Peirce says, in a flash.

We can see an analogy of this in the ontological manifestation of firstness: chance. In order to explain the multitudinous novelty of the cosmos, Peirce insists on the reality of chance spontaneity in events. If chance were merely a word we use to describe our ignorance of how things take place, if, in fact, everything is absolutely determined and necessary and occurs according to a rule (of which we are ignorant), then we would be left without a way to explain novelty, creation, and evolution. Such a determinism would "block the road of inquiry," as Peirce says, insofar as it posits some ultimate metaphysical entity whose origin cannot be explained, much as some religious people do with God. So chance, corresponding to firstness, is totally undetermined, just as abduction is in the realm of logical inference.

Given all this, the fact that one of the greatest logicians of all time nowhere formalizes the abductive process as a strictly logical procedure seems, well, perfectly logical. The real philosophical significance of the nature of abduction is its metaphysical implication. Peirce speaks on occasion of the relationship between mind and reality. For example: inquiry can only arrive at the truth if there is "sufficient affinity between the reasoner's mind and nature's to render guessing not altogether hopeless" (CP 1.121). Although he says that abduction is just guessing, it cannot be merely that, or else we would still be in caves eating our lunch over a fire. Abduction is guessing, but the fact is that we guess right more often than not. What can explain this?

The "affinity" between mind and nature that Peirce speaks of reflects his idealistic monism, his thesis of continuity, or what he calls synechism, and his doctrine that matter is but effete mind. Peirce is anti-Cartesian and antidualist to the core. There is no mind/body split but rather a continuity of all being. Matter is simply mind whose habits of inference have become so "hide-bound" or crystallized that they have lost the capacity to change. His logic or metaphysics is not one of substances but rather of relations (as we see in his categories). What something is is a function of what it does (pragmatism), and this in turn is a function of the relations it holds at any given time (an idea to be found in complexity theory, connectionism, systems theory, etc.). It is "logical" then that abduction be understood in these terms, as the result of this affinity between mind and nature. If dualism were correct, there would have to be some rational decision procedure for abduction so as to avoid mere random guessing. But if the mind has developed under the laws that govern the universe, it is reasonable to suppose that the mind has a tendency to alight on true hypotheses concerning the universe.

Although this may sound mystical to some, this is not all Peirce has to say about abduction. There are certain things we can do to expedite our journey down abduction's path. In addition to choosing hypotheses that have experiential consequences and that are capable of explaining the phenomenon and taking away its surprising character, there are economic considerations to take into account (EP 2, 107–9). Peirce mentions three: cost, the value of the thing proposed, and its effect upon other projects:

- *Cost*: Those hypotheses that would cost very little to test should be preferred, for even though they have little to recommend them on other grounds they can be quickly dispatched, thus clearing the ground and concentrating the attention on more promising ones.

- *Value*: This has to do with considerations that lead us to believe that a given hypothesis may be true, of which Peirce mentions two kinds—the instinctive and the reasoned.

  (a) Peirce says that we *instinctively* arrive at the correct hypothesis. Given his belief that the most adequate way to explain the fact that we arrive quickly at the right hypothesis instead of drudging through one after the other is to hypothesize that the human mind is akin to the truth, we should favor those hypotheses at which we arrive instinctively. "The existence of a natural instinct for truth is, after all, the sheet anchor of science."

  (b) "If we know any positive facts which render a given hypothesis objectively probable, they recommend it for inductive testing."

- *Impact of the hypothesis on other projects*: It is rare for a given hypothesis to completely explain the phenomenon under question, for which reason we should consider how the hypothesis might relate to other questions we may be considering. For Peirce this consideration leads us to value three different qualities in hypotheses: caution, breadth, and incomplexity.

  (a) Peirce adduces the game of twenty questions to illustrate the quality of *caution*. Someone thinks of an object and the other players can ask twenty questions susceptible of a yes or no answer in order to determine its identity. The point is to ask skillful questions, and for Peirce the most efficient way of doing this is by bisecting the possibilities exactly in half. Assuming that a million objects are commonly known to all the world, questions where yes and no were equally probable would be capable of identifying the right object out of a collection numbering 2^{20}. "Thus, twenty skillful hypotheses will ascertain what two hundred thousand stupid ones might fail to do. The secret of the business lies in the caution which breaks a hypothesis up into its smallest logical components."

  (b) The question of *breadth* concerns the applicable extension of hypotheses. Those hypotheses should be favored, when balanced of course against other considerations of economy, which offer explanations for the same phenomenon appearing in other contexts. Other things being equal, we should make our hypotheses as broad as possible.

  (c) *Incomplexity* is sort of like Peirce's version of Ockham's razor. Though more complicated hypotheses may take us nearer the truth in a shorter amount of time, the use of a simpler hypothesis, although it ends up not panning out, may be instructive with reference to the formation of the next hypothesis.

5 New Perspectives

I would like to add here another suggestion, not mentioned by Peirce, but inspired by something he says. I already quoted the following: "The abductive suggestion comes to us like a flash. It is an act of *insight*, although of extremely fallible insight."

Immediately following this he says: "It is true that the different elements of the hypothesis were in our minds before; but it is the idea of putting together what we had never before dreamed of putting together which flashes the new suggestion before our contemplation." I am sure that we have all had this "aha" experience before. In our work we come upon some anomaly, a strange set of facts that does not fit into the expectations of our current constellation of beliefs. We work hard on the problem but with no luck, and frustrated, we leave it and move on to something else. Then, reading some article on an unrelated matter or talking with a colleague about his or her work, we suddenly have a flash of insight. What we were reading or talking about allowed us to see the anomalous facts in a new light, from a new perspective. The facts remain the same. What changes is how we relate or interpret these facts, or as Peirce says, "the idea of putting together what we had never before dreamed of putting together." We suddenly *see* the problem in a new light.

This metaphor of sight is not casual. We understand sight as being a mode of perception, and in what I have said I have likened abduction to a form of perception, a way of seeing or perceiving anomalous facts from a new perspective. Peirce himself links perception and abduction in the following comment. He says: "Abductive inference shades into perceptual judgment without any sharp line of demarcation between them" (CP 5.181). This is an important passage because it associates two things that we normally distinguish. When we hear the phrase "abductive inference" we think of something cognitive, logical, the proposal of a conceptual theory to mediate our understanding of empirical facts. "Perception," on the other hand, connotes something direct and brute, an immediate access to the world. There may be some who think that we have only to open our eyes and perceive the world to see how it is, but Peirce would not agree. The images in Fig. 4 have been used in psychology to show how even perception, or more properly perceptual judgment, is mediated and interpretative.

The point here is that perception itself is interpretative. If we change *how* we see we change *what* we see. So, what Peirce means when he says that abductive inference shades into perceptual judgment is that abduction is a process closer in its nature to perception than to a rational process like deduction. What we are looking for when we try to generate a hypothesis is a new way of seeing the facts, a new mode of perception if you will.

So, how do we change from seeing the rabbit to seeing the duck? In order to answer this we need to understand why we see either the rabbit or the duck in the

 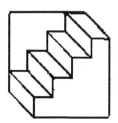

Fig. 4 Examples of Perception as Interpretative

first place. What determines this? The answer, for Peirce, is context. We normally understand context as a spatiotemporal arrangement of facts in a given situation, but for Peirce the important thing, that which determines the interaction between two things or the interpretation by one of the other, is the relation between these facts, or what he would call habits of inference. The constellation of beliefs that each of us has forms the backbone of the habits by which each one of us interprets and understands the world around us. But for Peirce, not only humans, but the world itself, is characterized by "habits of inference," by particular forms of reacting to its environment. This is a reflection of his idealistic monism of which I wrote earlier. So, we open our eyes and see the world in a certain way because a certain context constrains us, that context being the relation of habits of inference between us and the particular part of the world in which we are interested.

Another way of expressing this idea of relation between habits of inference is to think of the model that Peirce's thought rejects. In this model we are rational beings trying to relate to and know an inert hunk of dead matter that is the world. This is the vision of Cartesian dualism that spawned the epistemological problem that the next three centuries of European philosophy tried to resolve. Peirce resolved it by rejecting dualism and conceiving of the being of the cosmos in terms of a continuum. Nature is not dead matter but rather a living mentality that operates according to its own habits of inference. When we investigate the world we come to a closer understanding of it by adapting our own habits of inference to those of Nature, by synchronizing the two if you will. When we are faced with an anomalous collection of facts, the two habits of inference are out of sync. Bringing them into sync is what abduction is all about.

Now let us return to our original question, how do we change from seeing the rabbit to seeing the duck? What we need is a way of seeing the facts before us in a new way. We have to change the context that is constraining our interpretation, i.e., our habits of inference, so that a new organization of the facts will make sense. Peirce says that humans, at least, achieve this reorganization by means of diagrammatic thought:

> With these two kinds of signs (symbols and indices) any proposition can be expressed; but it cannot be reasoned upon, for reasoning consists in the observation that where certain relations subsist certain others are found, and it accordingly requires the exhibition of the relations reasoned within an icon. . . . It appears that all deductive reasoning, even simple syllogism, involves an element of observation; namely, deduction consists in constructing an icon or diagram the relations of whose parts shall present a complete analogy with those of the parts of the object of reasoning, of experimenting upon this image in the imagination, and of observing the result so as to discover unnoticed and hidden relations among the parts. (EP1, 227)

Peirce speaks here of the imagination, of manipulating the elements represented in an icon or diagram so as to discover previously hidden or unseen relations. It is the new representation thus generated that flashes or suggests the abductive inference. He gives an example of this in an unpublished manuscript [as quoted in Hoffmann (1997)]. The "ten point theorem" was a famous problem of geometry whose solution was found by von Stadt in the nineteenth century. The problem was framed in terms of a two-dimensional representation, but von Stadt showed that the theorem is provable when it is represented in terms of three-dimensional projective geometry. Von Stadt had done much work in perspective geometry and the relation between two- and three-dimensional representations. When he came to this problem of the ten points, the familiar context of his previous work greatly facilitated the creation of a new representation of, or new way of seeing, the elements in the two-dimensional problem.

We could call it a stroke of luck that he had this background experience and that he happened upon the ten-point problem. It is clear that he followed no principled procedure to find problems fruitfully susceptible to the application of his context. How to determine the relevance of a context to a specific problem? That question remains, and I at least see no formalizable solution. In this increasingly specialized and complex world it is clear that there is no longer room for renaissance men capable of juggling all the world's knowledge; there is just too much information to be held heuristically in one mind. For this reason Peirce never tires of insisting on the importance of the community of inquirers for the advancement of knowledge. It is in dialogue with others, especially interdisciplinary dialogue, that new ideas emerge and solve the problems we face. We may not have the context appropriate for a given problem, but our colleague working in another field just might.

6 Conclusions

I have not referred directly here to sapience or sapient systems but rather to an important quality or characteristic that such systems should be able to exhibit—that of forming fruitful hypotheses to advance their knowledge of the world around them. Peirce's basic argument against the possibility of formalizing this ability is metaphysical in nature. The pervasive and coherent application of his categorial scheme throughout his philosophical thought leads us, heuristically, to attribute to abduction the qualities characteristic of firstness and thus to consider it as undetermined. If a hypothesis could be determinately inferred from antecedents, science would not be a process of discovery but merely one of an unfolding explanation. In spite of this, we have considered various strategies for coaxing abduction along its path. Although a rational ordering of abductive processes is very unlikely, if not impossible, perhaps the aforementioned strategies can be formally implemented into sapient systems.

References

Aliseda, A. (1997) *Seeking Explanations Abduction in Logic, Philosophy of Science and Artificial Intelligence*. Doctoral Dissertation. Philosophy Department. Stanford University. Also published by the Institute for Logic, Language and Computation, University of Amsterdam, The Netherlands, 1997.

Aravindan, C., and Dung, P.M. (1994) Belief Dynamics, abduction and databases, in MacNish c. and Pearce, D (eds.) *Logics in Artificial Intelligence. European Workshop JELIA'94*, pp. 66–85. Lecture Notes in Artificial Intelligence 838. Springer-Verlag.

Fisch, "Introductory Note," in Sebeok, *The Play of Musement*. Advances in Semiotics Series. Bloomington: Indiana University Press, 1982.

Hoffmann, M. (1997) "Is There a Logic of Abduction?" Published on the internet at http://www.uni-bielefeld.de/idm/personen/mhoffman/papers/abduction-logic.html 1997.

Kakas, A.C., Kowalski, R., and Toni, F. (1995) Abductive Logic Programming. Journal of Logic and Computation 2 (6) 719–770.

Konolige, K. (1996). "Abductive Theories in Artificial Intelligence", in Brewka, G. (ed.) Principles of Knowledge Representation. CSLI Publications, Stanford University.

Sebeok, T. (ed.), *A Perfusion of Signs*, Bloomington: Indiana, 1977, pp. 22–39.

On Plasticity, Complexity, and Sapient Systems

Carlos Rubén de la Mora-Basáñez, Alejandro Guerra-Hernández,
V. Angélica García-Vega, and Luc Steels

Abstract Sapient agents have been characterized as a subclass of intelligent agents capable of "insight" and "sound judgment." Although several engineering issues have been established to characterize sapient agents, biological referents also seem necessary to understand the cognitive functionality of such systems. Small-world and scale-free networks, the so-called complex networks, provide a new mathematical approach to anatomical and functional connectivity related to cognitive processes. We argue that complex cognitive functions require such complex connectivity, which results from epigenetic development through experiences. Particularly we claim that agents will show complex functionality only if a complex arrangement of their knowledge is achieved. In this chapter, we propose a model in which situated agents evolve knowledge networks holding both small-world and scale-free properties. Experimental results using pragmatic games support explanations about the conditions required to obtain such networks relating degree distribution and sensing; clustering coefficient and biological motivations; goals; acquired knowledge; and attentional focus. This constitutes a relevant advance in the understanding of how low-level connectivity emerges in artificial agents.

1 Introduction

In the context of artificial intelligence (AI), an intelligent agent (Franklin and Graesser 1997; Russell and Norvig 1995; Wooldridge and Jennings 1995); is usually defined as a temporal persistent autonomous system situated within an environment, sensing and acting in pursuit of its own agenda to achieve its goals, possibly influencing the environment. Russell and Subramanian (1995) argue that an advantage of such definition is that it allows room to consider different kinds of agents, including rational agents and even those that are not supposed to have such cognitive faculties.

Because the generality of this definition covers a variety of agents with quite different properties, sapient agents have been characterized as a subclass of intelligent

C.R. de la Mora-Basáñez
Artificial Intelligence Laboratory, Vrije Universiteit Brussel, Brussels, Belgium
e-mail: carlos@arti.vub.ac.be

R.V. Mayorga, L.I. Perlovsky (eds.), *Toward Artificial Sapience,*
© Springer 2008

agents with "insight" and the capability of "sound judgment." From an engineering perspective, Skolicki and Arciszewski (2003) propose seven approaches to distinguish sapient agents from the entire class of intelligent agents. In terms of knowledge representation, it is assumed that sapient agents are defined as knowledge systems. They must be capable of abstracting knowledge and adapting its behavior to drive further knowledge acquisition; making long-term decisions; and exploiting the representation space, as well as conducting exploration; making strategic decisions that may not be entirely justified by local results; and recognizing emergent patterns and avoiding undesired attractors in the representation space, while, if necessary, using various search methods to reach a given attractor.

Even when the issues referred to are useful to differentiate the subclass of sapient agents, we argue that both biological and social referents are also required to do the same. Biological inspiration has been always present in AI, although not always explicitly, with the aim of emulating complex cognitive behaviors. In particular, behavior-based AI (Brooks 1990; Smithers 1992; Steels and Brooks 1995) emphasizes the necessity of working with autonomous, embodied, and situated systems, always arguing biological referents. Brooks et al. (1998) considers embodiment, development, social interaction, and sensorial integration as methodologies to construct humanoids. Zlatev and Balkenius (2001) identify embodiment, situatedness, and development as the main issues to built epigenetic robots. Prince (2002) considers the ability to construct potential complex skills based on developmental architectures, sensory motor integration, and imitation. McIntyre et al. (2002) consider the need for structural issues, as well as other external factors to achieve adequate dynamics and then an appropriated development, e.g., social, individual, and environmental stability and group size, among others. All these approaches consider development an important issue. Some of them do it from the point of view of developmental psychology, following Piaget like Drescher (1991) and Stojanov (2001). Others add social interactions, mainly in language research (Steels 1996a, 1997) or neurobiological modeling (Montague and Dayan 1998).

However, a better conceptualization is required. Some of these issues are not well defined or even have different connotations, as embodiment (Ziemke 2001), autonomy (Collier 2000), or even the epigenetic concept (Lederberg 2001, Levenson and Sweatt 2005). Moreover, there is a lack of global measures mainly because, being biologically inspired models, their validation involves comparisons with the functionality of observed systems, but also because only recently a kind of universal way of organization in connectivity has been found, the so-called complex networks: small-world and scale-free networks.

Properties explained by complex networks include: fault tolerance, attack vulnerability, redundancy in transmission of information, integration, and segregation. More importantly, they explain that complex functionality, e,g., cognitive functionality, requires complex physical connectivity. In this chapter we claim that sapient agents require an epigenetic development displaying complex network topology in order to perform complex cognitive functionality.

The chapter is organized as follows: Section 2 introduces the concept of networks and their properties. The study of complex networks is proposed as a way to approach the complex cognitive functionality resulting from brain connectivity, emphasizing that the understanding of the mechanisms giving place to complex connectivity are not well known. Section 3 introduces the concept of epigenetics and proposes some requirements for sapient agents in order to develop a mechanism equivalent to epigenetic organizations. Section 4 introduces the methodology of pragmatic games, a model in which an artificial situated agent develops a knowledge of networks exhibiting complex properties based on the epigenetic mechanism proposed in the previous section. Results, presented in Section 5, support explanations about the conditions required to obtain networks with the expected properties, relating degree distribution and sensing: clustering coefficient and biological motivations, goals, acquired knowledge, and attentional focus. Conclusions are offered in Section 6.

2 Networks

Networks are invaluable mathematical objects able to represent a wide variety of phenomena and processes (Barabási and Bonabeau 2003), which makes this mathematical abstraction an appropriate formalism by which to characterize and analyze many real life problems, in both a static and a dynamic way. For example:

- Social networks are defined as sets of people showing a specific pattern of contacts or interactions, e.g., friendship, business, marriage, and scientific collaboration. Newman (2003) referred to early papers on social networks of friendship patterns in small groups, social circles of women, and social circles of factory workers. However, social networks were difficult to establish, inaccurate, and sometimes subjective. Nowadays, digital files make it easier to establish relationships in a reliable way, as in collaboration networks, e.g., scientists or actors. These networks are well documented on the Internet. Other reliable social relationships are established by e-mail or telephone.
- Information networks are also called knowledge networks. One of the first studies of this kind of network was made by *Alfred Lotks*, who in 1929 discovered the so-called law of scientific productivity, establishing that the distribution of the number of papers written by individual scientists follows a power law. This result was extended to the arts and humanities. Another example of an information network is the World Wide Web (WWW), obtained by joining web pages through hyperlinks. This network shows very interesting properties, as a power-law degree distribution. Other examples include the network citation between US patents, peer-to-peer networks, and word classes in a thesaurus.
- Technological networks are designed for distribution of some commodity or resource, such as electricity or information. Examples include the electric power grid, airline routes, roads, railways, pedestrian traffic, telephone, and delivery services. A widely studied network of this kind is Internet, joining computers through physical connections.

- Biological networks include the metabolic pathways representing metabolic substrates and products, where directed edges appear if a metabolic reaction relates substrates and products. Another example is the protein interaction network. Since we are interested in the development of systems that display complex cognitive functionality, e.g., sapient agents, brain functional connectivity is a network in this class of special interest. Brain functional connectivity is approached in this chapter with the tools provided by the study of complex networks.

Despite the nature of networks, they can be defined in terms of graphs. A graph is a pair of sets $G = \{P, E\}$, where P is a set of n nodes $p_1, \ldots, p_n$ and E is a set of edges that connect two elements of P. Graphs are directed if the direction is specified for all of the links. If relationships between nodes runs in both senses, the graph is called indirected. Directed edges are also called arcs or arrows. Degree is the number of edges connected to a vertex. In a directed graph, is necessary specify the in, out, or all-degree, considering, respectively, the arcs in-coming, out-going, or the addition of the two. Component is the set of vertices that can be reached between them along the edges. In a directed graph, the component to which a vertex belongs is that set of vertices that can be reached from it by paths running along the edges of the graph. The geodesic or minimal path is the shortest path through the network from one vertex to another. It is possible for there to be more than one geodesic path. The diameter of a network is the length of the longest geodesic path. The evolution of a graph is understood as the historical process of constructing the graph.

2.1 Complex Networks

Erdös and Rényi (1960) introduced a new way of characterizing networks, considering graphs with a large number of elements and, studying the probabilistic space of all the graphs having n nodes and n edges. They used macrovariables to statistically analyze the growth of these networks as the result of stochastic processes. Such random networks were considered appropriate for describing many real problems having many nodes and links, including road maps.

Very recently it was discovered that many interesting phenomena and processes involving huge numbers of nodes do not have random topology, but rather complex network topology (Watts 1999; Barabási 2002; Albert and Barabási 2002; Newman 2003). The parameters characterizing such topologies are like macrovariables describing the whole network and representing a fingerprint of its complexity. Complex networks were not considered so important until 1998, when a relationship among networks as different as the collaboration graph of film actors, the power grid of the western United States, and the neural network of the worm *Caenorhabditis elegans* were found, showing that they are not completely random, neither completely regular, but somewhere in between. Such networks were called small-world networks by Watts and Strogatz (1998) and Watts (1999), who introduced two measures to determine how far toward randomness or near to order a network is. Interesting networks were found between randomness and complete order.

Barabási and Albert (1999) showed that a power law could be obtained from the degree distribution of complex networks and that this property is rooted in their growth mechanism. Such networks are called scale free. Observe that in random networks, the degree distribution follows a bell curve. This random departure creates the difference between random and complex networks.

Phenomena with small-world and scale-free properties include: the WWW (Albert et al. 1999), metabolic networks (Jeong et al. 2000), human language (Ferrer-i-Cancho and Sole 2001), scientific collaboration networks (Barabási 2002), brain networks in mammalians (Sporns and Chialvo 2004), and functional brain networks in humans (Eguiluz et al. 2005).

The study of complex networks is an active field devoted to understanding complex phenomena, focusing in three aspects: Finding statistical properties to characterize the structure and behavior of complex networks; trying to create models of networks to explain the meaning of such parameters; and predicting network behavior, based on their topological properties and local rules for nodes and links.

2.2 Complex Networks and Brain Connectivity

Brains have evolved as efficient networks whose structural connectivity allows a large repertoire of functional states. Recently, it has been shown that functional connectivity in the human cerebral cortex presents topological properties both of small-world and scale-free networks (Eguiluz et al. 2005). Although this was known for other animals (Sporns and Chialvo 2004), it is the first time in which statistically significant results showned that this happens in a variety of individuals performing different tasks.

Sporns and Chialvo (2004) reflected on the relevance of research on the structure and dynamics of such networks as a way, to contribute to our understanding of brain and cognitive functionality. They established three major modalities of brain networks:

- Anatomical connectivity is the set of physical or structural (synaptic) connections linking neuronal units at a given time. The relevant data can range over multiple spatial scales, from local circuits to large-scale networks of interregional pathways. Anatomical connection patterns are relatively static at shorter time scales (second to minutes), but can be dynamic at longer time scales (hours to days), e.g., during learning or development.
- Functional connectivity captures patterns of deviations from statistical independence between distributed and often spatially remote neuronal units, measuring their correlation/covariance, spectral coherence, or phase locking. Functional connectivity is time dependent (hundreds of milliseconds) and "model free," i.e., it measures statistical interdependence (mutual information) without explicit reference to causal effects. Different methodologies for measuring brain activity will generally result in different statistical estimates of functional connectivity.

- Effective connectivity describes the set of causal effects of one neural system over another. Thus, unlike functional connectivity, effective connectivity is not model free, but requires the specification of a causal model, including structural parameters. Experimentally, effective connectivity can be inferred through perturbations or through the observation of the temporal ordering of neural events. Other measures estimating causal interactions can also be used.

Functional and effective connectivity are time dependent. Statistical interactions between brain regions change rapidly, reflecting the participation of varying subsets of brain regions and pathways in different cognitive conditions and tasks.

Structural, functional, and effective connectivity are mutually interrelated. Clearly, structural connectivity is a major constraint on the kinds of patterns of functional or effective connectivity that can be generated in a network.

Structural inputs and outputs of a given cortical region, its connectional fingerprint, are major determinants of its functional properties. Conversely, functional interactions can contribute to the shaping of the underlying anatomical substrate, either directly through activity (covariance)-dependent synaptic modification or, over longer time scales, through affecting perceptual, cognitive, or behavioral capabilities and thus its adaptation and survival.

The scale-free properties in the brain explain the coexistence of functional segregation and integration, redundancy, and efficiency in information transmission. The power law in degree distribution affects the functional impact of brain lesions, being vulnerable to damage on a few highly connected nodes, and explains the small impact of random lesions on damage. Cortical areas in mammalian brains exhibit attributes of complex networks. The distribution of functional connections and the probability of finding a link vs. distance are both scale free. Furthermore, the characteristic path length is small and the clustering coefficient is high when compared with random graphs. Short path length captures potential functional proximity between regions. High clustering measures the degree to which a particular area is part of local collective dynamics. Frequent connectivity in all of the shortest paths linking areas explains structural stability and the efficient working of cortical networks.

2.3 Complex Networks and Complex Cognitive Functionality

Human language is an important example of complex cognitive functionality with complex networks properties mounted on complex connectivity (the brain itself). This connectivity allows the fast and robust construction of a huge variety of sentences from a limited number of discrete units (words). Sole et al. (2006) enumerate and compare three kinds of language networks:

- Co-ocurrence networks can be built relating words that co-occur using directed graphs, capturing syntactic relations useful on speech production processes.
- Syntactic networks are built of pieces forming part of higher structures and joining them due to syntax dependence, as taking arcs beginning in complements

and ending in the nucleus of a phrase (verbs). These networks are related to grammatical structure.
- Semantic networks try to capture the meaning carried in linguistic productions. Meaning relations between words can be established in several ways: antonymy, homonymy, hypernymy, meronymy, and polisemy: "Links can be defined by free meaning association, opening the window to psycho-linguistic processes."

All of these networks are shown to have complex connectivity, with power law degree distributions ($\gamma \sim 2.2$ to -3.0), high clustering coefficients ($C/C_{rand} \sim 10^3$), and short pathlengths. Hub deletion has the effect of losing optimal navigation in co-occurrence networks, articulation loss in the case of syntactic networks, and conceptual loss plasticity in the case of semantic networks.

Graphs of word interactions show small-world properties (high clustering coefficient) and scale-free distributions ($\gamma \sim 1.5$ to -2.0) (Ferrer-i-Cancho and Sole 2001). Based on the significance profile of small subgraphs from different languages, common local structure in word adjacency networks is also observed (Milo et al. 2004). This allows the definition of universal classes of networks by local motif statistics (Milo et al. 2002).

A dynamics within an appropriate connectivity enables approaching some particular brain functionalities. For example, short-term memory, can be envisaged dynamically when bursts are sustained in a small-world network (Cohen 2004). This is possible because the probability of the percolation of loops in such networks is higher than in random networks.

2.4 Complex Networks Growth and Evolution

However, the kinds of mechanism giving place to complex connectivity are not well understood. Growth algorithms have been proposed for the emergence of small-world and scale-free networks. Unfortunately such algorithms are not biologically realistic. Chialvo (2004) noted that they do not represent good models for the development of cortical networks.

Especially intriguing is the role that experience might play in network growth. From a biological perspective, we know that this development in brain is the result of an epigenetic mechanism. On the other hand, "the ontogeny of language is strongly tied to underlying cognitive potentials and also is a product of the exposure of individuals to normal language use. What it is clear is that unless a minimal (scale-free) neural substrate is present, consensus between individuals might not be enough to trigger the emergence of a fully developed grammar" (Sole et al. 2006).

Sapient agents are expected to display complex cognitive functionality. It is clear that complex functionality is mounted in complex connectivity. Our claim is that we need to understand how complex connectivity can emerge on situated agents and how experience affects this connectivity. In what follows, we propose an epigenetic mechanism useful for understanding some basic considerations on how this processes can be achieved by sapient agents.

3 Epigenetic Mechanism and Plasticity

Plasticity refers to the ability of the nervous system to change (Gazzaniga et al. 2002). These changes refer mainly to modifications in connectivity that allow learning to contend with novel situations. Such changes result from an epigenetic mechanism or, more specifically, a synaptogenesis. In order to develop a mechanism equivalent to epigenetic organization, a sapient agent requires:

1. An innate process emulating epigenesis, triggered as a function of the experience of the agent. We call this process a closure mechanism.
2. A set of biological innate distinguishable states, called biological motivations as in the sense of Batali and Grundy (1996), are required to start the closure mechanism. These biological motivations are inborn affective states as those considered by Sheutz and Sloman (2001) and Scheutz (2001).
3. A kind of distinguishability to discriminate the degree of epigenetic formation. It is used to mimic the natural process, which requires definite steps in order to recruit memory: identification, consolidation, and eventual long-term storage (Levenson and Sweatt 2005). In a rough abstraction, we can talk about states of incorporation of experiences in the epigenetic organization or closure states.
4. Multimodality is required in order to allow integration and segregation, as shown later by the results of our experiments.
5. To interact with an environment as a situated system.
6. To incorporate new sensorial states by making them distinguishable after experience.
7. A maximum degree of relationship between two nodes. Each one of them corresponds to a kind of rule of the form $State_1 \rightarrow action \rightarrow State_2$, being schemes for Drescher (1991), or facts for Foner and Maes (1994); here we use the last term. The set of all of the obtained facts constitutes the knowledge acquired by the agent.

The acquired knowledge is represented as an evolving network processed by the closure mechanism emulating epigenesis, when the agent performs complex learning of a complex network of relationships.

It is thought that epigenetic mechanisms have an important role in synaptic plasticity and memory formation. If this is true, episodes in our daily life can be stored 'permanently' in a step-by-step process. Acquisition, consolidation, and long-term memory registering are carried out by epigenetic development. These mechanisms are very general, and are also observed in systems as, far removed from humans as plants (vernalization), having to 'remember' not to flower over the whole winter or in mother cells being marked to transmit specificity to daughters (Levenson and Sweatt 2005).

4 Pragmatic Games

Pragmatic games (Mora-Basáñez et al. 2004) inspired in language games (Steels 1996a,b) are used to explore the ideas expressed in the previous section. They offer a methodology by which a situated agent is immersed in similar but not identical repetitive situations to perform complex spatial learning. Although these games resemble subsets of Drescher's (1991) experiments, they have different objectives and dynamics, and the results are analyzed differently. Using these games we are able to control, test, and measure the epigenetic development. We pretend to isolate learning of complex relationships, excluding any appetitive or aversive reinforcement and any conditioning. The experiments were designed to involve memory use, acquisition, consolidation, and long-term establishment, but not in an integrated way. Three pragmatic games (Fig. 1) have been defined:

- *Focusing game.* One agent having only one eye and its visual field. The game starts by setting an object within an environment in a random place. The eye moves randomly, once the fovea "sees" the object, the game is restarted.
- *Grasping game.* One agent having one eye, as in the focusing game, and also one hand. The game restarts when the hand reaches the object.
- *Feeding game.* One agent having one eye, one hand, and a mouth. When the hand passes over the object, the agent closes its hand and the object is attached to it. The random movements continue until the hand (with the object) reaches the mouth. At that moment, the game restarts.

The knowledge acquired by the agents while performing complex learning is represented as an evolving network of affective states, processed by the mechanism emulating epigenesis. The proposed closure mechanism, together with the morphology of the agent, and the specific interrelation within the environment (games), represents the minimal conditions discriminating the games that produce complex networks and those that do not. In what follows, the elements of these games are explained in detail.

4.1 Environment

The environment or "world" consists of a simple 7×7 grid (large square in Fig. 1), including one agent and one 1×1 object (red circle).

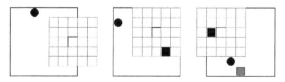

Fig. 1 Pragmatic games: from left to right focusing (visual field), grasping (hand and visual field), and feeding (mouth, hand, and visual field) games. In all games the object is the circle

4.2 Agent

Our agent has 77 bit sensors: 75 for a 5×5 (the grid in Fig. 1) red (R), green(G), and blue (B) sensitive visual field; one for a 1×1 blue "hand" and one for a 1×1 green "mouth."

The agent has four actuators: two for the eye and two for the hand. Each actuator has three possible states: do nothing, up/right, and down/left. The mouth is always fixed. An agent's actuation is then specified by a set of four values ($e_x, e_y, h_x, h_y \in \{-1, 0, 1\}$). The agent moves randomly, choosing one of the three possible states of each one of the actuators, considering these states random variables under uniform distribution. Eventually, the agent can "redo" the last movement by performing the opposite movement performed by each actuator.

The agent has a set of distinguishable innate affective states (Sheutz 2001) called biological motivations, which are mapped to a five-bit vector: three bits for detecting RGB in the fovea; one for the hand holding an object, and other for the presence of the object in the mouth. Therefore, there are 32 possible biological motivations, although in our simulations fewer than ten are experienced. These biological motivations do not have any appetitive or aversive character; they are only distinguishable. At the beginning they are not related to any sensorial state; this relation must be established by the closure mechanism, which causes the network to grow up.

4.3 Closure Mechanism

Every time the agent experiences a particular biological motivation, this motivation and the sensing state (77-bit string) is saved. Thus, every biological motivation has an associated record of sensing vectors. This process does not affect the network. Any biological motivation can give way to an affective state or to a potential affective state, which is then incorporated into the network by two mechanisms:

1. Detecting affective states from biological motivations. After a certain number of iterations (500 in our simulations), the system tries to determine if biological motivations have a specific associated sensing state. The affective state represents the set of sensing bits always present in the associated record when the biological motivation has been experienced.
2. Detecting potential affective states. If the sensing state at time t corresponds to an affective state, then a node corresponding to the sensing state at time $t - 1$ is incorporated, as well as the directed arc between the nodes (representing the actuation). The new node has the possibility of evoking an affective state.

A potential affective state could become affective if its frequency exceeds some value. If the values are too small, noise can be learned. If the values are too big, then it takes more time to learn. This also happens for other parameters of the model.

The arcs joining nodes can be incorporated into the network in two ways:

1. When a potential affective state is reached, it is linked to the previous state. If the previous state does not have an associated node, it is created.
2. When the agent experiences two consecutive sensing states and their associated nodes exist (affective states or potential affective states), then a link is created between them.

Arcs are labeled as frequent or codified. Once an arc exists between two nodes, some statistics (frequency and actuation) are updated if it is traversed. Its label is then computed in the following way:

1. If the frequency of occurrence for an arc is higher than a given value, it is labeled as a frequent arc. The distribution of probabilities for the the actuators is computed from the history and saved in the arc in the form: { $p(e_x = -1)$, $p(e_x = 0)$, $p(e_x = 1)$ }, { $p(e_y = -1)$, $p(e_y = 0)$, $p(e_y = 1)$ }, { $p(h_x = -1)$, $p(h_x = 0)$, $p(h_x = 1)$ }, { $p(h_y = -1)$, $p(h_y = 0)$, $p(h_y = 1)$ }. The distributions for each actuator are normalized.
2. If one of the three probabilities in each one of the four triplets of a frequent arc is higher than a threshold, the triplet is replaced with one code, representing the associated winning movement for the correspondent actuator. For example, if the distribution of probabilities for the eye in the x direction is { $p(e_x = -1)$, $p(e_x = 0)$, $p(e_x = 1)$ } = { 0.1, 0.3, 0.7 }, then the triplet is replaced by a 1, meaning that the associated movement for this actuator is considered as being 1 unit in the x direction. This is why the arcs holding this condition are named codified arcs, since the nodes joining the arc have more than a random probability to be joined by performing the codified movement.

4.4 Closure States

Given two consecutive iterations, the agent experiences two sensing states: S_{t-1} and S_t, verifying that there are related nodes in the network. More precisely, the agent checks whether each sensing state has or has not got an associated node in the network; and whether each has associated potential affective states or associated affective states in the network. In the same way, it checks if the performed act has has or has not got an associated arc in the network; has an associated arc in the network, but not frequently; has an associated frequent arc in the network; or has an associated arc suitable to be codified. So, there are $2^3 \times 2^4 \times 2^3$ possible closure states.

If a labeled arc has affective states as source and target nodes, it is called a fact. This is considered the most refined state for the closure mechanism. It contrasts with the Drescher's (1991) perspective, which considers reliability as the way to verify the arc's functionality.

4.5 Attentional Focus

Attentional focus is a number between [0, 1], representing the probability to undo the last performed movement. Thus, a 0.5 attentional focus means that the agent has a 50% probability of revisiting the last sensorial state. Each one of the pragmatic games is performed using different attentional focus values: 0.0, 0.25, 0.50, and 0.75. The 0.0 value is equivalent to a random movement, whereas 1.0 was not used because it means an infinite loop between two sensing states. These attentional focus values are fixed during all the experiments.

5 Results

Experiments on plasticity showed that the networks evolved by the situated agents—and then their properties—depend on the game played and the epigenetic mechanism. They also showed that wiring is made in terms of experiences. First, the complexity of interactions between the agent and its environment was found relevant to evolve complex networks, relating degree distribution and sensing. Second, biological motivations affect the clustering coefficient of the obtained networks. Third, attentional focus affects the number of goals achieved and the amount of knowledge acquired by the agent.

5.1 Degree Distribution and Sensing

The possibility of obtaining a power law for the degree distribution is the fingerprint to distinguish whether a network is complex or not. This property reflects the character of having few highly connected nodes (hubs), and a lot of them few connected. This allows tolerance to random fails, but vulnerability if the failure affects a hub.

There is a substantial difference between unimodal and multimodal games. In the unimodal game (focusing) the resulting network is by no means complex, but in multimodal games (grasping and feeding games) a power law emerges (Fig. 2).

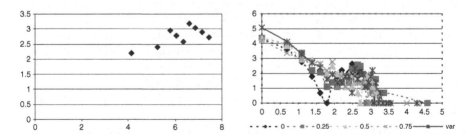

Fig. 2 Degree distribution for focusing game at left (*degree* × *frec*) and grasping game at right (ln *degree* × ln *frec*). The unimodal–multimodal character of the game affects the complexity of the resulting network

This is not a result of the implemented epigenetic mechanism, but of the richness of the interaction. The only difference between grasping and focusing games is the 1×1 moving hand around the world, absent in the focusing game. It is not only the complexity of the environment that matters, but the complexity of the interactions. To have enough rich networks, multimodality is required.

5.2 Clustering Coefficient and Biological Motivations

The clustering coefficient gives a measure of the possibility of being part of a local collective dynamics. In some way, it measures the integration of elements in a network. It is shown that the clustering coefficient in multimodal game is high when compared with a random graph (Fig. 3).

It is also shown that this measure depends on the mechanism itself and, in particular, on consideration of biological motivations (Fig. 4).

5.3 Goals, Acquired Knowledge, and Attentional Focus

The number of games played can be understood as the number of goals achieved by the agents. The experiments show that the rate of growth in the number of goals with time is similar for all the games. A lower focus, as expected, is associated with a higher probability to advance, resulting in more games played (Fig. 5).

However, this tendency is different when the amount of knowledge acquired is considered. As noted earlier, a fact is identified as two affective states connected by a labeled arc. The number of facts is a measure of the quantity of knowledge acquired. It depends on the focus value, but its effect varies with the game played.

In the unimodal game more goals and knowledge are attained by the agent for lower focus values. In the multimodal games the opposite effect is observed. This seems to be the source of the exploration/exploitation trade-off in learning agents. If the game is multimodal, the agent requires different behavior to achieve goals and acquire knowledge, but this does not hold in the unimodal game (Fig. 6).

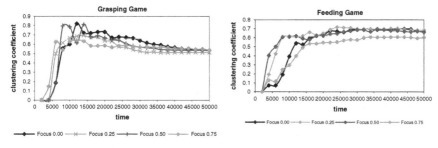

Fig. 3 Clustering coefficient in focusing game (left) and feeding game (right) is high when compared with an equivalent random graph

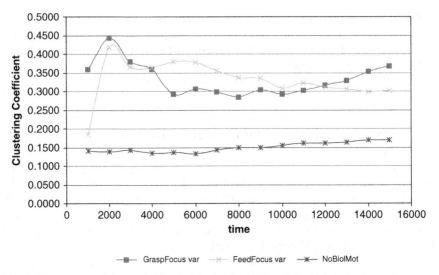

Fig. 4 Clustering coefficient and biological motivations. When biological motivations are not considered (NoBioMot) in the epigenetic mechanism to evolve the network, the clustering coefficient is very low

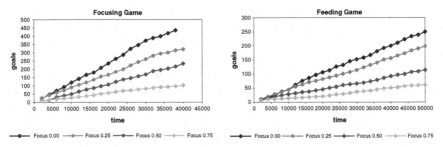

Fig. 5 The number of pragmatic games played (goals) by the agent in time has similar behavior when the focus is changed, both for focusing and feeding games

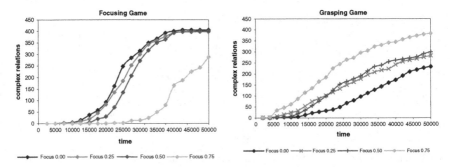

Fig. 6 The knowledge acquired depends on the game played and the focus value

6 Conclusions

We used pragmatic games as a methodology to study knowledge development in agents. The acquired knowledge is represented as an evolving network, processed by a mechanism emulating epigenesis, which is enacted by experiences. The acquired knowledge is complex in the sense that it relates spatial rules in the appropriate way. Nodes represent affective states (related to sensing states) and links are actuations relating affective states. The proposed epigenetic mechanism includes innate biological motivations and the incorporation of nodes and links in steps. Network analyses and measures are applied to the corpus of acquired knowledge.

In our experiments, the clustering coefficient is large (a small-world property) when compared with random graphs. This result is due to the proposed epigenetic mechanism, particularly because the innate biological motivations starting the process give way to initial hubs to evolve the network.

Knowledge networks in games involving multimodal agents exhibit power law distributions (a scale-free property), whereas the games played by our unimodal agents do not. This means that in our experiments complex learning arises independently of the complexity of the environment, but is dependent on the interactions the agent has with it. Connectivity distribution in our unimodal game is finite and well defined, no matter the size of the eye. If the hand is introduced, the number of states increases significantly, and a complex network emerges.

In order to observe how agent behavior might affect the acquired knowledge, a behavior modulator, called attentional focus, was introduced. If we consider the number of played games as the number of goals achieved by the agent, we observe that the focus value has the same impact for both unimodal and multimodal games, i.e., a lower focus value results in more achieved games. However, the number of facts incorporated in the network depends on the modality of the game. For the unimodal game, a lower focus value results in a larger number of facts, but for the multimodal games the inverse relation was observed. Thus, the modality of the game seems to be the source of the exploitation-exploration trade-off in learning agents.

The proposed epigenetic mechanism is suitable, in the sense that the topology of the generated networks representing the acquired knowledge evolves showing complex network properties. These results suggest that sapient agents must consider biological motivations in their epigenetic mechanisms and must be multimodal. The properties that characterize artificial agents emerge naturally from complex connectivity. For an artificial agent, complex topology represents the potential to exhibit complex functionality, i.e., the dynamics that becomes exploitation of the acquired knowledge.

Future work will consider cognitive autonomy, which enables the agent to adapt its behavior to maximize knowledge acquisition, so that the amount of acquired knowledge becomes a behavior modulator. The effect of the relationship between knowledge and behavior will be quantified and analyzed in terms of complex network properties.

References

Albert, R., Jeong, H., and Barabási, A-L. (1999). The diameter of the World Wide Web, *Nature*, 401, 130–131.

Albert, R., and Barabási, A-L. (2002). Statistical mechanics of complex networks, *Reviews of Modern Physics*, 74, 47.

Barabási, A-L., and Albert, R. (1999). Emergence of scaling in random networks, *Science*, 286, 509–512.

Barabási, A-L. (2002). *Linked: The New Science of Networks*, Perseus.

Barabási, A.-L., Jeong, H., Ravasz, R., Néda, Z., Vicsek, T., and Schubert, A. (2002). On the topology of the scientific collaboration networks, *Physica A*, 311, 590–614.

Barabási, A-L., and Bonabeau, E. (2003). Scale-Free Networks, *Scientific American*, 288, 60–69.

Batali, J., and Grundy, W.N. (1996) Modeling the evolution of motivation, *Evolutionary Computation* 4(3), 235–270.

Brooks, R.A. (1990). Elephants don't play chess, *Robotics and Autonomous Systems* 6(28), 3–15.

Brooks, R.A., Breazeal, C., Marjanovic, M., Scassellati, B., and Williamson, M. (1998). The cog project: Building a humanoid robot, *Computation for Metaphors, Analogy and Agents*, C. Nehaniv (ed.), Berlin, LNAI 1562, 52–87

Chialvo, D.R. (2004). Critical brain networks, *Physica A*, 340(4), 756–765, September.

Cohen, P. (2004). Small world networks key to memory, *New Scientist*, 182, p. 12.

Collier, J. (2000). Autonomy and process closure as the basis for functionality, *Annals of the New York Academy of Sciences*, J.L.R. Chandler and G. Van der Vijver (eds.), 901, 280–290, New York.

Drescher, D.L. (1991). *Made-Up Minds: A Constructivist Approach to Artificial Intelligence*, MIT Press, Cambridge, MA.

Eguiluz V.M., et al. (2005). Scale-free brain functional networks, *Physical Review. Letters*, 92, p. 018102.

Erdős, P., and Rényi, A. (1960). On the evolution of random graphs, Mathematics Institute Publication Hungarian Academy of Science, 5, 17–60.

Ferrer-i-Cancho R., and Sole, R.V., (2001) The small world of human language, *Proceedings of the Royal Society of London, Series* B, *Biological Sciences*, 268(1482), 2261–2265.

Foner, L. and Maes, P. (1994). Paying attention to what's important: Using Focus of attention to improve unsupervised learning, *The Third International Conference on the Simulation of Adaptive Behavior* (SAB94), pp. 256–265.

Franklin, S., and Graesser, A. (1997). Is it an agent, or just a program?, *Intelligent Agents III, LNAI* 1193, 21–36, Springer-Verlag.

Gazzaniga, M.S., et al.(2002). *Cognitive Neuroscience: The Biology of the Mind*, W.W. Norton, New York London.

Jeong H., et al. (2000). The large-scale organization of metabolic networks, *Nature*, 407, 651–654.

Lederberg, J. (2001). The meaning of epigenetics, *The Scientist* 15(18), 6.

Levenson, J.M., and Sweatt, D. (2005). Epigenetic mechanisms in memory formation, *Nature* 6, 109–119.

McIntyre, A., Kaplan, F. and Steels, L. (2002). Crucial factors in the origins of word-meaning. In: A. Wray, (ed.). *The Transition to Language*, Oxford, UK, Oxford University Press. pp. 252–271.

Milo, R., et al. (2002). Network motifs: Simple building blocks of complex networks, *Science* 298, 824–827.

Milo, R., et al. (2004). Superfamilies of evolved and designed networks, *Science* 303, 1538–1542.

Montague, P.R., and Dayan, P. (1998). Neurobiological modeling: Squeezing top down to meet bottom up, *A Companion to Cognitive Science*. W. Bechtel and G. Graham (eds.), Basil Blackwell, Oxford, UK pp. 526–542.

Mora-Basáñez, C.R. de la Gersherson, C., and García-Vega, V.A. (2004). Representation development and behavior modifiers, *Advances in Artificial Intelligence*: Iberamia 2004, Lecture Notes in Artificial Intelligence, 3315, 504–513, Berlin.

Newman, M.E.J. (2003). The structure and function of complex networks, *SIAM Review*, 45(2), 167–256.

Prince, C.G. (2002). Introduction: The Second International Workshop on Epigenetic Robotics, *Lund University Cognitive Studies* 94, Lund, Sweden.

Russell, S.J. , and Norvig, P. (1995). *Artificial Intelligence: A Modern Approach*, Prentice Hall, Enstlwood Clifts, NJ.

Russell, S.J., and Subramanian, D. (1995). Provably bounded-optimal agents, *Journal of Artificial Intelligence Research*, 2, 575–609, May.

Scheutz, M., (2001) The evolution of simple affective states in multi-agent environments, *Proceedings of AAAI Fall Symposium* 01, AAAI Press, USA.

Sheutz, M., and Sloman, A. (2001). Affect and agent control: Experiments with simple affective states, *Proceedings of IAT-01*, pages 200–209, World Scientific.

Skolicki, Z., and Arciszewski, T. (2003). Sapient agents—Seven approaches, *Proceedings of International Conference Integration of Knowledge Intensive Multi-Agent Systems: KIMAS'03: Modeling, Exploration, and Engineering*, Boston.

Smithers, T. (1992). Taking eliminative materialism seriously: A methodology for autonomous systems research, *toward a practice of autonomous systems: Proceedings of the First European Conference on Artificial Life*, F.J. Varela and P. Bourgine (eds.), MIT Press / Bradford Book, pp. 31–40.

Sole, R.V., et al. (2006). Language networks: Their structure, function and evolution, Santa Fe Institute Working Paper 05-12-042, Santa Fe, CA.

Sporns, O., and Chialvo, D.R. (2004). Organization, development and function of complex rain networks, *Trends in Cognitive Sciences*, 8, 418–425.

Steels, L., and Brooks, R. A. (1995). *The Artificial Life route to Artificial Intelligence: Building Situated embodied agents*, Lawrence Erlbaum Ass.

Steels, L. (1996a) Emergent behavior lexicons, *From Animals To Animats 4: Proceedings of the Fourth International Conference on Simulation of Adaptive Behavior, SAB'96. Complex Adaptive Systems*, pp. 562–567, MIT Press, Cambridge, MA.

Steels, L. (1996b). Self-organizing vocabularies, *Proceedings of Alife* V, C. Langton and T. Shimohara (eds), pages 179–184, Nara Japan.

Steels, L. (1997). Synthesising the origins of language and meaning using co-evolution, self-organisation and level formation, *Approaches to the Evolution of Language: Social and Cognitive Bases*, J. Hurford, C. Knight, and M. Studdert-Kennedy (eds.), Edinburgh University Press, UK.

Stojanov, G. (2001). Petitagé: A case study in developmental robotics, *Proceedings of the First International Workshop on Epigenetic Robotics: Modeling Cognitive Development in Robotic Systems, Lund University Cognitive Studies* 85, Lund, Sweden.

Watts, D., and Strogatz, S. (1998). Collective dynamics of "small-world" networks, *Nature*, 393, 440–442.

Watts, D. (1999). Small-worlds. *The Dynamics of Networks between Order and Randomness, Princeton Studies in Complexity*, Princeton University Press.

Wooldridge, M., and Jennings, N.R. (1995). Intelligent agents: Theory and practice, *The Knowledge Engineering Review*, 10(2), 115–152.

Ziemke, T. (2001). Are robots embodied?, *Proceedings of the First International Workshop on Epigenetic Robotics: Modeling Cognitive Development in Robotic Systems, Lund University Cognitive Studies* 85 Lund, Sweden.

Zlatev, J., and Balkenius, C. (2001). Introduction: Why 'epigenetic robotics?,' *Proceedings of the First International Workshop on Epigenetic Robotics: Modeling Cognitive Development in Robotic Systems*, Lund University Cognitive Studies, 85 pp 1–4 Lund, Sweden.

Sapience, Consciousness, and the Knowledge Instinct (Prolegomena to a Physical Theory)

Leonid I. Perlovsky

Abstract The chapter describes a mathematical theory of sapience and consciousness: higher mental abilities including abilities for concepts, emotions, instincts, understanding, imagination, intuition, beauty, and sublimity. The knowledge instinct drives our understanding of the world. Aesthetic emotions, our needs for beauty and sublimity, are related to the knowledge instinct. I briefly discuss neurobiological grounds as well as difficulties encountered since the 1950s by previous attempts at mathematical modeling of the mind. Dynamic logic, the mathematics of the knowledge instinct, is related to cognitive and philosophical discussions about the mind and sapience.

1 Introduction: Abilities of the Mind

The mind understands the world around it by relying on internal representations, the models of the world that were learned previously, an hour ago, earlier in life, in childhood, and, ultimately, on inborn genetic information. These internal models of the mind are related to Plato's ideas (Plato IV BC; Perlovsky 2001), Aristotelian forms (Aristotle IV BC; Perlovsky 1996a), the Kantian ability for understanding (Kant 1781; Perlovsky 2006a), Jungian archetypes (Jung 1934; Perlovsky 2001), and various mechanisms of concepts discussed in artificial intelligence, psychology, cognitive science, and neural networks (Grossberg 1982). Mind conjures up concept-models that correspond to objects and situations in the world; as a result, there appear phenomena, internal mind's perceptions (or representations, which could be conscious or unconscious to varying degrees). Concepts (say, a word "chair," written or spoken) are very different from objects (a chair one sits on). In our brains there are inborn structures that have been developed over hundreds of millions of years of evolution specifically to enable fast learning (in childhood) to combine a spoken, written, drawn, imagined, and real chair into a single concept-model. Let us note that the "real chair" is what is seen by our eyes, but also what is sensed as

L.I. Perlovsky
Harvard University Cambridge, MA, USA, Air Force Research Laboratory Sensors Directorate
e-mail: leonid.seas.harvard.edu

R.V. Mayorga, L.I. Perlovsky (eds.), *Toward Artificial Sapience,*
© Springer 2008

a "seat" by the sitting part of our body. Therefore chair is a bodily-sensed-spatio-thought concept. The process of comparing concept-models to objects around us is neither simple nor straightforward. Kant (1790) called the ability to find correspondence between concepts and objects judgment and identified this ability as the foundation for all higher spiritual abilities of our mind—or sapience.

Ability for concept-models was evolved during evolution to enhance survivability; it works together with other mechanisms developed for this purpose, primarily instincts and emotions. Instincts are like internal sensors that generate signals in neural networks to indicate the basic needs of an organism, say hunger (Piaget 2000). Connection of instincts and concepts is accomplished by emotions. In a usual conversation, "emotions" refer to a special type of behavior: agitation, higher voice pitch, bright eyes, but these are just displays of emotions. Emotions are evaluations—"good-bad." Evaluations not according to concepts of good and bad, but directly instinctive evaluations better characterized in terms of pleasure or pain. An emotion evaluates a degree to which a phenomenon (objects or a situation) satisfies our instinctual needs. Emotions are signals in neural pathways that carry information about object values from instinct-related brain areas to perceptual, cognitive, decision-making and behavior-generating areas. Emotions "mark" perceived phenomena with their values for instinct satisfaction. There are inborn as well as learned emotional responses. A mathematical description of the "marking" of concepts by emotions was first obtained by Grossberg and co-workers in the late 1980s, e.g., Grossberg and Levine (1987). Every instinct generates evaluative emotional signals indicating satisfaction or dissatisfaction of that instinct. Therefore emotions are called evaluative signals. These signals affect the process of comparing concept-models to objects around us (which explains why a hungry person "sees food all around"). So, instinctual needs affect our perception and cognition through emotions; and concept-models originally formed in evolution and culture are intended for survival and thus for instinct satisfaction. This intentionality of the mind has been a subject of much discussions and controversy (Searle 1992). Many emotions originate in ancient parts of the brain, relating us to primates and even to lower animals (Adelman 1987). Ability for concepts includes learning and recognition (i.e., creating and remembering models as well as recognizing objects and situations more or less corresponding to earlier learned models). The short description in this section did not touch on many of the mind's properties, a most important one being behavior. This chapter is primarily concerned with just one type of behavior—the behavior of learning and recognition.

The next section briefly reviews mathematical approaches to describing the mind proposed since the 1950s and discusses difficulties encountered along the way. Then I formulate a mathematical theory providing a foundation for an initial description of the mind abilities discussed earlier and extend it to consciousness and higher cognitive abilities, abstract concepts, and abilities for beauty and sublimity. Arguments are presented, as to why feelings of beautiful and sublime are inseparable aspects of sapience. Concluding sections discuss relationships between the theory and concepts of the mind that originated in multiple disciplines as well as future directions of experimental programs and theoretical development toward a physical theory of sapience.

2 Computational Intelligence Since the 1950s

Perception and cognition require the association of subsets of signals corresponding to objects with representations of objects in the mind (or in an algorithm). A mathematical description of this seemingly simple association-recognition-understanding process was difficult to develop. A number of difficulties encountered during the past 50 years were summarized under the notion of combinatorial complexity (CC) (Perlovsky 1998). CC refers to multiple combinations of various elements in a complex system; e.g., recognition of a scene often requires concurrent recognition of its multiple elements, which might be encountered in various combinations. CC is prohibitive because the number of combinations is very large: for instance, consider 100 elements (not too large a number); the number of combinations of 100 elements is 100^{100}, exceeding the number of all elementary particle events in the life of the universe; no computer would ever be able to compute that many combinations.

In self-learning pattern recognition and classification research in the 1960s the problem was named "the curse of dimensionality" (Bellman 1961). Adaptive algorithms and neural networks, it seemed, could learn solutions to any problem 'on their own,' if provided with a sufficient number of training examples. It turned out that the required number of training examples for self-learning required training using objects *in context*, *in combination* with other objects, and therefore was often combinatorially large. Self-learning approaches encountered *CC of learning requirements*.

Rule-based artificial intelligence was proposed in the 1970s to solve the problem of learning complexity (Minsky 1975; Winston 1984). An initial idea was that rules would capture the required knowledge and eliminate the need for learning. However, in the presence of variability, the number of rules grew; rules became contingent on other rules; combinations of rules had to be considered; rule systems encountered *CC of rules*.

Model-based systems were proposed in the 1980s to combine the advantages of self-learning and rule systems. The knowledge was to be encapsulated in models, whereas unknown aspects of particular situations were to be learned by fitting model parameters (Singer et al. 1974). Fitting models to data required selecting data subsets corresponding to various models. The number of subsets, however, is combinatorially large. A general algorithm for fitting models to the data, multiple hypothesis testing (Perlovsky et al. 1998) is known to face CC of computations. Model-based approaches encountered *computational CC* (N and NP complete algorithms).

It turned out that CC was related to the type of logic underlying various algorithms (Perlovsky 1996a). Formal logic is based on the "law of the excluded middle," according to which every statement is either true or false and there is nothing in between. Therefore, algorithms based on formal logic have to evaluate every little variation in data or internal representations as a separate logical statement (hypothesis); a large number of combinations of these variations causes CC. In fact, CC of algorithms based on logic is related to Gödel theory, a manifestation of the inconsistency of logic in finite systems (Perlovsky 1996b). Multivalued logic and fuzzy logic were proposed to overcome limitations related to the law of the excluded third (Kecman 2001). Yet the mathematics of multivalued logic is no different in principle from formal logic: "excluded third" is substituted by "excluded $n+1$." Fuzzy logic encountered a difficulty related to the degree of fuzziness. If too much fuzziness is specified, the solution does not achieve the necessary accuracy; if too little, becomes similar to formal logic. Complex systems require different degrees of fuzziness in various elements of system operations. Searching for the appropriate degrees of fuzziness among combinations of elements again would lead to CC. Is logic still possible after Gödel? Bruno Marchal (2005) reviewed the contemporary state of this field and it appears that logic after Gödel is much more complicated and much less logical than was assumed by the founders of artificial intelligence. Moreover, CC is still unsolved within logic.

Various manifestations of CC are all related to formal logic and Gödel theory. Rule systems rely on formal logic in a most direct way. Self-learning algorithms and neural networks rely on logic in their training or learning procedures: every training example is treated as a separate logical statement. Fuzzy logic systems rely on logic for setting degrees of fuzziness. CC of mathematical approaches to the mind is related to the fundamental inconsistency of logic.

3 Mechanisms of the Mind and the Knowledge Instinct

Although logic does not work, the mind does work. Let us turn to the mechanisms of the mind discussed in psychology, philosophy, cognitive science, and neurobiology. Possibly, we will find inspiration for developing mathematical and physical theories of the mind. The main mechanisms of the mind include instincts, concepts, emotions, and behavior, and each can be described mathematically. Among the mind's higher abilities, the most directly accessible to consciousness are concepts. Concepts are like internal models of the objects and situations in the world. This analogy is quite literal; e.g., during visual perception of an object, a concept-models in our memory projects an image onto the visual cortex, which is matched there to an image projected from the retina (this simplified description will be refined later).

Instincts emerged as survival mechanisms long before concepts. Grossberg and Levine (1987) separated instincts as internal sensors indicating the basic needs from instinctual behavior, which should be described by appropriate mechanisms. Accordingly, I use word instincts to describe mechanisms of internal sensors: e.g., when blood sugar goes below a certain level an instinct "tells us" to eat. Such separation of instinct as internal sensor from instinctual behavior helps to explain many cognitive functions.

Instinctual needs are conveyed to conceptual and decision-making centers of the brain by emotional neural signals. Whereas in colloquial usage, emotions are often understood as facial expressions, higher voice pitch, or exaggerated gesticulation, these are outward signs of emotions, serving for communication. A more fundamental role of emotions within the mind system is that emotional signals evaluate concepts for the purpose of instinct satisfaction (Grossberg and Levine 1987). As discussed in the next section, this emotional mechanism is crucial for breaking out of the "vicious cizcle" of combinatorial complexity.

An important aspect of our minds is that concept-models always have to be adapted. The same object is never same: distance, angles, lighting, and other objects around always change. Therefore, concept-models always have to be adapted to the concrete conditions around us. An inevitable conclusion from mathematical analysis is that humans and higher animals have a special instinct responsible for cognition. In thousands of publications describing adaptive algorithms, there is always some quantity-structure within the algorithm, that measures a degree of correspondence between the models and the world; this correspondence is maximized.

Clearly, humans and animals engage in exploratory behavior, even when basic bodily needs, like eating, are satisfied. Biologists and psychologists discussed various aspects of this behavior. David Berlyne (1960, 1973) discussed curiosity in this regard; Leon Festinger (1957) introduced the notion of cognitive dissonance and described many experiments on the drive of humans to reduce dissonance. Until recently, however, it was not mentioned among basic instincts on a par with the instincts for food and procreation. The reasons were that it was difficult to define and that its fundamental nature was not obvious. The fundamental nature of this mechanism is related to the fact that our knowledge always has to be modified to fit the current situation. Knowledge is not just a static state; it is rather in a constant process of adaptation and learning. Without adaptation of concept-models we will not be able to understand the ever-changing surrounding world. We will not be able to orient ourselves or satisfy any of our bodily instincts. Therefore, we have an inborn need, a drive, an instinct to improve our knowledge, which I call *the knowledge instinct*.

Evaluating satisfaction or dissatisfaction of the knowledge instinct involves emotional signals that are not directly related to bodily needs. Therefore, they are spiritual or aesthetic emotions. I would like to emphasize that aesthetic emotions are not peculiar to the perception of art; they are inseparable from every act of perception and cognition. The mind involves a hierarchy of multiple levels of concept-models, from simple perceptual elements (like edges or moving dots), to concept-models of objects, to relationships among objects, to complex scenes, and up the hierarchy... toward the concept-models of the meaning of life and the purpose of our existence. The ability to perceive beauty is related to the highest levels of this hierarchy. The tremendous complexity of the mind is due to the hierarchy, yet a few basic principles explain the fundamental mechanisms of the mind at every level of the hierarchy.

4 Modeling Field Theory and Dynamic Logic

Modeling field theory (MFT) is a neural architecture mathematically implementing mechanisms of the mind discussed above (Perlovsky 2001). MFT is a multilevel, heterohierarchical system. The mind is not a strict hierarchy; there are multiple feedback connections among nearby levels; hence the term heterohierarchy. At each level in MFT there are concept-models encapsulating the mind's knowledge, which generate so-called top-down neural signals, interacting with input bottom-up signals. These interactions are governed by the knowledge instinct, which drives concept-models learning, adaptation, and formation of new concept-models for better correspondence to the input signals.

We enumerate neurons at a given hierarchical level, by index $n = 1, \ldots, N$. These neurons receive bottom-up input signals, $\mathbf{X}(n)$, from lower levels in the processing hierarchy. $\mathbf{X}(n)$ is a field of bottom-up neuronal synapse activations, coming from neurons at a lower level. MFT describes each neuron activation as a set of numbers, $\mathbf{X}(n) = \{X_d(n), d = 1, \ldots, D\}$. Top-down, or priming signals to these neurons are sent by concept-models, $\mathbf{M}_h(\mathbf{S}_h, n)$; we enumerate models by index $h = 1, \ldots, h$. Each model is characterized by its parameters, $\mathbf{S}_h = \{S_h^a, a = 1, \ldots, A\}$. Models *represent* signals in the following way: Say, signal $\mathbf{X}(n)$ is coming from sensory neurons activated by object h, characterized by parameters $\mathbf{S}_h$. Model $\mathbf{M}_h(\mathbf{S}_h, n)$ predicts a value $\mathbf{X}(n)$ of a signal at neuron n. For example, during visual perception, a neuron n in the visual cortex receives a signal $\mathbf{X}(n)$ from the retina and a priming signal $\mathbf{M}_h(\mathbf{S}_h, n)$ from an object concept-models h. A neuron n is activated if both a bottom-up signal from lower-level input and top-down priming signal are strong. Various models compete for evidence in the bottom-up signals, while adapting their parameters for a better match as described below. This is a simplified description of perception. The MFT premise is that the same laws describe the basic interaction dynamics at each level. Perception of minute features or everyday objects and cognition of complex abstract concepts are due to the same mechanism, described below.

Learning is driven by the knowledge instinct. Mathematically, it increases a similarity measure between the sets of models (knowledge) and bottom-up neural signals, $L(\{\mathbf{X}\}, \{\mathbf{M}\})$. The similarity measure is a function of model parameters and associations between the input bottom-up signals and top-down concept-models signals. For concreteness I refer here to an object perception using a simplified terminology, as if perception of objects in retinal signals occurs at a single level.

In constructing a mathematical description of the similarity measure, it is important to acknowledge two principles (which are almost obvious). First, the visual field content is unknown before perception occurred and, second, it may contain any of a number of objects. Important information might be contained in any bottom-up signal; therefore, the similarity measure is constructed so that it accounts for all bottom-up signals, $\mathbf{X}(n)$,

$$L(\{\mathbf{X}\}, \{\mathbf{M}\}) = \prod_{n \in N} l(\mathbf{X}(n)). \tag{1}$$

This expression contains a product of partial similarities, $l(\mathbf{X}(n))$, over all bottom-up signals; therefore it forces the mind to account for every signal (if even one term in the product is zero, the product is zero, the similarity is low, and the knowledge instinct is not satisfied); this is a reflection of the first principle. Second, before perception occurs, the mind does not know which object gave rise to a signal from a particular retinal neuron. Therefore a partial similarity measure is constructed so that it treats each model as an alternative (a sum over models) for each input neuron signal. Its constituent elements are conditional partial similarities between signal $\mathbf{X}(n)$ and model $\mathbf{M}_h$, $l(\mathbf{X}(n)|h)$. This measure is "conditional" on object h being present; therefore, when combining these quantities into the overall similarity measure, L, they are multiplied by $r(h)$, which represents a probabilistic measure of object h actually being present. Combining these elements with the two principles noted above, one constructs a similarity measure as follows:

$$L(\{\mathbf{X}\}, \{\mathbf{M}\}) = \prod_{n \in N} \sum_{h \in H} r(h) \, l(\mathbf{X}(n)|h). \tag{2}$$

The structure of (2) follows standard principles of probability theory: a summation is taken over alternatives, h, and various pieces of evidence, n, are multiplied. This expression is not necessarily a probability, but it has a probabilistic structure. If learning is successful, it approximates a probabilistic description and leads to near-optimal Bayesian decisions. The name "conditional partial similarity" for $l(\mathbf{X}(n)|h)$ [or simply $l(n|h)$] follows the probabilistic terminology. If learning is successful, $l(n|h)$ becomes a conditional probability density function (pdf), a probabilistic measure that the signal in neuron n originated from object h. Then L is a total likelihood of observing signals $\{\mathbf{X}(n)\}$ coming from objects described by models $\{\mathbf{M}_h\}$. Coefficients $r(h)$, called priors in probability theory, contain preliminary biases or expectations. Expected objects h have relatively high $r(h)$ values; their true values are usually unknown and should be learned, like other parameters $\mathbf{S}_h$. However, in general, $l(n|h)$ are not pdfs, but fuzzy measures of signal $\mathbf{X}(n)$ belonging to object h.

We note that in probability theory, a product of probabilities usually assumes that evidence is independent. Expression (2) contains a product over n, but it does not assume independence among the various signals $\mathbf{X}(n)$. There is dependence among signals owing to models: each model $\mathbf{M}_h(\mathbf{S}_h, n)$ predicts expected signal values in many neurons n.

During the learning process, concept-models are constantly modified. Here we consider a case in which functional forms of models, $\mathbf{M}_h(\mathbf{S}_h, n)$, are all fixed and learning adaptation involves only model parameters, $\mathbf{S}_h$. More complicated structural learning of models is considered in Perlovsky (2004, 2006b). From time to time a system forms a new concept, while retaining an old one as well. Alternatively, old concepts are sometimes merged or eliminated, which requires a modification of the similarity measure (2), the reason being that more models always result in a better fit between the models and the data. This is a well-known problem, which is addressed by reducing similarity (2) using a "skeptic penalty function," $p(N, M)$, which grows with the number of models M. For example, an asymptotically unbiased maximum likelihood estimation leads to multiplicative $p(N, M) = \exp(-N_{\text{par}}/2)$, where N_{par} is the total number of adaptive parameters in all models (Perlovsky 2001).

The learning process consists of estimating model parameters $\mathbf{S}$ and associating signals with concepts by maximizing the similarity (2). Note that all possible combinations of signals and models are accounted for in expression (2). This can be seen by expanding a sum in (2) and multiplying all the terms, which would result in H^N items, a huge number. This is the number of combinations between all signals (N) and all models (H). Here is the source of CC of many algorithms discussed in the previous section.

Fuzzy dynamic logic (DL) solves this problem without CC (Perlovsky 2006c). The crucial aspect of DL is matching vagueness or fuzziness of similarity measures to the uncertainty of knowledge of the model parameters. Initially, parameter values are not known, and uncertainty of models is high, as is the fuzziness of the similarity measures. In the process of learning, models become more accurate, the similarity measure becomes more crisp, and the value of the similarity increases. This is the mechanism of dynamic logic. Mathematically it is described as follows: First, assign any values to unknown parameters, $\{S_h\}$. Then, compute association variables $f(h|n)$,

$$f(h|n) = r(h)\, l(\mathbf{X}(n)|h) / \sum_{h' \in H} r(h')\, l(\mathbf{X}(n)|h'). \tag{3}$$

This looks like the Bayes formula for a posteriori probabilities; if the $l(n|h)$ in the result of learning become conditional likelihoods, the $f(h|n)$ become Bayesian probabilities for signal n originating from object h. In general, $f(h|n)$ can be interpreted as fuzzy class membership functions. The rest of the dynamic logic operations are defined as follows:

$$df(h|n)/dt = f(h|n) \sum_{h' \in H} [\delta_{hh'} - f(h'|n)] \cdot [\partial \ln l(n|h')/\partial \mathbf{M}_{h'}] \partial \mathbf{M}_{h'}/\partial \mathbf{S}_{h'} \cdot d\mathbf{S}_{h'}/dt,$$
$$\tag{4}$$

where

$$d\mathbf{S}_h/dt = \sum_{n \in N} f(h|n)[\partial \ln l(n|h)/\partial \mathbf{M}_h] \partial \mathbf{M}_h/\partial \mathbf{S}_h, \tag{5}$$

$$\delta_{hh'} = 1 \text{ if } h = h', 0 \text{ otherwise}. \tag{6}$$

Parameter t is the time of the internal dynamics of the MF system (a number of dynamic logic iterations). Gaussian shape functions can often be used for conditional partial similarities,

$$l(n|h) = G(\mathbf{X}(n)|\mathbf{M}_h(\mathbf{S}_h, n), \mathbf{C}_h). \tag{7}$$

Here G is a Gaussian function with mean $\mathbf{M}_h$ and covariance matrix $\mathbf{C}_h$. Note that *a* Gaussian assumption, which assumes that the signal distribution is Gaussian, is often used in statistics; This is not the case in (7), where the signal is not assumed to be Gaussian. Equation (7) is valid if *deviations* between the model $\mathbf{M}$ and signal

$\mathbf{X}$ are Gaussian; these deviations are usually due to many random causes and, therefore, Gaussian. If there is no information about functional shapes of conditional partial similarities, (7) is still a good choice, as it is not a limiting assumption: a weighted sum of Gaussians in (2) can approximate any positive function, like similarity.

Covariance matrices, $\mathbf{C}_h$, in (7) are estimated like other unknown parameters. Their initial values should be large, corresponding to uncertainty in knowledge of models, $\mathbf{M}_h$. As parameter values and models improve, covariances are reduced to intrinsic differences between models and signals (due to sensor errors or model inaccuracies). As covariances get smaller, similarities get crisper, closer to delta functions; association variables (3) get closer to crisp $\{0, 1\}$ values, and DL solutions converge to crisp logic. This process of concurrent parameter improvement and convergence of similarity to a crisp logical function is an essential part of DL, the mechanism that combines fuzzy and crisp logic. The dynamic evolution of fuzziness from large to small is the reason for the name "dynamic logic."

Theorem 1. *Equations (3) through (6) define a convergent dynamic MF system with stationary states defined by* $\max_{\{Sh\}} L$.

This theorem was proved in Perlovsky (2006c). It follows that the stationary states of an MF system are the maximum similarity states satisfying the knowledge instinct. When partial similarities are specified as probability density functions (pdf), or likelihoods, the stationary values of parameters $\{\mathbf{S}_h\}$ are asymptotically unbiased and efficient estimates of these parameters (Cramer 1946). A computational complexity of the MF method is linear in N.

The dynamic logic is therefore a convergent process. It converges to the maximum of similarity, and thus satisfies the knowledge instinct. If likelihood is used as similarity, parameter values are estimated efficiently (i.e., in most cases, parameters cannot be better learned using any other procedure). Moreover, as part of the above theorem, it is proven that the similarity measure increases at each iteration. A psychological interpretation is that the knowledge instinct is satisfied at each step: a modeling field system with dynamic logic *enjoys* learning.

Here we illustrate operations of dynamic logic using an example of tracking targets below noise, which can be an exceedingly complex problem. A single scan does not contain enough information for detection. If a target signal is below noise, it cannot be detected in a single scan; one must combine information from multiple scans. Detection should be performed concurrently with tracking, using several radar scans. A standard approach for solving this kind of problem, which has already been mentioned, is multiple hypotheses tracking (Perlovsky et al. 1998). Since a large number of combinations of subsets and models should be searched, one faces the problem of combinatorial complexity.

Figure 1 illustrates detecting and tracking targets below noise; in this case six scans were used concurrently for detection and tracking and a predetection threshold was set so that only about 500 points are to be considered in the six scans. Figure 1a

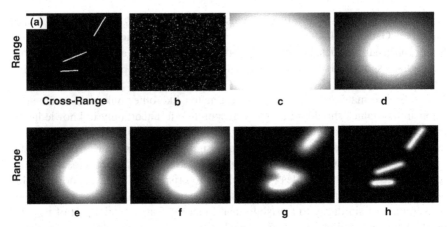

Fig. 1 Detection and tracking targets below clutter: (a) true track positions in 0.5 km × 0.5 km data set; (b) actual data available for detection and tracking (signal is below clutter, signal-to-clutter ratio is about −2 dB for amplitude and −3 dB for Doppler; six scans are shown on top of one other). Dynamic logic operation: (c) an initial fuzzy model, the fuzziness corresponding to the uncertainty of knowledge; (d) to (h) show increasingly improved models at various iterations (total of 20 iterations). Between (c) and (d) the algorithm fits the data with one model and uncertainty is somewhat reduced. There are two *types* of models: one uniform model describing clutter (not shown), and linear track models with large uncertainty; the number of track models, locations, and velocities are estimated from the data. Between (d) and (e) the algorithm tried to fit the data with more than one track model and decided that it needs two models to 'understand' the content of the data. Fitting with two tracks continues till (f); between (f) and (g) a third track is added. Iterations stopped at (h), when similarity stopped increasing. Detected tracks closely correspond to the truth (a). Complexity of this solution is low, about 10^6 operations. Solving this problem by multiple hypothesis tracking would take about 10^{1500} operations, a prohibitive complexity

shows true track positions in 0.5 km × 0.5 km data set; Fig. 1b shows the actual data available for detection and tracking (the signal is below clutter; the signal-to-clutter ratio is about −2 dB for amplitude and −3 dB for Doppler; the six scans are shown on top of each other. The following figures (c) through (h) illustrate operations of dynamic logic: (c) an initial fuzzy model, the fuzziness corresponding to the uncertainty of knowledge; (d) to (h) increasingly improved models at various iterations (a total of 20 iterations). Between (c) and (d) the algorithm fits the data with one model, and uncertainty is somewhat reduced. There are two types of models: one uniform model describing clutter (not shown), and linear track models with large uncertainty; the number of track models, locations, and velocities are unknown and are estimated from the data. Between (d) and (e) the algorithm tried to fit the data with more than one track model and decided that it needs two models to 'understand' the content of the data. Fitting with two tracks continues till (f); between (f) and (g) a third track is added. Iterations stopped at (h), when similarity stopped increasing. Detected tracks closely correspond to the truth (a). Complexity of this solution is low, about 10^6 operations. Solving this problem by multiple hypothesis tracking with exhaustive search would take about $M^N = 10^{1500}$ operations, a prohibitively large number, exceeding the number of all the events in the universe.

5 Hierarchy, Differentiation, and Synthesis

I have already described a single processing level in a hierarchical MFT system. At each level of a hierarchy there are input signals from lower levels, models, similarity measures, Eq. (2); emotions, which are changes in similarity, Eq. (2); and actions. Actions include adaptation, behavior satisfying the knowledge instinct—maximization of similarity, Eqs. (3) through (6). An input to each level is a set of signals $\mathbf{X}(n)$ or, in neural terminology, an input field of neuronal activations. The results of signal processing at a given level are activated models, or concepts h recognized in the input signals n. These models along with the corresponding instinctual signals and emotions may activate behavioral models and generate behavior at this level.

The activated models initiate other actions. They serve as input signals to the next processing level, where more general concept-models are recognized or created. Output signals from a given level, serving as input to the next level, could be model activation signals, a_h, defined as

$$a_h = \sum_{n \in N} f(h|n). \tag{8}$$

The hierarchical MF system is illustrated in Fig. 2. Within the hierarchy of the mind, each concept-models finds its "mental" meaning and purpose at a higher level (in addition to other purposes). For example, consider a concept-models "plate." It has a "behavioral" purpose of using a plate, say, for eating (if this is required by the body), which is the "bodily" purpose at the same hierarchical level. In addition, it has a "purely mental" purpose at a higher level in the hierarchy, a purpose of helping to recognize a more general concept, say of a "dining hall," which model contains many plates.

Models at higher levels in the hierarchy are more general than models at lower levels. For example, at the very bottom of the hierarchy, if we consider the vision system, models correspond (roughly speaking) to retinal ganglion cells and perform similar functions; they detect simple features in the visual field. At higher levels, models correspond to functions performed at V1 and higher up in the visual cortex, i.e., detection of more complex features, such as contrast edges, their directions, elementary moves, objects, etc. Visual hierarchical structures and models have been studied in detail (Grossberg 1982; Zeki 1993). At still higher cognitive levels, models correspond to relationships among objects, to situations, and relationships among situations, etc. Still higher up are even more general models of complex cultural notions and relationships, like family, love, and friendship, and abstract concepts, like law, rationality, etc. The contents of these models correspond to the cultural wealth of knowledge, including the writings of Shakespeare and Tolstoy. Mechanisms of the development of these models are reviewed later. At the top of the hierarchy of the mind, according to Kantian analysis (Kant 1790, 1798), are models of the meaning and purpose of our existence, unifying our knowledge, and the corresponding behavioral models aimed at achieving this meaning.

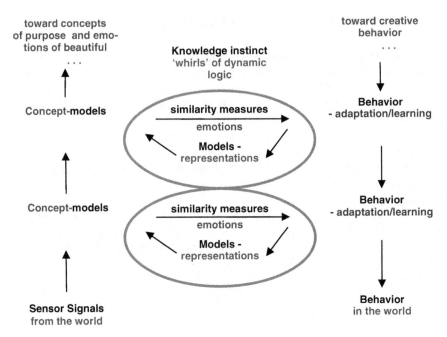

toward concepts
of purpose and emo-
tions of beautiful
. . .

Concept-**models**

Concept-**models**

Sensor Signals
from the world

Knowledge instinct
'whirls' of dynamic
logic

similarity measures
emotions
Models -
representations

similarity measures
emotions
Models -
representations

toward creative
behavior
. . .

Behavior
- adaptation/learning

Behavior
- adaptation/learning

Behavior
in the world

Fig. 2 Hierarchical MF system. At each level of a hierarchy there are concept-models, similarity measures/emotions, and actions (including adaptation, maximizing the knowledge instinct/similarity). High levels of partial similarity measures correspond to concepts recognized at a given level. Concept activations are output signals at this level and they become input signals to the next level, propagating knowledge up the hierarchy

Two aspects of the knowledge instinct are differentiation and synthesis. Differentiation or creation of more diverse concept-models with more concrete meanings was described in previous sections. Another aspect of the knowledge instinct is synthesis, creating a unified whole of the diversity of knowledge and meanings. Each model finds its more abstract, more general meaning at higher levels of the hierarchy. So each object model finds its more general meanings in situation concepts, where the object may occur. The higher up the hierarchy the more abstract and general the concept-models. These more general models are usually more fuzzy and less concrete than object models. One reason is that abstract concept-models cannot be directly perceived in the world, unlike object models, which can be matched to direct sensory perceptions. One can obtain an illustration of vagueness of abstract concept-models by closing one's eyes and imagining a familiar object, say a chair. An imagined chair is usually vague as compared to a perception of an actual chair in front of our eyes. More concrete object models are more accessible by consciousness; they are more amenable to conscious manipulations than abstract, fuzzy, less conscious models higher in the hierarchy.

An important aspect of synthesis is our symbolic ability, an ability to use language for designation and description of abstract concepts. Symbolic ability as described by MFT is considered elsewhere (Perlovsky 2006a,b).

6 Consciousness and Sapience

Elementary processes of perception and cognition are described mathematically in this chapter by Eqs. (3–6); these processes maximize knowledge. Knowledge is measured by the similarity between concept-models and the world. In these processes a large number of concept-models compete for incoming signals, models are modified and new ones are formed, and, eventually, connections are established between signal subsets on the one hand, and concept-models on the other. Perception refers to processes in which the input signals come from sensory organs and concept-models correspond to objects in the surrounding world. Cognition refers to higher levels in the hierarchy where the input signals are activation signals from concepts cognized (activated) at lower levels, whereas concept-models are more complex, abstract, and correspond to situations and relationships among lower-level concepts.

Perception and cognition are described by dynamic logic. Their salient mathematical property is a correspondence between uncertainty in models and vagueness-fuzziness in associations $f(h|n)$. During perception, as long as model parameters do not correspond to actual objects, there is no match between models and signals; many models match many objects poorly, and associations remain fuzzy. Eventually, one model (h') wins a competition for a subset $\{n'\}$ of input signals $\mathbf{X}(n)$, when parameter values match object properties; $f(h'|n)$ values become close to 1 for $n \in \{n'\}$ and 0 for $n \notin \{n'\}$. Upon convergence, the entire set of input signals $\{n\}$ is divided into subsets, each associated with one object model. Initial fuzzy concepts become crisp, approximately obeying formal logic. The general mathematical laws of perception, cognition, and high-level abstract thinking are similar.

The dynamic aspect of the working of the mind, described by dynamic logic, was first given by Aristotle (IV BC), who described thinking as a learning process in which an a priori form-as-potentiality (fuzzy model) meets matter (sensory signals) and becomes a form-as-actuality (a crisp concept of the mind). He pointed out an important aspect of dynamic logic—reduction of fuzziness during learning: Form-potentialities are fuzzy (do not obey logic), whereas form-actualities are logical. Logic is not the basic mechanism of the working of the mind, but an approximate result of the mind working according to dynamic logic.

The three famous volumes by Kant, *Critique of Pure Reason, Critique of Judgment*, and *Critique of Practical Reason* (Kant 1781; 1788; 1790) describe the structure of the mind similarly to MFT. Pure reason or the faculty of understanding contains concept-models. The faculty of judgment, or emotions, establishes correspondences between models and data about the world acquired by sensory organs (in Kant's terminology, between general concepts and individual events). Practical reason contains models of behavior. Kant was the first to recognize that emotions are an inseparable part of cognition. However, he missed the dynamic aspect of thinking, a pervading need for adaptation and considered concepts as given a priori. The knowledge instinct is the only missing link in Kantian theory.

Thinking involves a number of subprocesses and attributes, some conscious and others unconscious. According to Carpenter and Grossberg (1987) every recognition and concept formation process involves a "resonance" between bottom-up and top-down signals. We are conscious only of the resonant state of models. In MFT, at every level in the hierarchy, the afferent signals are represented by the input signal field $\mathbf{X}$ and the efferent signals are represented by the modeling field signals $\mathbf{M}_h$; resonances correspond to high-similarity measures $l(n|h)$ for some subsets of $\{n\}$ that are "recognized" as concepts (or objects) h. This mechanism, leading to the resonances Eqs. (3–6), is a thought process in which subsets of signals corresponding to objects or situations are understood as concepts; signals acquire meanings and become accessible by consciousness.

Why is there consciousness? Why would a feature like consciousness appear in the process of evolution? The answer to this question contains no mystery: consciousness directs the will and results in a better adaptation for survival. In simple situations, when only minimal adaptation is required, an instinct directly wired to action is sufficient, and unconscious processes can efficiently allocate resources and will. However, in complex situations, when adaptation is complicated, various bodily instincts might contradict one another. Undifferentiated unconscious psychic functions result in ambivalence and ambitendency; every position entails its own negation, leading to an inhibition. This inhibition cannot be resolved by an unconscious that does not differentiate among alternatives. Direction is impossible without differentiated conscious understanding. Consciousness is needed to resolve an instinctual impasse by suppressing some processes and allocating power to others. By differentiating alternatives, consciousness can direct a psychological function to a goal.

Most organism functioning is not accessible to consciousness; blood flow, breathing, workings of heart and stomach are unconscious, at least as long as they work appropriately. The same is true about most of the processes in the brain and mind. We are not conscious of neural firings, or fuzzy models competing for evidence in retinal signals, etc. We become conscious of concepts only during resonance, when a concept model matches bottom-up signals and becomes crisp. To put it more accurately, crisper models are more accessible by consciousness. Taylor (2005) emphasizes that consciousness requires more than a resonance. He relates consciousness to the mind being a control mechanism of the mind and body. Part of this mechanism is a prediction model. When this model predictions differ from sensory observations, the difference may reach a resonant state, of which we become consciousness. In evolution and in our personal psychic functioning the goal is to increase consciousness. But this is largely unconscious, because our direct knowledge of ourselves is limited to consciousness. This fact creates a lot of confusion about consciousness.

A detailed, scientific analysis of consciousness has proven difficult. For a long time it seemed obvious that consciousness completely pervades our entire mental life, or at least its main aspects. Now we know that this idea is wrong, and the main reason for this misconception has been analyzed and understood: We are conscious only about what we are conscious of, and it is extremely difficult to notice anything else.

Jaynes (1976) noted the following misconceptions about consciousness: consciousness is nothing but a property of matter, or a property of living things, or a property of neural systems. These three 'explanations' attempted to dismiss consciousness as an epiphenomenon, an unimportant quality of something else. They are useless because the problem is in *explaining* the relationships of conscious-ness to matter, to life, and to neural systems. These dismissals of consciousness are not very different from saying that there is no consciousness; but, of course, this statement refutes itself. (If somebody makes such a statement unconsciously, there is no point of discussing it.) A dualistic position is that consciousness belongs to the world of ideas and has nothing to do with the world of matter. But the scien-tific problem *is* in explaining consciousness as a natural science phenomenon, i.e., to relate consciousness and the material world. Searle (1992) suggested that any explanation of consciousness has to account for it being real and based on physical mechanisms in the brain. Among the properties of consciousness requiring expla-nation he listed unity and intentionality. (We perceive our consciousness as being *unified* in the space of our perceptions and in the time of our life; consciousness is about something; this 'about' points to its *intentionality*.)

Searle (1997) reviewed recent attempts to explain consciousness and came to the conclusion that little progress was made during the 1990s. Penrose (1994) sug-gested that consciousness cannot be explained by known physical laws of matter. His arguments descend from Gödel's proofs of the inconsistency and incomplete-ness of logic. However, as I have already mentioned, this only proves that the mind is not a system of logical rules (Perlovsky 1996b).

Roughly speaking, there are three conscious/unconscious levels of psychic con-tents: (1) contents that can be recalled and made conscious voluntarily (memories); (2) contents that are not under voluntary control, which we know about because they spontaneously irrupt into consciousness; and (3) contents inaccessible to con-sciousness, which we know about through scientific deduction. But consciousness is not a simple phenomenon; it is a complicated differentiated process. Jung (1934) differentiated four types of consciousness related to experiences of feelings (emo-tions), thoughts (concepts), sensations, and intuitions. In addition to these four psy-chic functions, consciousness is characterized by attitude: introverted, concentrated mainly on the inner experience, or extroverted, concentrated mainly on the outer experience. Interplay of various conscious and unconscious levels of psychic func-tions and attitudes results in a number of types of consciousness; interactions of these types with individual memories and experiences make consciousness depen-dent on the entire individual experience producing variability among individuals. An idea that better differentiated, crisper concept-models are more conscious is close to Jung's views. Mechanisms of other types of consciousness are less understood and their mathematical descriptions belong to future. Future research should also address emergence in evolution of different types of consciousness, elaborating on Jungian ideas.

In modeling field theory properties of consciousness are explained as being due to a special model, closely related to what psychologists call ego or self. Conscious-ness, to a significant extent, coincides with the conscious part of these archetype-models. A conscious part of self belongs to ego, but not everything within ego (as defined by Freud) is conscious. Individuality as a total character distinguishing one individual from others is a main characteristic of Ego. Not all aspects of individuality are conscious, so the relationships among the models discussed can be summarized to some extent, as:

Consciousness $\in$ Individuality $\in$ Ego $\in$ Self $\in$ Psyche.

Consciousness-model is a subject of free will; it possesses, controls, and directs free will. This model accesses conscious parts of other models. Among properties of consciousness discussed by Searle, which are explained by the properties of the consciousness model are the following.

Totality and undividedness of consciousness are important adaptive properties needed to concentrate power on the most important goal at every moment. This is illustrated, e.g., by clinical cases of divided consciousness and multiple personalities, resulting in maladaptation up to a complete loss of functionality. Simple consciousness operates with relatively few concepts. Humans need more differentiation for selecting more specific goals in more a complex environment. The scientific quest is to explain these opposing tendencies of consciousness: how does consciousness pursue undividedness and differentiation at the same time? There is no mystery: the knowledge instinct together with the hierarchical structure of the mind hold the key to the answer. Whereas every level pursues differentiation, totality belongs to the highest levels of the hierarchy. Future research will have to address these mechanisms in their fascinating details.

Intentionality is a property of referring to something else, and consciousness is about something. Many philosophers refer to this "aboutness" as intentionality. In everyday life, when we hear an opinion we do not just collate it in our memory and relate to other opinions (like a pseudoscientist in a comedy); this would not lead very far. We wish to know the aims and intentions associated with this opinion. Mechanisms of perceiving intent vs. specific words were studied by Valerie Reyna and Charles Brainerd (1995), who discuss the contrast between *gist* and *verbatim* systems of memory and decision making. Often, we perceive the *intent* of what is said better than specific words, even if the words are chosen to disguise the intent behind causal reasoning. The desire to know and the ability to perceive the goal indicates that in psyche, the *final standpoint or purpose* is more important than the *causal* one. This intentionality of psyche was emphasized by Aristotle (IV BC) in his discussions of the end cause of forms of the mind. Intentionality of consciousness is more fundamental than "aboutness"; it is *purposiveness*.

The intentional property of consciousness led many philosophers during the last decades to believe that intentionality is a unique and most important characteristic of consciousness: according to Searle (1992) only conscious beings can be intentional. But, the mechanism of the knowledge instinct leads to an opposing conclusion. Intentionality is a fundamental property of life: even the simplest living being is a result of long evolution and its every component, say a gene or a protein, has a purpose and intent. In particular, every concept model has evolved with an intent or purpose to recognize a particular type of signal (event, message, concept) and to act accordingly (e.g., send a recognition message to other parts of the brain and to behavioral models). Aristotle was the first to explain the intentionality of the mind in this way; he argued that intentionality should be explained through the a priori contents of the mind. Possibly, future developments of mechanisms of the knowledge instinct will explain the mind's intentionality and purposiveness in its complexity.

Is there any specific relationship between consciousness and intentionality? If so, it is just the opposite of Searle's hypothesis of intentionality implying consciousness. Affective, subconscious, lower-bodily-level emotional responses are concerned with immediate survival, utilitarian goals, and are therefore *intentional in the most* straightforward way. A higher-intellectual-level consciousness is not concerned with immediate survival, but with an overall understanding of the world, with knowledge and beauty. It can afford to be impartial, abstract, and less immediately intentional than the rest of the psyche; its intentions might be directed toward meanings and purposes of life. As I discuss below, the highest creative aspect of individual consciousness and the abilities of perceiving beautiful and sublime are intentional without any specific, lower-level utilitarian goal; they are intentional toward self-realization, toward future self beyond current self. The current mathematical theories reviewed in this chapter allow us to manipulate these metaphorical descriptions more accurately to obtain solutions to long-standing philosophical problems. Moreover, we can identify directions for concrete studies of these metaphors in future mathematical simulations and laboratory experiments.

Unity of consciousness refers to conscious mental states being parts of a unified sequence and simultaneous conscious events are perceived as unified into a coherent picture. Searle's unity is close to what Kant called "the transcendental unity of apperception." In MFT, this internal perception is explained as are all perceptions as being due to a property of the special model involved in consciousness, called ego by psychologists. The properties of the ego model explain the properties of consciousness. When certain properties of consciousness seem difficult to explain, we should follow Kant's example and turn the question around to ask: Which properties of the ego model would explain the phenomenological properties of consciousness?

Let us begin the analysis of the structures of the ego model and the process of its adaptation to the constantly changing world from evolutionary-preceding simpler forms. What is the initial state of consciousness: an undifferentiated unity or a "booming, buzzing confusion" (James 1890)? Or, let us take a step back in evolutionary development and ask, what is the initial state of the preconscious psyche? Or, let us move back even further toward evolution of sensory systems and perception. When building a robot for a factory floor, why provide it with a sensor? Obviously, such an expensive thing as a sensor is needed to achieve specific goals: to sense the environment with the purpose of accomplishing specific tasks. Providing a robot with a sensor goes together with an ability to utilize sensory data.

Similarly, in the process of evolution, sensory abilities emerged together with perception abilities. A natural evolution of sensory abilities could not result in a "booming, buzzing confusion," but would have to result in evolutionary advantageous abilities to avoid danger, attain food, etc. Primitive perception abilities (observed in primitive animals) are *limited* to a few types of concept-objects (light-dark, warm-cold, edible-nonedible, dangerous-attractive...) and are directly 'wired' to proper actions. When perception functions evolve further, beyond imme-diate actions, it is through the development of complex internal concept-models, which unify simpler object-models into a unified and flexible model of the world. Only at this point of possessing relatively complicated differentiated concept-models composed of a large number of submodels, can an intelligent system expe-rience a "booming, buzzing confusion" if it faces a new type of environment. A primitive system is simply incapable of perceiving confusion: It perceives only those 'things' for which it has concept-models and if its perceptions do not correspond to reality, it just does not survive without experiencing confusion. When a baby is born, it undergoes a tremendous change of environment, most likely without much conscious confusion. The original state of consciousness is undifferentiated unity. It possesses a single modality of a primordial undifferentiated self-world.

The initial unity of psyche limited abilities of the mind, and further development proceeded through differentiation of psychic functions or modalities (concepts, emotions, behavior); they were further differentiated into multiple concept-models, etc., which accelerated adaptation. Differentiation of consciousness is a relatively recent process (Perlovsky 2006d).

Consciousness is about aspects of concept-models (of the environment, self, past, present, future plans, and alternatives) and emotions to which we can direct our attention. As already mentioned, MFT explains consciousness as a specialized ego model. Within this model, consciousness can direct attention at will, and this conscious control of will is called free will. A subjective feeling of free will is a most cherished property of our psyche. Most of us feel that this is what makes us different from inanimate objects and simple forms of life. Moreover, this property is a most difficult one to explain rationally or to describe mathematically. But, let us see how far we can go toward understanding this phenomenon. We know that raw percepts are often not conscious. As noted earlier, e.g., in the visual system, we are conscious about the final processing stage, the integrated crisp model, and unconscious about intermediate processing. We are unconscious about eye receptive fields, about details of visual perception of motion and color as far as it takes place in our brain separately from the main visual cortex, etc. (Zeki 1993). In most cases, we are conscious only of the integrated scene, crisp objects, and so on.

These properties of consciousness follow from properties of concept-models; they have conscious (crisp) and unconscious (fuzzy) parts, which are accessible and inaccessible to consciousness, i.e., to the Ego model. In prescientific literature about mechanisms of the mind there was a popular idea of a homunculus, a little mind inside our mind, which perceived our perceptions and made them available to our mind. This naive view is amazingly close to the actual scientific explanation. The fundamental difference is that the scientific explanation does not need an infinite chain of homunculi inside homunculi. Instead, there is a hierarchy of mind models with their conscious and unconscious aspects. The higher in the hierarchy, the less the conscious differentiated aspect of the models. Until at the top of the hierarchy there are mostly unconscious models of the meaning of our existence (which I dis-cuss later).

Our internal perceptions of consciousness due to the ego model 'perceive' crisp conscious parts of other models similar to models of perception 'perceive' objects in the world. The properties of consciousness as we experience them, such as continuity and identity of consciousness, are due to properties of the ego model. What is known about this consciousness model? Since Freud, a certain complex of psychological functions has been called ego. Jung considered ego to be based on a more general model or archetype of self. Jungian archetypes are psychic structures (models) of a primordial origin, which are mostly inaccessible to consciousness, but determine the structure of our psyche. In this way, archetypes are similar to other models, e.g., receptive fields of the retina are not consciously perceived, but determine the structure of visual perception. The self archetype determines our phenomenological subjective perception of ourselves, and structures our psyche in many different ways, which are far from being completely understood. An important phenomenological property of self is the perception of uniqueness and indivisibility (hence, the word *individual*).

Many contemporary philosophers consider the subjective nature of consciousness to be an impenetrable barrier to scientific investigation. Chalmers (1997) differentiated hard and easy questions about consciousness as follows. Easy questions, which will be answered better and better, are concerned with brain mechanisms: which brain structures are responsible for consciousness? Hard questions, about which no progress can be expected, are concerned with the subjective nature of consciousness and *qualia*, subjective feelings associated with every conscious perception. Nagel (1974) described it dramatically with a question: "What is it like to be a bat?" But I disagree. I do not think these questions are hard. They are not mysteries; they are just the wrong questions for a scientific theory. Newton, while describing the laws of planetary motion, did not ask: "What is it like to be a planet?" (Even so, something like this feeling *is* a part of scientific intuition.) The subjective nature of consciousness is not a mystery. It is explained by the subjective nature of the concept-models of which we are conscious. The subjectivity is the result of combined apriority and adaptivity of the consciousness model, the unique genetic a priori structures of psyche together with our unique individual experiences. I consider the only hard questions about consciousness to be *free will* and *the nature of creativity*.

Let us summarize. Most of the mind's operations are not accessible to consciousness. We definitely know that neural firings and connections cannot be perceived consciously. In the foundations of the mind there are material processes in the brain inaccessible to consciousness. Jung (1934) suggested that conscious concepts are developed by the mind based on genetically inherited structures, archetypes, which are inaccessible to consciousness. The mind mechanisms, described in MFT by dynamic logic and fuzzy models, are not accessible to consciousness. Grossberg (1982) suggested that only signals and models attaining a resonant state (i.e., signals matching models) could reach consciousness. It was further detailed by Taylor (2005); we are conscious about our modelswhen our model anticipation of reality contradicts sensory signals. Final results of dynamic logic processes, resonant states characterized by crisp models, and corresponding signals are accessible to consciousness.

7 Higher Cognitive Functions

Imagination involves excitation of a neural pattern in a sensory cortex in the absence of an actual sensory stimulation. For example, visual imagination involves excitation of visual cortex, say, with closed eyes (Grossberg 1982; Zeki 1993). Imagination was long considered a part of the thinking process; Kant (1790) emphasized the role of imagination in the thought process, and called thinking "a play of cognitive functions of imagination and understanding." Whereas pattern recognition and artificial intelligence algorithms of the recent past could not relate to this (Minsky 1988; Penrose 1994), the Carpenter and Grossberg (1987) resonance model and the MFT dynamics both describe imagination as an inseparable part of thinking. Imagined patterns are top-down signals that *prime* the perception cortex areas (*priming* is neural terminology for enabling neurons to be more readily excited). In MFT, the imagined neural patterns are given by models $\mathbf{M}_h$.

As discussed earlier, visual imagination can be "internally perceived" with closed eyes. The same process can be mathematically modeled at higher cognitive levels, where it involves models of complex situations or plans. Similarly, models of behavior at higher levels of the hierarchy can be activated without actually propagating their output signals down to actual muscle movements and to actual acts in the world. In other words, behavior can be imagined and evaluated along with its consequences, which is the essence of plans. Sometimes, imagination involves detailed alternative courses of action considered and evaluated consciously. Sometimes, imagination may involve fuzzy or vague, barely conscious models, which reach consciousness only after they converge to a "reasonable" course of action, which can be consciously evaluated. From a mathematical standpoint, this latter mechanism is the only possible, because conscious evaluation cannot involve all possible courses of action; it would lead to combinatorial complexity and impasse. It remains to be proven in brain studies, which will identify the exact brain regions and neural mechanisms involved.

MFT adds details to the Kantian description of the working of the mind in agreement with neural data: thinking is a play of top-down higher-hierarchical-level imagination and bottom-up lower-level understanding. Kant identified this "play" described by [Eqs. (3–6)] as a source of aesthetic emotion. Kant used the word "play," when he was uncertain about the exact mechanism; this mechanism, according to our suggestion, is the knowledge instinct and dynamic logic.

Aesthetic emotions and the instinct for knowledge. Perception and cognition, recognizing objects in the environment and understanding their meaning is so important for survival that a special instinct evolved for this purpose. This instinct for learning and improving concept-models I call the instinct for knowledge. In MFT it is described by maximization of the similarity between the models and the world, [Eq. (2)]. We perceive emotions related to satisfaction-dissatisfaction of this instinct as harmony-disharmony (between our understanding of how things ought to be and how they actually are in the surrounding world). According to Kant (1790) these are aesthetic emotions (emotions that are not related directly to satisfaction or dissatisfaction of bodily needs).

The instinct for knowledge makes little kids, cubs, and piglets jump around and play fight. Their inborn models of behavior must adapt to their body weights, objects, and animals around them long before the instincts of hunger and fear will use the models for direct aims of survival. Childish behavior just makes the work of the knowledge instinct more observable; to varying degrees, this instinct continues acting throughout our lives. We are always bringing our internal models into correspondence with the world. In adult life, when our perception and understanding of the surrounding world is adequate, aesthetic emotions are barely perceptible: the mind just does its job. Similarly, we do not usually notice adequate performance of our breathing muscles and satisfaction of the breathing instinct. However, if breathing is difficult, negative emotions immediately reach consciousness. The same is true about the knowledge instinct and aesthetic emotions. If we do not understand our surroundings, if objects around us do not correspond to our expectations, negative emotions immediately reach consciousness. We perceive these emotions as disharmony between our knowledge and the world. Thriller movies exploit the instinct for knowledge: they are mainly based on violating our expectations; their personages are shown in situations, in which knowledge of the world is inadequate for survival.

Let me emphasize again, aesthetic emotions are not peculiar to art and artists; they are inseparable from every act of perception and cognition. In everyday life we usually do not notice them. Aesthetic emotions become noticeable at higher cognitive levels in the mind hierarchy, when cognition is not automatic, but requires conscious effort. Damasio's (1994) view of emotions defined by visceral mechanisms, as far as discussing higher cognitive functions, seems erroneous in taking secondary effects for the primary mechanisms. People often devote their spare time to increasing their knowledge, even if it is not related to their job and a possibility of promotion. Pragmatic interests could be involved: knowledge makes us more attractive to friends and might help find sexual partners. Still, there is a remainder, a pure joy of knowledge, aesthetic emotions satisfying the knowledge instinct.

Beauty and sublimity. Cognitive science is at a complete loss when trying to explain the highest human abilities, the most important and cherished abilities to create and perceive beautiful and sublime experiences. Their role in the working of the mind is not understood. MFT explains that simple harmony is an elementary aesthetic emotion related to improvement of object models. Higher aesthetic emotions are related to the development and improvement of more complex "higher" models at higher levels of the mind hierarchy. The highest forms of aesthetic emotion are related to the most general and most important models near the top of the hierarchy. According to Kantian analysis (Kant 1790, 1798), among the highest models are models of the meaning of our existence, of our purposiveness or intentionality, and beauty is related to improving these models.

Models at the top of the mind hierarchy, models of our purposiveness, are largely fuzzy and unconscious. Some people, at some points in their lives, may believe that their life purpose is finite and concrete, e.g., to make a lot of money or build a loving family and bring up good children. These models are aimed at satisfying powerful instincts, but not the knowledge instinct, and they do not reflect the highest human aspirations. Everyone who has achieved a finite goal of making money or raising good children knows that this is not the end of his or her aspirations. The reason is that everyone has an ineffable feeling of partaking in the infinite, while at the same time knowing that our material existence is finite. This contradiction cannot be resolved. For this reason, models of our purpose and meaning cannot be made crisp and conscious; they will forever remain fuzzy and partly unconscious.

Everyday life gives us little evidence with which to develop models of meaning and purposiveness of our existence. People are dying every day and often from random causes. Nevertheless, life itself demands belief in one's purpose; without such a belief it is easier to get drunk or take drugs than to read this article. These issues are not new; philosophers and theologians have expounded them from time immemorial. The knowledge instinct theory gives us a scientific approach to the eternal quest for meaning. We perceive an object or a situation as beautiful when it stimulates improvement of the highest models of meaning. Beauty is what "reminds" us of our purposiveness. This is true about perception of beauty in a flower or in an art object. Just as an example, R. Buckminster Fuller, an architect, best known for inventing the geodesic dome wrote: "When I'm working on a problem, I never think about beauty. I think only how to solve the problem. But when I have finished, if the solution is not beautiful, I know it is wrong" (http://www.quotationspage.com/quote/26209.html). The MFT explanation of the nature of beautiful helps in understanding the exact meaning of this statement and resolves a number of mysteries and contradictions in contemporary aesthetics (Perlovsky 2002, 2006d).

The feeling of spiritually sublime is similar yet different from beautiful. Whereas beauty is related to improvement of the models of *cognition*, sublimity is related to improvement of the models of *behavior* realizing the highest meaning in our lives. Beauty and sublimity are not finite. MFT tells us that mathematically, improvement of complex models is related to choices from among an infinite number of possibilities. A mathematician may consider 100^{100}, or a million to the millionth power as a finite number. But for a physicist, a number that exceeds all elementary events in the life of the universe is infinite. A choice from infinity is infinitely complex and contains infinite information. Therefore, choices of beauty and sublimity contain infinite information. This is not a metaphor, but exact mathematical fact. Beauty is at once objective and subjective. It really exists. Cultures and individuals cannot exist without the ability for beauty, yet it cannot be described by any finite algorithm or set of rules.

Beauty of a physical theory, sometimes discussed by physicists, is similar in its infinity to beauty in an artwork. For a physicist, beauty of a physical theory is related to improving the models of the meaning in our understanding of the universe. This satisfies a scientist's quest for the purpose, which he identifies with the purpose in the world.

Intuition. Intuitions include inner perceptions of object models, images produced by them, and their relationship with objects in the world, including higher-level models of relationships among simpler models. Intuitions involve fuzzy unconscious concept-models that are in a state of being formed, learned, and being adapted toward crisp and conscious models (say, a theory). Conceptual contents of fuzzy models are undifferentiated and partly unconscious. Similarly, conceptual and emotional contents of these fuzzy mind states are undifferentiated; concepts and emotions are mixed up. Fuzzy mind states may satisfy or not satisfy the knowledge instinct in varying degrees before they become differentiated and accessible to consciousness, hence the vague complex emotional-cognitive feel of an intuition. Contents of intuitive states differ among people, but the main mechanism of intuition is the same among artists and scientists. Composer's intuitions are mostly about sounds and their relationship to psyche. Painter's intuitions are mostly about colors and shapes and their relationship to psyche. Writer's intuitions are about words or, more generally, about language and its relationship to psyche. Mathematical intuition is about structure and consistency within a theory and about relationships between the theory and a priori content of psyche. Physical intuition is about the real world, the first principles of its organization, and the mathematics describing it.

Creativity is an ability to improve and construct new concept-models. To a small degree it is present in everyday perception and cognition. Usually the words "creativity," "creative," or "discovery" are applied to improving or creating new concept-models at higher cognitive levels, concepts that are important for the entire society or culture. A crisp and specific model can only match a specific content; therefore it cannot lead to creation of new content. Creativity and discovery, according to Section 5, involve vague, fuzzy models, which are made more crisp and clear. It occurs, therefore, at the interface between consciousness and unconscious. A similar nature of the creative process, involving consciousness and unconscious, was discussed by Jung (1921). Creativity usually involves intuition, as discussed above: fuzzy undifferentiated feelings-concepts.

Creativity is driven by the knowledge instinct. Two main mechanisms of creativity, the components of the knowledge instinct, are differentiation and synthesis. Differentiation is a process of creating new, more specific, and more detailed concept-models from simpler, less differentiated, and less conscious models. Mathematical mechanisms of differentiation were discussed in Section 5. The role of language in differentiation of cognition was discussed in (Perlovsky, 2006b), as noted, this research is in its infancy and a subject of future work.

Synthesis is a process of connecting detailed crisp concept-models to the unconscious, instincts, and emotions. The need for synthesis comes from the fact that most of our concept-models are acquired from language. The entire conceptual content of the culture is transmitted from generation to generation through language; cognitive concept-models cannot be transmitted directly from brain to brain. Therefore, concepts acquired from language have to be used by individual minds to create cognitive concepts. The mechanism of integrating cognition and language (Perlovsky 2006b) explains that language concepts could be detailed and conscious, but not necessarily connected to equally detailed cognitive concepts, to emotions, and to the knowledge instinct. Connecting language and cognition involves differentiating cognitive models; developing cognitive models, which differentiation and consciousness approach that of language models. Every child acquires language between the ages of one and seven, but it takes the rest of life to connect-abstract language models to cognitive concept-models, to emotions, instincts, and to life's needs. This is the process of synthesis; it integrates language and cognition, concepts and emotions, conscious and unconscious, instinctual and learned. Current research directions discussed in (Perlovsky 2006b) are just touching on these mechanisms of synthesis, which is largely an area for future research.

Another aspect of synthesis, essential for creativity, is developing a unified whole within psyche, a feel and intuition of purpose and the meaning of existence. It is necessary for concentrating will, for survival, for achieving individual goals, and in particular for satisfying the knowledge instinct by differentiating knowledge. Concept-models of purpose and meaning, as discussed, are near the top of the mind hierarchy; they are mostly unconscious and related to feelings of beautiful and sublime. A condition of synthesis is correspondence among a large number of concept-models. A knowledge instinct as discussed in Section 3 is a single measure of correspondence among all the concept-models and all the experiences-data about the world. This is, of course, a simplification. Certain concept-models have high value for psyche (e.g., religion, family, success, political causes) and they affect recognition and understanding of other concepts. This is a mechanism of differentiation of the knowledge instinct. Satisfaction of the knowledge instinct therefore is not measured by a single aesthetic emotion, but by a large number of aesthetic emotions. The entire wealth of our knowledge should be brought into correspondence with itself, which requires manifold of aesthetic emotions. Differentiation of emotions is engendered by music (Perlovsky 2008), but that is beyond the scope of this chapter.

There is an opposition between differentiation and synthesis in individual minds as well as in the collective psyche, which leads to complex evolution of cultures. Differentiated concepts acquire meaning in connection with the instinctual and unconscious in synthesis. In the evolution of the mind, differentiation is the essence of the development of the mind and consciousness, but it may bring about a split between conscious and unconscious, between emotional and conceptual, between language and cognition. Differentiated and refined models existing in language may lose their connection with cognitive models, with people's instinctual needs. If the split affects the collective psyche, it leads to a loss of the creative potential of a community or a nation. This was the mechanism of death of great ancient civilizations. The development of culture, the very interest of life requires *combining differentiation and synthesis*. Evolution of the mind and cultures is determined by this complex nonlinear interaction: One factor prevails, then another (Perlovsky 2008). This is an area for future research.

Teleology, causality, and the knowledge instinct. Teleology explains the universe in terms of purposes. In many religious teachings, it is a basic argument for the existence of God: If there is purpose, an ultimate Designer must exist. Therefore, teleology is a hot point of debate between creationists and evolutionists: Is there a purpose in the world? Evolutionists assume that the only explanation is causal. Newton's laws gave a perfect causal explanation for the motion of planets: A planet moves from moment to moment under the influence of a gravitational force. Similarly, today, science explains motions of all particles and fields according to causal laws, and there are exact mathematical expressions for fields, forces, and their motion. Causality explains what happens in the next moment as a result of forces acting in the previous moment. Scientists accept this causal explanation and oppose teleological explanations in terms of purposes. The very basis of science, it seems, is on the side of causality, and religion is on the side of teleology.

However, at the level of first physical principles this is wrong. The contradiction between causality and teleology does not exist at the very basic level of fundamental physics. The laws of physics, from classical Newtonian laws to quantum superstrings, can be formulated equally as causal or as teleological. An example of a teleological principle in physics is energy minimization: particles move so that energy is minimized, as if particles in each moment know that their purpose is to minimize the energy. The most general physical laws are formulated as minimization of Lagrangian. Causal dynamics, motions of particles, quantum strings, and superstrings are determined by minimizing Lagrangian (Feynman and Hibbs 1965). A particle under force moves from point to point as if it knows its final purpose—to minimize Lagrangian. Causal dynamics and teleology are two sides of the same coin.

The knowledge instinct is similar to these most general physical laws: evolution of the mind is guided by maximization of knowledge. A mathematical structure of similarity (2) is similar to a Lagrangian, and it plays a similar role; it bridges the causal dynamic logic of cognition and the teleological principle of maximum knowledge. Similarly to basic physics, dynamics and teleology are equivalent: Dynamic logic follows from maximization of knowledge and vice versa. Ideas, concept-models, change under the 'force' of dynamic logic, as if they know their purpose—Maximum knowledge. One does not have to choose between scientific explanation and teleological purpose: Causal dynamics and teleology are equivalent.

8 Experimental Evidence, Prediction, and Testing

The mind is described in psychological and philosophical terms, whereas the brain is described in terms of neurobiology and medicine. Within scientific exploration the mind and brain are different description levels of the same system. Establishing relationships between these descriptions is of great scientific interest. Today we approach solutions to this challenge (Grossberg 2000), which eluded Newton in his attempt to establish a physics of "spiritual substance" (Westfall 1983). Detailed discussion of established relationships between the mind and the brain is beyond the scope of this chapter. I briefly mention the main known and unknown facts and give references for further reading. Adaptive modeling abilities are well studied with adaptive parameters identified with synaptic connections (Koch and Segev 1998; Hebb 1949); instinctual learning mechanisms have been studied in psychology and linguistics (Piaget 2000; Chomsky 1981; Jackendoff 2002; Deacon 1998). General neural mechanisms of the elementary thought process (which are similar in MFT and ART (Carpenter and Grossberg 1987)) include neural mechanisms for bottom-up (sensory) signals, top-down imagination model signals, and the resonant matching between the two; these have been confirmed by neural and psychological experiments (Grossberg 1988; Zeki 1993; Freeman 1975). Ongoing research addresses relationships between neural processes and consciousness (Koch 2004; Carpenter and Grossberg 1987). Relating MFT to brain mechanisms in detail is a subject of current as well as future research.

Ongoing and future research will confirm, disprove, or suggest modifications to the specific mechanisms considered in Sections 5 and 6. These mechanisms include model parameterization and parameter adaptation, reduction of fuzziness during learning, and the similarity measure described by Eq. (2) as a foundation of the knowledge instinct and aesthetic emotion. Other mechanisms include, on one hand, relationships between psychological and neural mechanisms of learning and, on the other, aesthetic feelings of harmony and emotions of beautiful and sublime. Future research will also investigate the validity of the dual integrated structure of concept-models described in (Perlovsky 2006b) as a foundation for interaction between cognition and language and for symbolic ability. A step in this direction will be to demonstrate in simulations that this mechanism actually integrates cognition and language without combinatorial complexity. Specific neural systems will need to be related to mathematical descriptions as well as to psychological descriptions in terms of subjective experiences and observable behavior. Ongoing simulation research addresses the evolution of models jointly with the evolution of language (Fontanari and Perlovsky 2004, 2005a,b). Also being investigated are the ways that MFT and the knowledge instinct relate to behavioral psychology and to the specific brain areas involved in emotional reward and punishment during learning (Levine and Perlovsky 2006). Interesting unsolved problems include: detailed mechanisms of interactions between cognitive hierarchy and language hierarchy (Perlovsky 2004, 2006b); differentiated forms of the knowledge instinct, the infinite variety of aesthetic emotions perceived in music, and their relationship to mechanisms of synthesis (Perlovsky 2008); and interactions of differentiation and synthesis in the development of the mind during cultural evolution. Future experimental research will have to examine, in detail, the nature of hierarchical interactions, including mechanisms of learning hierarchy, to what extent the hierarchy is inborn vs. adaptively learned, and the hierarchy of the knowledge instinct.

Acknowledgments I am grateful to D. Levine, R. Deming, R. Linnehan, and B. Weijers, for discussions, help, and advice, and to AFOSR for supporting part of this research under the Lab. Task 05SN02COR, PM Dr. Jon Sjogren.

References

Adelman, G. (1987). *Encyclopedia of Neuroscience*. Birkhaüser, Boston, MA.

Aristotle (IV BC). Metaphysics, tr. W. D. Ross, in: *Complete Works of Aristotle*, J. Barnes (ed.), Princeton, NJ, 1995.

Bellman, R.E. (1961). *Adaptive Control Processes*. Princeton University Press, Princeton, NJ.

Berlyne, D. E. (1960). *Conflict, Arousal, and Curiosity*, McGraw-Hill, New York

Berlyne, D. E. (1973). *Pleasure, Reward, Preference: Their Nature, Determinants, and Role in Behavior*, Academic Press, New York.

Carpenter, G.A, and Grossberg, S. (1987). A massively parallel architecture for a self-organizing neural pattern recognition machine. *Computer Vision, Graphics and Image Processing*, 37, 54–115.

Chalmers, D.J. (1997). *The Conscious Mind: In Search of a Fundamental Theory*, Oxford University Press, 1997.

Chomsky, N. (1981). In *Explanation in Linguistics*, N.Hornstein and D.Lightfoot (eds.), Longman, London.

Cramer, H. (1946). *Mathematical Methods of Statistics*, Princeton University Press, Princeton NJ.

Damasio, A.R. (1994). *Descartes' Error: Emotion, Reason, and the Human Brain*. Grosset/Putnam, New York.

Deacon, T.W. (1998). *The Symbolic Species: The Co-Evolution of Language and the Brain*, Norton.

Festinger, L. (1957). *A Theory of Cognitive Dissonance*, Stanford University Press, Stanford, CA.

Feynman, R.P. and Hibbs, A.R. (1965). *Quantum Mechanics and Path Integrals*. McGraw-Hill, New York.

Fontanari, J.F., and Perlovsky, L.I. (2004). Solvable null model for the distribution of word frequencies. *Physical Review E* 70, 042901.

Fontanari, J.F., and Perlovsky, L.I. (2005a). Evolution of communication in a community of simple-minded agents. IEEE International Conference on Integration of Knowledge in Intensive Multi-Agent Sys., Waltham, MA.

Fontanari, J.F., and Perlovsky, L.I. (2005b). Meaning Creation and Modeling Field Theory. IEEE International Conference on Integration of Knowledge in Intensive Multi-Agent Sys., Waltham, MA

Freeman, W.J. (1975) *Mass Action in the Nervous System*. Academic Press, New York.

Grossberg, S. (1982). *Studies of Mind and Brain*, D. Reidel, Dordrecht, Holland.

Grossberg, S., and Levine, D.S. (1987). Neural dynamics of attentionally modulated Pavlovian conditioning: blocking, inter-stimulus interval, and secondary reinforcement. *Psychobiology*, **15**(3), 195–240.

Grossberg, S. (1988). *Neural Networks and Natural Intelligence*. MIT Press, Cambridge, MA.

Grossberg, S. (2000). Linking mind to brain: the mathematics of biological intelligence. *Notices of the American Mathematical Society*, 471361–1372.

Hebb, D. (1949). *Organization of Behavior*, J.Wiley & Sons, New York.

Jackendoff, R. (2002). *Foundations of Language: Brain, Meaning, Grammar, Evolution*. Oxford University Press.

James, W. (1890) *The Principles of Psychology*. Dover Books, New York, 1950.

Jaynes, J. (2000). *The Origin of Consciousness in the Breakdown of the Bicameral Mind*. Houghton Mifflin Co., Boston, MA; 2nd Ed.

Jung, C.G. (1921). *Psychological Types. In the Collected Works*, v.6, Bollingen Series XX, Princeton University Press, Princeton, NJ, 1971.

Jung, C.G (1934) *Archetypes of the Collective Unconscious, in: The Collected Works*, v.9,II, Princeton University Press, Princeton, NJ, 1969.

Kant, I. (1781) *Critique of Pure Reason,* tr. J.M.D. Meiklejohn, Wiley, New York, 1943.

Kant, I. (1788). *Critique of Practical Reason*, tr. J.H Bernard, 1986, Hafner.

Kant, I. (1790). *Critique of Judgment,* tr. J.H.Bernard, Macmillan, London, 1914.

Kant, I. (1798). *Anthropology from a Pragmatic Point of View*. Tr. M.J. Gregor. Kluwer, Boston, 1974.

Kecman, V. (2001). *Learning and Soft Computing: Support Vector Machines, Neural Networks, and Fuzzy Logic Models (Complex Adaptive Systems)*. The MIT Press, Cambridge, MA.

Koch, C., and Segev, I. (eds.), (1998). *Methods in Neuronal Modeling: From Ions to Networks* MIT Press, Cambridge, MA.

Koch, C. (2004). *The Quest for Consciousness: A Neurobiological Approach*, Roberts & Company.

Levine, D., and Perlovsky, L. (2006). The knowledge instinct, reward, and punishment. To be published.

Marchal, B. (2005) Theoretical Computer Science and the Natural Sciences. *Physics of Life Reviews*, **2**(3), pp. 1–38.

Minsky, M.L. (1975). A Framework for Representing Knowlege, in *The Psychology of Computer Vision*, P. H. Whinston (ed.), McGraw-Hill, New York.

Minsky, M. (1988). *The Society of Mind*. MIT Press, Cambridge, MA.

Nagel, T. (1974). What is it like to be a bat? *Philosophical Review*, **11**, 207–212.

Penrose, R. (1994). *Shadows of the Mind*. Oxford University Press, Oxford.

Perlovsky, L.I. (1996a). Fuzzy Logic of Aristotelian For Perlovsky, L.I. (1996a) Proceedings of the Conference on Intelligent Systems and Semiotics '96. Gaithersburg, MD, v.1, pp. 43–48.

Perlovsky, L.I. (1996b). Gödel Theorem and Semiotics. Proceedings of the Conference on Intelligent Systems and Semiotics '96. Gaithersburg, MD, v.2, pp. 14–18.

Perlovsky, L.I. (1998). Conundrum of combinatorial complexity. *IEEE Trans. PAMI*, **20**(6), 666–670.

Perlovsky, L.I., Webb, V.H., Bradley, S.R. and Hansen, C.A. (1998). Improved ROTHR detection and tracking using MLANS. *AGU Radio Science*, **33**(4), 1034–44.

Perlovsky, L.I., (2001). *Neural Networks and Intellect*, Oxford University. Press, New York.

Perlovsky, L. (2002). Aesthetics and mathematical theories of intellect (Russian). *Iskusstvoznanie*, **2**(02), 558–594, Moscow.

Perlovsky, L.I. (2004). Integrating language and cognition. *IEEE Connections* (Feature article), **2**(2), 8–12.

Perlovsky, L.I. (2006a). Toward physics of the mind: Concepts, emotions, consciousness, and symbols. *Physics of Life Reviews*, **3**(1), 23–55.

Perlovsky, L.I. (2006b). Symbols: Integrated cognition and language, in *Computational Semiotics*, A. Loula and R. Gudwin (ed.). The Idea Group, PA.

Perlovsky, L.I. (2006c). Fuzzy dynamic logic. New Mathematics and Natural Computation, **2**(1), 43–55.

Perlovsky, L. (2008). *The Knowledge Instinct*. Basic Books. New York, NY.

Piaget, J. (2000) *The Psychology of the Child* Tr. H.Weaver, Basic Books.

Plato (IV BC) *Parmenides*, in: L. Cooper, *Plato*, Oxford University Press, New York, 1997.

Reyna, V.F., and Brainerd, C.J. (1995). Fuzzy-trace theory: An interim synthesis. *Learning and Individual Differences*, **7**(1), 1–75.

Searle, J. (1992). *The Rediscovery of the Mind* MIT Press, Cambridge, MA.

Searle, J.R. (1997). "The mystery of consciousness." *New York Review of Books*, NY.

Singer, R.A., Sea, R.G. and Housewright, R.B. (1974). Derivation and evaluation of improved tracking filters for use in dense multitarget environments, *IEEE Transactions on Information Theory*, IT-20, 423–432.

Taylor, J. G. (2005). Mind And Consciousness: Towards A Final Answer? *Physics of Life Reviews*, **2**(1), 57.

Westfall, R.S. (1983). *Never at Rest: A Biography of Isaac Newton*. Cambridge University Press, Cambridge.

Winston, P.H. (1984). *Artificial Intelligence*. 2nd edition, Addison-Wesley, Reading, MA.

Zeki, S. (1993). *A Vision of the Brain*. Blackwell, Oxford.

A Real-Time Agent System Perspective of Meaning and Sapience

Ricardo Sanz, Julita Bermejo, Ignacio López, and Jaime Gómez

Abstract Wisdom and sapience have traditionally been considered desirable traits in humans, but the use of the terms is decaying, due perhaps to an arising relativism that lessens the value of others' knowledge. This chapter proposes an interpretation of *sapience* in terms of meaning generation and knowledge exploitation in social groups of knowledge-based agents. Sapient agents are able to generate useful meanings for other agents beyond their own capability to generate self-meanings. This makes sapient agents especially valuable entities in agent societies because they engender interagent reliable third-person meaning generation that provides some functional redundancy, which contributes to the enhancement of individual and social robustness and global performance. This chapter describes some musings concerning sapience and meaning generation in the context os the ASys theory of autonomous cognitive systems.

1 Introduction

Knowledge-based systems have been a matter of research and development for years. From the logic-based problem solvers of the 1960s to the expert systems of the 1980s or contemporary model-based systems, the nature of exploitable knowledge has been a core issue in artificial intelligence. Construction of well-performing systems seems to require the codification of suitable knowledge in suitable forms for agent activity.

In a sense, there has been an increasing awareness that having knowledge—whatever its form—is not enough. To perform adequately, agents need to acquire an *understanding* of their action context so they can decide rationally about the proper action to be taken and the proper knowledge to be used in deciding about it. This means that agents should interpret information coming from their sensors and generate meanings from this information to be used in the action decision-making process. This issue of *situation awareness* has been raised many times

R. Sanz
UPM Autonomous Systems Lab, Universidad Politécnica de Madrid, Madrid, Spain
e-mail: Ricardo.Sanz@upm.es

R.V. Mayorga, L.I. Perlovsky (eds.), *Toward Artificial Sapience,*
© Springer 2008

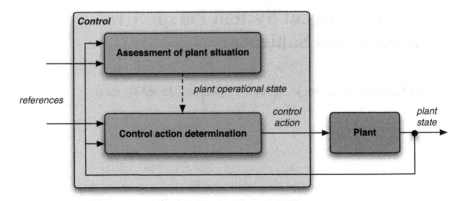

Fig. 1 Two-level phasing of situated intelligent systems: (1) plant situation awareness, and (2) control action generation; from Sanz (1990)

and even addressed specifically in the design of intelligent system architectures (see, e.g., Fig. 1).

While this brief analysis directly gets into the old debate about data, information, knowledge, and meaning, we will not contribute to it extensively, but it will be somehow necessary to clarify some of the terms used in the analysis of wisdom and sapience that follows (e.g., intelligence, meaning or knowledge).

(Mayorga 2005) proposed a differentiation between *intelligence* and *wisdom* based on the inner architecture of action. He sees "intelligence" as related to an "analysis" → "action" process, whereas "wisdom" is seen as related to "analysis," "synthesis," → "action" process.

Although we are not going to enter the debate about the definition of intelligence [see Sanz et al. (2000)] forss a partial account of our views, which we can summarize as *utility maximization in knowledge-based action*), it is none the less necessary to analyze the nature of the knowledge involved in action generation and propose a model for third-person meaning generation that will provide a simple interpretation of the concepts of "wisdom" and "sapience."

To achieve this objective, first we present a model of first-person meaning generation. Next, we apply this model to a cross-agent meaning generation process.

Other authors, (e.g., Tien, 2003) consider that wisdom is just a further step in the data → information → knowledge ladder (see Fig. 2). Or as Landauer (1998) puts it in his meaning hierarchy, the ladder is data → information → knowledge → understanding. Tuomi (1999) proposes an alternative hierarchy of information and meaning going from unfiltered data to high level wisdom related to compassion (see Fig. 5).

While meaning (semantics) is critical for purposeful action, few psychological theories have taken the study of meaning as the foundation of a working theory of the mind (Combs 2000). Hardy (1998) says that the generation of meaning is produced by the continuous closed causal link between an internal context (what she calls the semantic constellations) and an external context (a meaning-

Fig. 2 Moving from
information to wisdom
according to Tien (2003)

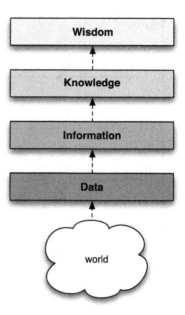

ful environment). Other's argue for a theory of meaning based on embodiment
(e.g., Barsalou, 1999; Glenberg, 1997; Lakoff, 1987). This alternative is based on
the idea that cognition is intimately connected with the functioning of the body
(Glenberg et al. 1999).

2 The Nature of Meaning

Beyond classical accounts of life-related information and meaning generation
(Oyama 1985), we focus on abstract cognitive agents with the—perhaps hopeless—
purpose of a theory that is applicable to both the analysis of extant cognitive agents
and to engineering processes of high-performance artificial agents, as those found
controlling the technical systems of today's world.

Some authors have proposed that *meaning* is just a list of features—like a frame
in classical AI—but there are compelling arguments from different sources against
this interpretation [see, e.g., Shanon (1988)]. Another classic alternative was to consider that the meaning of symbols is a semantic network, but this leads to a recursive search of meaning that finally ends in the symbol-grounding problem (Harnad
1990). A third solution is based on the symbols taking on meaning by referring to
entities outside the agent. That is, perception is seen as the core engine of meaning assignment to internal symbols, which corresponds to the views of interactivist
schools. But the recurrent discussion about the necessity of embodiment disappears
when constructors become aware that minds necessarily run on virtual machines
and hence the existence and awareness of an extant body is both unavoidable and

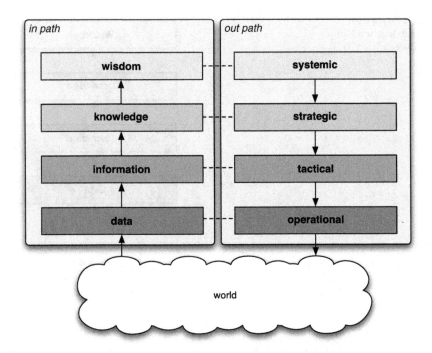

Fig. 3 The in and out paths of a situated system show the range of decision-making activities coupled with the different information levels

useful for enhancing behavior. All this happens over a dual layered structure of in and out steps (see Fig. 3).

In most of these interpretations, however, there is a big pending issue: they usually lack support of a core feature of meanings: *meanings can capture the dynamics of entities in their contexts.* Meanings are not constrained to statics; they also express change (actual or potential).

If we can say that X captures the meaning of a concrete piece of information, it is because X provides a sensible account of the relation of the agent with the originator—the causal agent—of the information in present and potentially future conditions.

As Meystel (2001) says, "the first fundamental property of intelligent systems architectures (the property of the existence of intelligence) can be visualized in the law of *forming the loop of closure*" (see Fig. 4). This loop of closure is seen in intelligent systems as composed by the world, sensors, world models, and behavior generators, the last three constituting parts of the agent. A fourth component is necessary to provide the goal-centered behavior of agents: the value judgment engine.

If we consider how behavior is generated, the value judgment component in RCS architecture (Albus and Barbera 2005) is critical (see Fig. 8). But this value judgment should not be made over raw or filtered sensor data (i.e., judging the present state of affairs) nor over the agent's present mental state. Value judgment

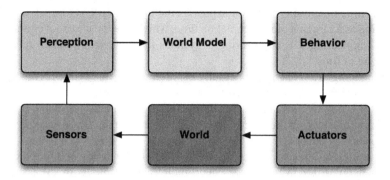

Fig. 4 The elementary loop of functioning—*loop of closure*—as described by Meystel (2003)

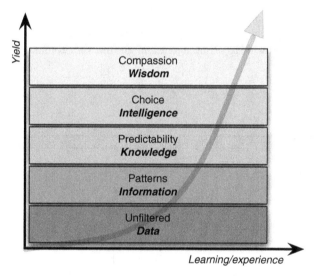

Fig. 5 The hierarchy of information/meaning (Tuomi 1999) when an agent is evolving from the experiential viewpoint (yield = intellectual dividends per effort invested).

is necessarily done over potential futures based on an agent's present mental state. Is this value judgment of potential future states what assigns meanings to facts of reality.

3 Meaning Generation in the ASys Model

The previous analysis shows that the core elements of a meaning generation engine are a predictor and a state value calculator. This is what the human brain does all the time to generate meanings: evaluation of causal impact of what we see. Meanings are generated by means of temporal utility functions.

A real-time time/utility function expresses the utility to the system of an action completion as a function of its completion time, which is at the core root of real-time systems engineering, i.e., engineering of systems that have requirements related to the passage of time.

The meaning of a concrete (externally or internally) perceived fact is the partitioning of potential future trajectories of the agent in its state space. For example, if I see that it is raining outside, this fact divides all my potential futures into two sets: in one I continue dry; in the other I get wet. This partitioning *is the meaning of the fact* "it is raining outside."

This interpretation of meaning as related to the dynamics of futures can be found in many different areas, e.g., neurobiology, psychology, or even software engineering. In order to help in this calculation of futures and future values, situated cognitive agents exploit the interaction with the world—and with other cognitive agents—to maximize behavior utility by driving such interaction by adaptive models of the reality they are dealing with (see Fig. 6). These models of a part of the reality—the plant under control in artificial systems—constitute the core of the real-world knowledge of the agent and are the very foundation of meaning calculation.

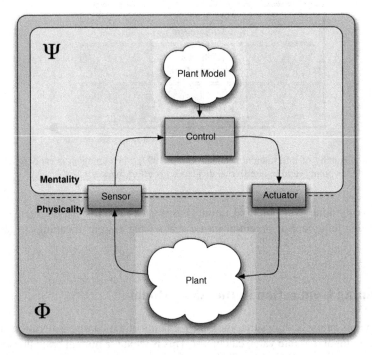

Fig. 6 Situated cognitive agents exploit the interaction with the world to maximize utility and this is achieved by means of driving such interaction by means of models of the reality—the plant under control in artificial systems—that constitute the very knowledge of the agent

4 Other Analyses of Meaning Generation

4.1 Freeman's Mental Dynamics

Walter Freeman (1997) identifies *meanings* with "the focus of an activity pattern that occupies the entire available brain." From his point of view there are no representations in the brain, only meanings. The brain is an engine for meaning generation—based on brain perceptual dynamics—and, simultaneously, an engine for action generation based on the same type of dynamics.

4.2 Gibson's Affordance Theory

According to the ecological psychologist James Gibson (1979), an *affordance* is an activity that is made possible—an *action possibility* so to say—by some property of an object. A valve affords flow control by being the right shape and size and being in the right place in the place where one needs to reduce the flow.

In some contexts, affordances are classified into three categories based on: sensory (unlearned sensory experience), perceptual (learned categorizations of sensory experience), or cognitive (thought-based) processes. There are even considerations about the possibilities of nonaware affordances. The most classic example of affordances involves doors and their handles (buildings, cars, etc.), but the world of control systems is full of these entities: actuators are embodiments of affordances.

4.3 Griswold's Program Meaning

In the area of tool-based software engineering, programmers look for automated methods to transform program specifications into final deployable packages. This is expected to solve the handcrafting bottleneck of manual programming. See, e.g., the work of Griswold and Notkin (1995) in the field of computer program transformation.

This implies having *meaningful transformations* of programs between different representations. The MDA proposal, e.g., considers transformations from UML-based platform-independent models into platform-dependent models, and then into concrete implementation-oriented languages (IDL, C + +, etc.).

All this transformation should be meaning preserving. But program meaning is not related to the actual wording of the code–that in model-centric software development may not even exist in some phases–but with the concrete program functionality (the program behavior) when it is executed over the appropriate platform, i.e., the platform that provides the required abstractions that the application was based on.

5 Meaning in Control Systems

From the former analysis, we can see that meaning cannot be associated with an isolated piece of information but rather with a set composed of the *information*, the *agent* for which the information is meaningful, and the *context* in which the agent operates. To summarize, the meaning of a piece of information is agent and context dependent, something that it is well known in psychology (Clark 1998).

Most researchers' creatures manipulate meanings without having an explicit theory, by means of ad hoc meaning generation processes embedded in the control architectures. These are based on a particular, hidden ontology and a value system that is implicit in the architecture [see, e.g., Steels (1998)].

Valuable engineering efforts are those oriented toward a clarification of the role that architecture plays in control systems and how is it possible to attain constructability of complex systems by means of scalable design patterns. This approach is especially well captured in the multiresolutional approach fostered by the control design pattern that Meystel (2003) calls the *elementary loop of functioning*. Is of importance in relation to the ASys theory of meaning. The incorporation of value judgment mechanisms over this elementary loop (see Fig. 7).

The elementary loop of functioning, when applied hierarchically, generates a multiresolutional ladder of meanings specifically focused on the controllable subspace of each control level. This approach partitions both the problem of meaning generation and the problem of action determination, leading to hierarchical control structures that have interesting properties of self-similarity.

This core design pattern approach is extended in the concept of a control node of the RCS control architecture (Albus 1992) (see Fig. 8). Beyond the model of the

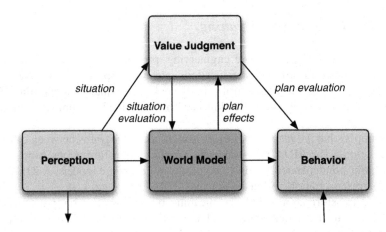

Fig. 7 Meystel's elementary loop of functioning incremented with a value judgment unit to generate meanings; this design matches what is proposed in the ASys theory about meaning generation. This structure corresponds to the elementary control node of the RCS intelligent control architecture (Albus 1992)

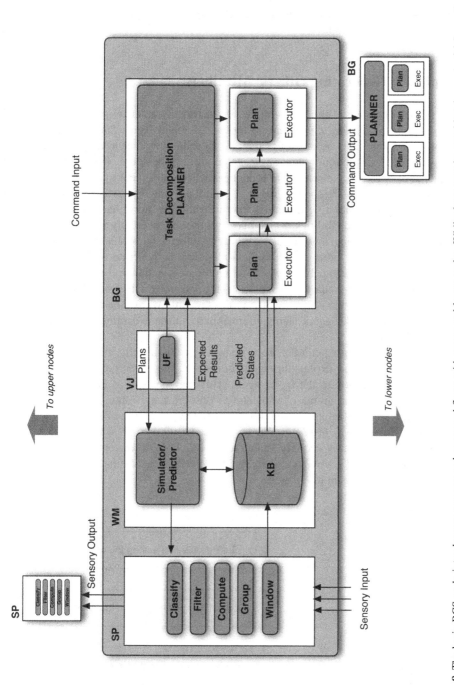

Fig. 8 The basic RCS node interchanges sensory and command flows with upper and lower nodes. While these may be considered *meaningful* flows, their meaning—*sensu stricto*—is limited to the originating node (Albus and Barbera 2005)

world and the sensing and acting units, this architecture considers the existence of a value judgment unit that evaluates both static and dynamic states derived from hypothetical plan execution.

6 Sapience: Generating Others' Meanings

To go to the core issue of the problem, i.e., the nature of sapience, we interpret it as the *capability of generating meanings for others*. Sapient agents can interpret the state of affairs and generate meanings that are valuable for other agents, i.e., like those generated by value judgment engines that are transpersonal. The attribution of sapience is *social* in the sense that it happens when the sapient agent is able to generate meanings that are socially valid, i.e., valid not only for one agent but for a group of agents. Generating meanings that are valid for more that one agent is beyond normal agent capabilities, which makes sapient agents really special.

To some extent, sapient systems can voluntarily select and use shared ontologies (those that are used by others) and prediction engines to generate meanings that are valid for them. This capability of shared ontology selection and use is largely sought (Mizoguchi and Ikeda 1996) in present-day research on distributed information systems (see, e.g., the efforts related to the semantic web). The sharing of an ontology is what enables agent teams to collaborate in the execution of task as a group (see Fig. 9).

Beyond the meaning calculation fact, sapient systems usually manifest themselves by means of their explanatory capabilities; i.e., they can communicate the results of the calculation to the target agent. This may be seen as clearly rejecting those fashionable accounts of sapience as obscure manifestations of mental capability. Explanation is hence strongly related to the perception of sapience [see Craik (1943) Brewer et al. (1998) or Wilson and Keil (1998)].

Obviously this vision is strongly related to the psychology concept of "theories of mind," but goes well beyond it in the sense that the "theory of mind" is typically restricted to agent-to-agent interaction.

Fig. 9 Multiagent systems can only operate if the ontologies are shared to be able to reconstruct meaning from messages coming from other agents

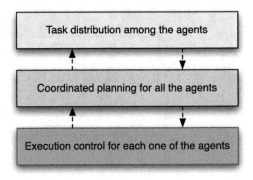

This view of sapience can be implicit or explicit (when the sapient system consciously uses the model of the other to calculate meanings). It is like having 'deliberative' sapience.

7 Meanings in Hive Minds

Of major interest for those of us who focus our research in the domain of complex distributed controllers is the capability of exploiting this sapience mechanics to improve the integration level of a distributed controller.

We may wonder to what extent meaning integration can lead to mind federation and the emergence of a single, unified controller: a hive mind. If meaning is globally integrated it implies that the different subsystems may be aware of what is going on that is affecting other subsystems. A kind of distributed consciousness emerges.

Some people have considered the possibility of shared or collective consciousness even for humans [see, e.g., Hardy 1998, Sheldrake 1988, or Laszlo 1996]. From this perspective, individuals can conjointly share a particular experience even from distance.

People dealing with practically independent environments can use other's previous experiences in similar situations to better understand the present state of affairs. These previous experiences are culturally shared, and when executed over similar virtual machines (Sloman and Chrisley 2003) can generate similar interpretations of reality that coalesce into coherent social behaviors that can be seen as a form of collective understanding.

Perhaps we can exploit this kind of social phenomenon in the implementation of advanced cognitive conscious modular controllers.

8 Conclusions

Agent's meanings are not static interpretations of agent-perceived data but do capture future trajectories of the agent in his state space in a particular context. This is strongly related to Putnam's (1975) causal theory of meaning.

Sapient systems are agents that have the capability of generating meanings for others, i.e., they can assess situations as other agents would do and suggest courses of action based on an other agents set of values.

Wisdom is hence nothing categorically different from what is available in conventional agent architectures, but a particular capability of an agent to use its own resources to think for others. Wisdom in hence attributed by others owing to this capability that goes beyond usual agent capabilities.

This understanding of meaning is strongly related to recent theories of consciousness and lead us to the possibility of achieving consciousness states in control systems (Sanz and Meystel 2002).

This approach to explicit management of meanings is currently under implementation in the SOUL Project (http://www.aslab.org/public/projects/SOUL/) in the authors' laboratory.

Acknowledgments The authors would like to acknowledge the support of the Spanish Ministry of Education and Science through the DPI C3 grant and the support of the European Commission through the IST ICEA grant.

References

Albus, J. S. (1992). A reference model architecture for intelligent systems design. In Antsaklis, P. and Passino, K. (ed.), *An Introduction to Intelligent and Autonomous Control*, pages 57–64. Kluwer Boston.

Albus, J. S., and Barbera, A. J. (2005). RCS: A cognitive architecture for intelligent multi-agent systems. *Annual Reviews in Control*, 29(1):87–99.

Brewer, W. F., Chinn, C. A., and Samarapungavan, A. (1998). Explanation in scientists and children. *Minds and Machines*, 8:119–136.

Clark, A. (1998). Twisted tales: Causal complexity and cognitive scientific explanation. *Minds and Machines*, 8:79–99.

Combs, A. (2000). Book review: Networks of meaning: The bridge between mind and matter, by Christine Hardy. *Nonlinear Dynamics, Psychology, and Life Sciences*, 4(1):129–134.

Craik, K. (1943). *The Nature of Explanation*. Cambridge University Press, Cambridge.

Freeman, W. J. (1997). A neurobiological interpretation of semiotics: meaning vs. representation. In *1997 IEEE International Conference on Systems, Man, and Cybernetics*, vol. 2, pages 12–15.

Gibson, J. J. (1979). *The Ecological Approach to Visual Perception*. Houghton Mifflin, Boston.

Glenberg, A. (1997). What memory is for. *Behavioral and Brain Sciences*, 1(20): 1–55.

Glenberg, A. M., Robertson, D. A., Jansen, J. L., and Johnson-Glenberg, M. C. (1999). Not propositions. *Journal of Cognitive Systems Research 1*, 1:19–33.

Griswold, W., and Notkin, D. (1995). Architectural tradeoffs for a meaning-preserving program restructuring tool. *IEEE Transactions on Software Engineering*, 21(4):275–287.

Hardy, C. (1998). *Networks of Meaning: The Bridge Between Mind and Matter*. Praeger/Greenwood, Westport, CT.

Harnad, S. (1990). The symbol grounding problem. *Physica D*, 42:335–346.

Lakoff, J. (1987). *Women, fire and dangerous things: What categories reveal about the mind*. University of Chicago Press, Chicago.

Landauer, C. (1998). Data, information, knowledge, understanding: computing up the meaning hierarchy. In *1998 IEEE International Conference on Systems, Man, and Cybernetics*, vol. 3, pages 2255–2260.

Laszlo, E. (1996). *The Whispering Pond*. Element Books, Rockport, MA.

Lawrence W. Barsalou. (1999). Perceptual Symbol Systems. *Behavioral and Brain Sciences*, 22:577–660.

Mayorga, R. V. (2005). Towards computational sapience (wisdom): A paradigm for sapient (wise) systems. In *IEEE International Conference on Integration of Knowledge Intensive Multi-agent Systems*, Boston.

Meystel, A. (2001). Multiresolutional representation and behavior generation: How do they affect the performance of intelligent systems. In *Tutorial at ISIC'2001*, Mexico D.F.

Meystel, A. M. (2003). Multiresolutional hierarchical decission support systems. *IEEE Transactions on Systems, Man and Cybernetics*, 33(1):86–101.

Mizoguchi, R., and Ikeda, M. (1996). Towards ontology engineering. Technical Report AI-TR-96-1, The Institute of Scientific and Industrial Research, Osaka University.

Oyama, S. (1985). *The Ontogeny of Information: Developmental Systems and Evolution*. Cambridge University Press, Cambridge.

Putnam, H. (1975). *Mind, Language and Reality*. Number 2 in Philosophical Papers. Cambridge University Press, Cambridge.

Sanz, R. (1990). *Arquitectura de Control Inteligente de Procesos*. PhD thesis, Universidad Politécnica de Madrid.

Sanz, R., MatLa, F., and Gal7n, S. (2000). Fridges, elephants and the meaning of autonomy and intelligence. In *IEEE International Symposium on Intelligent Control, ISIC'2000*, Patras, Greece.

Sanz, R., and Meystel, A. (2002). Modeling, self and consciousness: Further perspectives of AI research. In *Proceedings of PerMIS '02, Performance Metrics for Intelligent Systems Workshop*, Gaithersburg, MD.

Shanon, B. (1988). Semantic representation of meaning: A critique. *Psychological Bulletin*, 104:7–83.

Sheldrake, R. (1988). *The Presence of the Past*. Random House, New York.

Sloman, A., and Chrisley, R. (2003). Virtual machines and consciousness. *Journal of Consciousness Studies*, 10(4-5):133–172.

Steels, L. (1998). The origins of syntax in visually grounded robotic agents. *Artificial Intelligence*, 103:133–156.

Tien, J. M. (2003). Toward a decision informatics paradigm: A real-time, information-based approach to decision making. *IEEE Transactions on Systems, Man, and Cybernetics-Part C: Applications and Reviews*, 33(1):102–112.

Tuomi, I. (1999). Data is more than knowledge. In *Proceedings of the 32nd Hawaii International Conference on System Sciences*.

von Uexk|ll, J. (1982). The theory of meaning. *Semiotica*, 42(1):25–82.

Wilson, R. A., and Keil, F. (1998). The shadows and shallows of explanation. *Minds and Machines*, 8:137–159.

Part II
Sapient Agents

Toward BDI Sapient Agents: Learning Intentionally

Alejandro Guerra-Hernández, and Gustavo Ortíz-Hernández

Abstract Sapient agents have been characterized as systems that learn their cognitive state and capabilities through experience, considering social environments and interactions with other agents or humans. The BDI (belief, desire, intention) model of cognitive agency offers philosophical grounds on intentionality and practical reasoning, as well as an elegant abstract logical semantics. However, the lack of learning and social competences of this model constitutes a serious limitation when sapient agents are the issue. This chapter discusses some ideas on intentional and social learning, that support the revision of practical reasons by the BDI agents. The resulting agents can learn, and then update, their plans' contexts to avoid forming intentions that eventually fail. Individual and social learning have been successfully attained in our own BDI interpreter based on dMARS, and ported to the Jason interpreter based on AgentSpeak(L). Multiagent consistency is guaranteed through a protocol based on cooperative goal adoption. These BDI learning agents seems closer to the intended characterization of sapient agents.

1 Introduction

Sapient agents have been characterized as systems that learn their cognitive state and capabilities through experience (Otterlo et al. 2003). Other features of such agents include the ability to consider social environments, interaction with other agents or humans, and the ability to deal with emotions. One of the best-known models of cognitive agency is the belief, desire, intention (BDI) approach. The relevance of this model can be explained in terms of its philosophical base on intentionality (Dennett 1987) and practical reasoning (Bratman 1987), as well as its elegant abstract logical semantics (Rao 1996, Rao and Georgeff 1998, Singh et al. 1999, Wooldridge 2000). However, if sapience is the issue, two well-known limitations of this model must be considered (Georgeff et al. 1999): its lack of learning and social competences. This chapter discusses some extensions to the BDI model (Guerra-Hernández et al. 2001,

A. Guerra-Hernández
Dept. de Inteligencia Artificial, Universidad Veracruzana, Xalapa, Veracruz, México
e-mail: aguerra@uv.mx

R.V. Mayorga, L.I. Perlovsky (eds.), *Toward Artificial Sapience,*
© Springer 2008

2004a,b, 2005), that enable intentional and social learning. By intentional learning, we mean that these agents can learn, and then update, their practical reasons (plans' contexts) to adopt an intention, particularly to correct experienced failures. By social learning, we mean that these agents can interact through collaborative goal adoption (Castelfranchi 1998) to learn intentionally and keep consistency in their multiagent system (MAS). The resulting BDI learning agents seem closer to the intended characterization of sapient agents.

The organization of the chapter is as follows: Since the BDI model is well known, Section 2 offers a very brief introduction to BDI agency, pointing out some relevant concepts and references. Section 3 discusses BDI learning agents' design issues. Section 4 focuses on a scale of learning agents, induced by their degree of awareness. Section 5 present some examples of BDI learning agents at the first two levels of the proposed scale: individual and collaborative learning. Finally Section 6 concludes and presents future work, including a new protocol based on incremental learning.

2 BDI Agency and Learning

Agents are usually characterized as systems that exhibit flexible autonomous behavior (Wooldridge 2000). BDI models of agency approximate this kind of behavior through two related theories about the philosophical concept of intentionality: Intentional systems are defined as entities that appear to be subject of beliefs, desires and other propositional attitudes (Dennett 1987); and the practical reasoning theory (Bratman 1987) is proposed as a common sense psychological framework to understand ourselves and others, based on beliefs, desires, and intentions conceived as partial, hierarchical plans. These related notions of intentionality provide us with the tools to describe agents at the right level of abstraction, i.e., adopting the intentional stance, and to design agents in a way that is compatible with such an intentional description, i.e., as practical reasoning systems.

Different aspects of intentionality and practical reasoning have been formally studied, resulting in the so-called BDI logics (Rao and Georgeff 1998). For a road map of the evolution of these formalisms, see Singh et al. (1999) and Wooldridge (2000). Implementations made use of refinement techniques, e.g., using specifications in Z language (Lightfoot 1991). A different approach is provided by AgentSpeak(L) (Rao 1996), a formal BDI model closer to the agent-oriented programming paradigm. Jason (Bordini and Hübner 2006) is an extended interpreter for AgentSpeak(L) implemented in Java. Originally our agents ran on a BDI architecture (Fig. 1) following dMARS specification in Z (Inverno et al. 1997). This architecture was implemented *ex nihilo* (Guerra-Hernández et al. 2001, 2004b) in Lisp. Recently, we have ported the approach to AgentSpeak(L), implementing it in Jason (Bordini and Hübner 2006).

When learning is considered independently of the implementation, (Fig. 2) we assume that the BDI interpreter corresponds to the performance element in the abstract learning architecture (Russell and Norvig 1995). The performance element

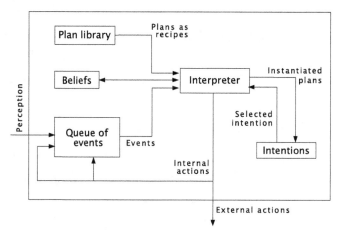

Fig. 1 A BDI architecture following dMARS specification

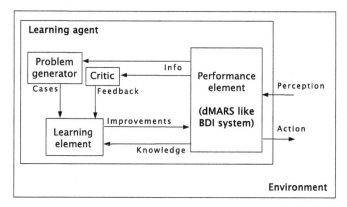

Fig. 2 Abstract learning architecture

is responsible for deciding what to do. The learning element is intended to provide modifications to the performance element to improve the behavior of the agent. The critic provides feedback about the performance of the agent, while the problem generator suggests cases or situations that constitute informative experiences for the learning element.

What do we mean by learning intentionally? Assume that the robots shown in the Fig. 3 are BDI agents. Suppose that r2 is thinking about what object it should take. Since it is deciding what to do, r2 is performing practical reasoning. Suppose r1 is figuring out what object r2 will take. Since it is modifying its beliefs, r1 is performing epistemic reasoning. Practical and epistemic reasoning are present explicitly in the BDI agents. They are activated by the achieve (!) and test (?) goals, respectively. Learning intentionally is related to practical reasoning.

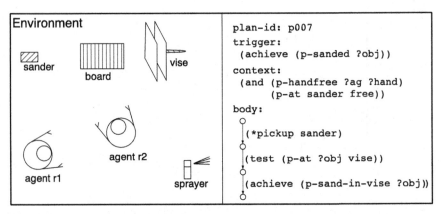

Fig. 3 Simple scenario of BDI agents and a plan

Practical reasoning leads to the adoption of intentions. For example, if an agent perceives the event `!p-sanded(board)`, it will look for relevant plans, i.e., the plans which trigger unifies the event. This is the case of the plan in the Fig. 3:

```
@p007
!p-sanded(Obj) : p-handfree(Ag, Hand) & p-at(sander, free)
    <- .pickup(sander);
       ?p-at(Obj, vise);
       !p-sanded-vise(Obj)}.
```

In what follows, AgentSpeak(L) syntax is adopted. Plans have the form `@Id trigger : context <- body`. Then, in order to form an intention, the agent will look for an applicable plan, i.e., a relevant plan whose context is a logical consequence of its current belief.

Although the agent seems to be performing a kind of epistemic reasoning to adopt its intentions, in fact it is only verifying if its practical reasons for adopting the plan as an intention are supported by its beliefs. From the role of beliefs in the theory of practical reasoning (Bratman 1987), e.g., the standard and filter of admissibility, it is clear that even when the beliefs justify the agent's behavior, they do it as part of a background frame that, together with prior intentions, constrains the adoption of new intentions. In doing so, beliefs are playing a different role than the one they play in epistemic reasoning. Particularly, practical reasons to act sometimes differ from epistemic reasons. This is the case for reasonableness of arbitrary choices in Buridan cases (situations equally desirable); e.g., it is practical reasonable for agent r2 to choose any plan in the set of relevant applicable plans to form an intention, even if there is no epistemic reason, no reason purely based on the beliefs of the agent, behind this choice. Sometimes this is called wishful thinking, and it is not epistemic reasonable for agent r1 to believe that agent r2 will take the sander in this way.

What is relevant here is that the contexts express practical reasons to act in some way and not in another face to desires. The context, together with the background frame of beliefs and prior intentions, supports the rational behavior of intentional agents. Contexts are the target concept, if BDI agents are going to learn about their practical reasons for satisfying desires.

3 Design Issues

Once the context of the plans has been identified as the target concept, all the other issues of the abstract learning architecture can be approached.

3.1 Representation

Representations in the BDI model are based on first-order formulas. If *at* is an atomic formula, then the well-formed formula (wff) of AgentSpeak(L) is given by the following grammar $\varphi ::= at|\neg at|\varphi \wedge \varphi'$. Beliefs are grounded atomic formulas, like Prolog facts. The extended interpreter Jason also considers disjunctions of the form $\varphi \vee \varphi'$. The context of the plans is expressed as a wff, which may include variables, e.g., `p-freehand(Ag, Hand) & p-at(sander, free)`. In dMARS, wffs of the form $at|\neg at$ are known as belief formulas, whereas those including disjunctions and conjunctions are known as situation formulas. This representation has two immediate consequences for the candidate learning methods: Given the first-order nature of the representation, propositional learning methods are discarded, and the fact that the context of plans is represented as a situation formulas demands disjunctive hypothesis, e.g., decision trees.

3.2 Feedback

Getting feedback from the BDI interpreter is almost direct, since it usually detects and processes success and failure of the execution of intentions. This is done by executing a set of internal actions, e.g., adding or deleting beliefs, and posting events, according to the result obtained in executions. Jason and any BDI interpreter can be extended with a special internal action that generates a log file of training examples for the learning task. Items to build these examples include: the beliefs characterizing the situation when the plan was selected to form an intention, the label of success or failure after the execution of the intention, the plan, and the agent identifications.

3.3 Background Knowledge

Although most of the time, agents do not use the knowledge they have for learning, this is not a good idea provided that BDI agents have very rich prior information. There are two possible sources of background knowledge. First, the plan library may be seen as background knowledge, since plans state expected effects that, from the perspective of the agent, must hold in the environment; i.e., the event e will be satisfied with the plan p execution, and this is the case if the context of p is a logical consequence of the beliefs of the agent. Second, we keep track of predicates and functions, as well as the signatures used to define the agents. This is used to specify the language for the target concept.

3.4 Top-Down Induction of Logical Decision Trees

Owing to the disjunctive nature of the context of plans, decision trees are adopted as the target representation. Top-down induction of decision trees is a widely used and efficient machine learning technique. As defined in the ID3 algorithm (Quinlan 1986) it approximates discrete target-value functions. Targets are represented as trees, corresponding to a disjunction of conjunctions of constraints on the attribute values of the instances. Each path from the decision tree root to a leaf corresponds to a conjunction of attribute tests, and the tree itself is the disjunction of these conjunctions. However, as one can guess, the ID3-like approaches have a propositional nature, where training examples are represented as a fixed set of attribute-value pairs. It is assumed that all the information available to be learned is in the examples, i.e., the background knowledge is not considered.

Logical decision trees upgrade the attribute-value representation to first-order, using the inductive logic programming (ILP) setting known as learning from interpretations (Blockeel and Raedt 1998). In this setting, each training example e is represented by a set of facts. Background knowledge can be given in the form of a Prolog program B. The interpretation that represents the example is the set of all ground facts that are entailed by $e \wedge B$, i.e., its minimal Herbrand model. Observe that instead of using a fixed-length vector to represent e, as in the case of an attribute-value pairs representation, a set of facts is used. This makes the representation much more flexible. Learning from interpretations can be defined as follows. Given: (i) a target variable Y; (ii) a set of labeled examples E, each consisting of a a set of definite clauses e labeled with a value y in the domain of Y; (iii) a language L; (iv) a background theory B, find a hypothesis $H \in L$ such that for all examples labeled with y: (i) $H \wedge e \wedge B \models label(y)$; and (ii) $\forall y' \neq y : H \wedge e \wedge B \not\models label(y')$.

The learning from interpretations setting, as the propositional case, exploits the local assumption, i.e., all the information that is relevant for a single example is localized in two ways: Information contained in the examples is separated from the information in background knowledge and information in one example is separated from information in other examples (Muggleton and Raedt 1994). The local assumption is relevant if we want the agents configuring their learning settings themselves.

Tilde (Blockeel et al. 2000) is a learning from interpretations system to induce logical decision trees, i.e., decision trees where every internal node is a first-order conjunction of literals. It uses the same heuristics as ID3 algorithms (gain-ratio and postpruning heuristics), but computations of the tests are based on the classical refinement operator under Θ-subsumption, which requires the specification of a language L stating which kind of tests are allowed in the decision tree.

4 Social Awareness

The awareness of other agents in the system seems to be indicative of a MAS hierarchy of increasing complexity. In a certain way, this hierarchy corresponds to the scale of intentionality discovered by Dennett (1987). Levels in the awareness hierarchy are as follows:

1. At the first level, agents act and learn from direct interaction with the environment. They are not explicitly aware of other agents in the MAS. However, the changes produced by other agents in the environment may be perceived by the learning agent. For example, in the scenario of Fig. 3, $r1$ can be specialized in painting objects, while $r2$ sands them. It is possible to program the painter robot without awareness of the sander, i.e., all $r1$ has to know is that once an object is sanded, it can be painted. The true isolated learning case with one agent may be seen as a special case of this level.
2. At the second level, agents act and learn from direct interaction with other agents using message exchange. For the example above, the sander robot can inform the painter robot that an object is already sanded. Alternatively, the painter agent can ask the sander robot for this information. Exchange of training examples in learning processes is also considered.
3. At the third level, agents act and learn from the observation of the actions performed by other agents in the system. This involves a different kind of awareness from that of level 2. Agents are not only aware of the presence of other agents, but they are also aware of their competences; hence the painter robot is able to perceive that the sander robot is going to sand the table. Observe that this seems to involve epistemic reasoning, e.g., adopting the belief that $r2$ will sand the object.

The purpose of our BDI agents while learning is to update the context of a plan after its execution has failed. If an agent can update this context after its own experience, no communication is needed and learning is performed at level 1 of the hierarchy. Otherwise, the agent will try to learn from the experience of other agents, starting a kind of collaborative goal adoption process (Castelfranchi 1998), where the agents in the MAS sharing the same plan cooperate with the goal of the learner agent because they are also interested in the results of its learning process, e.g., inducing the updated context of the shared plan. The group of agents interested in a learning goal may be seen as an emerging social structure, where the roles of learner and supervisors are dynamically assigned. An incremental version of this protocol (Bourgne et al. 2007) is discussed in future work.

5 BDI Learning Agents

In order to test the AgentSpeak(L) implementation of our intentional learning approach, we decided to use the well-known MAS examples, e.g., those in Jason's distribution. The idea is to modify some contexts in the plan library of the agents

Table 1 Some beliefs and a plan in the blocks world

Beliefs	Plan
on(b,a).	@stack
clear(b).	+!stack(X,Y) : clear(Y) & holding(X) <-
clear(c).	-clear(Y); -holding(X);
onTable(a).	+armEmpty; +on(X,Y);
onTable(c).	.print("Stacking ",X," on ", Y).
armEmpty.	

and observe whether they are able to learn a new context and how this new context compares with the original one. The example used in this section is the well-known blocks world. Table 1 (analogous to Fig. 3) shows a situation in this environment represented by a set of beliefs and a plan for stacking a block. The context of the plan `stack` constrains the plan to be applicable only if the destination is clear (`clear(Y)`) and the agent is holding the block to be stacked (`holding(X)`). What would happen if our definition for this plan did not consider the atom `holding(X)`? The plan would fail (the agent cannot forget (–) what it did not believe) and the agent should reconsider its practical reasons for adopting this plan as an intention.

5.1 Centralized Learning (level 1)

Suppose the plan `stack` failed because of the reasons explained above. We want the agent trying to learn why the plan failed, if there were practical reasons to adopt it as an intention. In order to execute the learning process, the agent posts the event `!pLearn(stack)` when detecting the failure of the plan. There is a relevant plan for this kind of event:

```
@learningPlan
+!pLearn(Plan) : flag(newExample)
   <- ia.makeSet(Plan);
      ia.execTilde(Plan);
      ia.updatePContex(Plan,C,V);
      ia.evalLearnedContext(Plan,C,V).
```

When the success or failure of an intention is detected, the agent keeps track of these executions as training examples. If at least one new example has been collected by the agent, it believes `flag(newExample)`, and the `learningPlan` becomes executable. While in dMARS failed plans are not intended again; this is not the case in Jason, where the agent can intend the plan again and collect more training examples. The internal action `ia.makeSet` configures the learning task of the agent, generating the files required by Tilde to learn: a knowledge base (`.kb`); the background knowledge (`.bg`); and the settings (`.s`), including the language bias *L*. The identifier `Plan` names these files, which are generated automatically by the agent as follows.

Each learning example is coded as a model of the learning from an interpretations paradigm. A model starts with a label that indicates the `success` or `failure` of the plan execution. Then a predicate `plan/2` is added to establish that the model is an instance of the execution of a particular plan by a particular agent. The model also contains the beliefs that the agent had when the plan was selected to form an intention. The label is added in the execution phase of the BDI interpreter. Table 2 shows some models generated for the plan `stack` by the agent `c1`.

Then the configuration file is generated. Following the example, it is named `stack.s`. The first part of this file is common to all configurations. It specifies the information printed while learning (talking); the minimal number of cases in a leaf; the format of the output (C4.5-like and as a logic program); and the classes for the target concept, i.e., either success or failure:

```
talking(0).
load(models).
minimal_cases(1).
output_options([c45,lp]).
classes([success, failure]).
```

The second part of the configuration file specifies the predicates to be considered while inducing the tree. The `rmode` command is used to define the language bias £ as follows: The '#' sign may be seen as a variable place holder that takes its constant values from the examples in the knowledge base. The '+' prefix means that the variable must be instantiated after the examples in the knowledge base. The way our agent generates this file relies on the agent definition. Table 3 shows the language bias for this example, generated automatically by agent `c1` based on its own definition.

The agent executes a modified noninteractive version of ACE (Blockeel et al. 2000) and automatically extracts the learned hypothesis from the `stack.out` file, to accordingly modify the definition of the plan. It is also possible to ask the user to modify the plans, showing him the obtained results:

Table 2 Training examples for the plan `stack`, collected by agent `c1`

begin(model(1)).	begin(model(2)).	begin(model(3)).	begin(model(4)).
failure.	success.	success.	success.
plan(c1,stack).	plan(c1,stack).	plan(c1,stack).	plan(c1,stack).
clear(b).	holding(c).	holding(b).	holding(c).
clear(c).	clear(b).	clear(b).	clear(a).
onTable(a).	clear(c)	clear(a).	clear(c).
onTable(c).	onTable(a).	clear(a).	clear(b).
on(b,a).	on(b,a).	onTable(a).	onTable(a).
armEmpty.	end(model(2)).	onTable(c).	onTable(b).
end(model(1)).		end(model(3)).	end(model(4))
begin(model(5)).	begin(model(6)).	begin(model(7)).	
success.	success.	failure.	
plan(c1,stack).	plan(c1,stack).	plan(c1,stack).	
holding(b).	holding(b).	clear(b).	
clear(b).	clear(b).	on(c,a).	
clear(c).	clear(c).	on(c,a).	
clear(a).	on(c,a).	on(b,c).	
onTable(a).	onTable(a).	onTable(a).	
onTable(c).	onTable(c).	onTable(c).	
end(model(5)).	armEmpty.	armEmpty.	
	end(model(6)).	end(model(7)).	

Table 3 Language bias in the configuration file

rmode(plan(Agent,Plan)).	rmode(clear(#)).
rmode(clear(X)).	rmode(clear(#)).
rmode(onTable(X)).	rmode(onTable(#)).
rmode(on(X,Y)).	rmode(on(#,+Y)).
rmode(armEmpty).	rmode(on(+X,#)).
rmode(holding(X)).	rmode(on(#,#)).
	rmode(holding(#)).

```
holding(X) ?
+--yes: [true]  5.0  [[true:5.0,false:0.0]]
+--no:  [false] 2.0  [[true:0.0,false:2.0]]
```

This example used seven models (Table 2) and the time of induction was 0.032 seconds, running on a Linux SuSe Intel Centrino 1.73 GHz. The result suggests a new plan context: `clear(Y) & holding(X)` (the original plan context!).

5.2 Decentralized Learning (Level 2)

Why should a BDI agent learning at level 1, try to communicate to learn (Guerra-Hernández et al. 2004a)? There are two situations in which an agent should consider communication while learning: when the agent is not able to start learning, i.e., it does not have enough examples or when it is not able to find a hypothesis to explain the failure of the plan in question. In both cases the learning agent may ask for more examples from other agents in the MAS.

Sharing examples in this way resembles other cases of distributed learning. Vertical fragmentation used to be a delicate issue in such settings, but not here since the examples are represented as labeled sets of definite clauses. Consider the training examples in Table 2. From the learning from interpretations perspective, these training examples are just models of a target concept, even if they are not homogeneous, e.g., model 1 has information about `armEmpty`, whereas model 2 does not. In propositional representations this implies that the attribute belongs to a different data source (vertical fragmentation). Avoiding this is very important: since our BDI learning agents face only horizontal fragmentation, the exchange of training examples is enough to achieve learning at level 2.

A group of agents is said to have the same *competence* for a given event if they share the same plan to deal with it. Competence in our approach is defined in terms of plans, because the event they deal with is already included in the plan definition. Competence induces two ways of asking help: a message including the label of the plan being learned is broadcast, and the agents sharing the same plan accept and process the message or the agent sends the message only to the agents with the same competence. We allow both options: The internal action `ia.setTolearningMode/3` takes the following as arguments: the plans for which learning is enabled (it is possible to specify `all`); the agents sharing the same competence (`all` means broadcasting); and some debug options; e.g., the action `ia.setTolearningMode([stack], [c2,c3], [verbose(true)])` means that the agent will learn about plan `stack` communicating with `c2` and `c3`, while giving some output details about the learning process.

In the Jason implementation, a learning agent at level 1 always tries to learn when a new example is acquired (`flag(newExample)`). So, the plan `pLearn` can only fail if the learning process does not produce an hypothesis. If this is the case, the agent posts the event `!gatherExamples`. There are two applicable plans for the triggering event `+!gatherExamples` (Table 4). First, the plan `gatherExamples_i` will iterate the whole list of agents asking each one for examples about `Plan`, while adopting answers from other agents in `List` as part of its own beliefs. After that, the agent tries to learn again (`gatherExamples_f`). Jason adopts Knowledge Query Meta Language (KQML) (Moreira et al. 2003) for communication.

The result obtained at level 2 is the same as that the obtained at level 1, the agent updates the context of the plan with the original definition. But observe that following the dMARS approach to failed plans, agent `c1` can achieve this result only at level 2. There is no way for it to collect the examples required to successfully learn the context alone. But even under the Jason approach enabling it to intend a failed plan again, the examples collected by a single agent seem to contribute little information. Also, observe that since BDI agents collect the training examples after their own experience, these examples are harder to obtain than in classic supervised machine learning, where they are previously collected by a supervisor, or in reinforcement learning, where agents explore the space of hypothesis while acting in a natural way. The use of ILP methods helps the agent since fewer examples may be needed to learn, provided that the background theory is relevant. Furthermore, situating the learning agent in a MAS at level 2, may help it to collect training examples faster, taking advantage of the experience of other agents. Table 5 shows the log of a descentralized learning process.

The result of a learning process is shared by the agents in the MAS. If the user or the agent modifies the plan definition according to the decision tree found, the change automatically affects all agents having this plan in their libraries. This justifies the cooperative goal adoption strategy: sharing examples is easy, whereas learning is not, but learning sometimes is not possible without cooperation, so cooperation becomes advantageous.

Table 4 Plans for gathering examples distributed in the MAS

```
@gatherExamplesf
+!gatherExamples([],Plan) : true

   <- !pLearn(Plan).
@gatherExamplesi
+!gatherExamples([Ag|T],Plan) : true

   <- .send(Ag, askAll, value([Plan,X,L,Y],example(Plan,X,L,Y)),List);
   !adoptList(List);
   !gatherExamples(T,Plan).
```

Table 5 Decentralized learning in the blocks world

```
[c1] saying: PLAN stack FAILED
[c1] saying: EXECUTE LEARNING FOR stack
[report] CURRENT EXAMPLES
[report] c1: example(stack,[clear(b),clear(c),onTable(a),
                   onTable(c),on(b,a),do,counter(1),
                   armEmpty],failure)
[c1] saying: CAN'T LEARN. CONTEXT IS clear(Y)
[c1] saying: NO NEW EXAMPLES, ASKING FOR HELP
...
[c1] saying: EXECUTE LEARNING FOR stack
[report] CURRENT EXAMPLES
[report] c1: example(stack,[clear(b),clear(c),onTable(a),onTable(c),
                   on(b,a),do,counter(1),armEmpty],failure)
[report] c1: example(stack,[holding(c),clear(b),clear(c),onTable(a),
                   on(b,a),do,counter(1)],success) [source(self)]
...
[report] c1: example(stack,[clear(b),clear(c),onTable(a),onTable(c),
                   on(b,a),do,counter(4),armEmpty],failure)
...
[showLearningRes] THE INDUCED TREE FOR stack IS:
[showLearningRes] holding(-A) ?
[showLearningRes] +--yes: [true] 5.0 [[true:5.0,false:0.0]]
[showLearningRes] +--no: [false] 4.0 [[true:0.0,false:4.0]]
[c1] saying: THE NEW CONTEXT FOR stack IS clear(Y) & ((holding(X)))
```

6 Results and Future Work

Our proposal for intentional learning in the context of BDI agency constitutes a relevant step toward sapience. Agents adopting this approach are able to perform a limited form of introspection: evaluate the validity of their practical reasons and modify such reasons trying to avoid failures. All of this in an autonomous way, as is required for sapient agents. Agents adopting the second level of social awareness exploit the interaction with other agents to learn, as is expected for a sapient agent. All of this exploiting social communication is based on speech acts. The BDI agents, extended in this way, seem closer to the intended characterization of sapient agents.

Of course learning about the practical reasons to adopt a plan as an intention is only one of the possible issues a sapient agent should learn about. What is relevant is that the kind of learning proposed here is performed according to the principles of intentionality and practical reasoning. Learning about other issues must take the same considerations into account.

Future work is related to the Smile ;-) protocol (Bourgne et al. 2007), an acronym for sound multiagent incremental learning. Each agent in the MAS is assumed to be able to learn from the information it perceives. An agent i is defined as $a_i = \langle B_i, K_i \rangle$, where B_i is the belief or knowledge state of agent i; and K_i is the information it perceives. It is assumed that all agents in the MAS shared some common knowledge, denoted by B_C so that $\forall i \ B_C \subseteq B_i$. Common knowledge introduces dependences among the agents: If an agent a_i updates its state B_i obtaining B_i', but also modifying B_C into B_C', then every agent a_j must update its state B_j to obtain B_j' so that $B_C' \subseteq B_j'$. An agent a_i updates its state B_i because it perceives new information K_i. The agents are supposed to be capable of verifying consistency between states and information, e.g., logical consequence. An agent a_i

is *a-consistent* if and only if $Cons(B_i, K_i)$ is true; i.e., the information it perceives is a logical consequence of its beliefs. An agent a_i is *mas-consistent* if and only if $Cons(S_i, K_i \cup K)$ is true, where $\forall j \neq i$ $K = \bigcup K_j$. A MAS is *consistent* if every agent in the system is *mas-consistent*.

The protocol depends on a consistency revision mechanism M with the following properties: it is *locally efficient* in the sense that an agent i can always update B_i; it is *additive* in the sense that $Cons(B_i, K_1) \land Cons(B_i, K_2) \implies Cons(B_i, K_1 \cup K_2)$; it is *coherent* in the sense that $\forall i, j, k$ $Cons(B_i, K_i) \land Cons(B_j, K_j) \implies (Cons(B_i, K_i \cup k) \iff Cons(B_j, K_j \cup k))$. M is said to be *a-consistent* and *mas-consistent* if it preserves such properties of the agent applying M. The consistency revision mechanism M is said to be *strong mas-consistent* if its application by an agent a_i preserves the *mas-consistency* of $\forall j \neq i$ a_j.

Bourgne et al. (2007) proved that *mas-consistency* can be ensured for the propositional case by the reiterative application of a mechanism M by the learner agent, followed by some interactions with other agents restoring the *a-consistence*, until no inconsistent information is produced in such interactions. The mechanism is triggered by an agent a_i receiving some information k that is inconsistent: $Cons(B_i, k) = False$. An interaction between a_i and some critic a_j is denoted by $I(a_i, a_j)$ and performed as follows: a_i sends a_j the updated common beliefs B'_C produced by the local application of M, i.e., a_i is *a-consistent*; a_j checks B'_j induced by the updated B'_C. if these modifications preserve its *a-consistency*, a_j adopts them, sending a_i its acceptance; otherwise it sends its refusal with some information k' s.t. $Cons(B'_j, k') = False$. The protocol finishes when no k' is produced by any agent. It is also suggested that if the response of the agents is minimal and serial (k' is one inconsistent example and the a_i sends B'_C sequentially to other agents), then the protocol minimizes the amount of information transmitted by the agents.

Our current approach uses a consistency revision mechanism M that is not locally efficient (Tilde). It forces the learning agent to collect all the training examples available to start learning. We are implementing an incremental version of the revision mechanism (TildeLDS), which will enable us to fully adopt Smile (B_C is the set of plans shared by the agents). The learning agent will be able to recover consistency locally and communicate the learned context to other agents to compute mas-consistency.

Acknowledgments The second author is supported by Conacyt scholarship 197819. The intentional learning approach was conceived with Amal El-Fallah Seghrouchni and Henry Soldano at Paris 13. Gauvain Bourgne has shared with us his work on Smile.

References

Blockeel, H., and de Raedt, L. (1998). Top-down induction of first-order logical decision trees. *Artificial Intelligence*, 101(1–2):285–297.

Blockeel, H., Dehaspe, L., Demoen, B., Gerda, J., Ramon, J., and Vandecasteele, H. (2000). Executing query packs in ILP. In: Cussens, J. and Frish, A. (eds.). *Inductive Logic Programming*,

10th International Conference, ILP2000, London, *LNAI* 1866:60–77, Springer-Verlag, Berlin and Heidelberg.

Bordini, R.H., and Hübner, J.F (2006). BDI agent programming in AgentSpeak using Jason. In Toni, F. and Torroni, P. (eds), *Proceedings of the Sixth International Workshop on Computational Logic in Multi-Agent Systems (CLIMA VI), London*, 27–29 June, 2005, Revised Selected and Invited Papers, *LNCS* 3900:143–164, Springer-Verlag, Berlin and Heidelberg.

Bourgne, G., El-Fallah-Seghrouchni, A. and Soldano, H. (2007). *SMILE: Sound Multi-agent Incremental LEarning ;-) AAMAS'07, May* 14–17, 2007, ACM, Honolulu, Hawai'i.

Bratman, M. (1987). *Intention, Plans, and Practical Reason*. Harvard University Press, Cambridge, MA and London.

Castelfranchi, C. (1998). Modelling social action for AI agents. *Artificial Intelligence*, 103(1998):157–182.

Dennett, D.C. (1987). *The Intentional Stance*. MIT Press, Cambridge MA.

Georgeff, M., Pell, B., Pollak, M. Tambe, M., and Wooldridge, M. (1999). The belief-desire-intention model of agency. In: Müller, J., Singh, M. and Rao, A. (eds.), *Proceedings of the Fifth International Workshop on Intelligent Agents: Agent, Theories, Architectures, and Languages* (ATAL-98). LNAI 1555:1–10, Springer Verlag, Berlin and Heidelberg.

Guerra-Hernández, A., El-Fallah-Seghrouchni, A., and Soldano, H. (2001). BDI multiagent learning based on first-order induction of logical decision trees. In: *Intelligent Agents Technology: Research and Development. Proceedings of the second Asia-Pacific Conference on IAT*, Maebashi, Japan, November, 2001, World Scientific, Singapre, pp. 160–169.

Guerra-Hernández, A., El-Fallah-Seghrouchni, A., and Soldano, H. (2004a) Distributed learning in intentional BDI multiagent systems. In: Baeza-Yates, R., Marroquín, J.L., and Chávez, E. (eds.), *Proceedings of the Fifth Mexican International Conference on Computer Science* (ENC'04), pages 225–232, IEEE Computer Society.

Guerra-Hernández, A., El-Fallah-Seghrouchni, A., and Soldano, H. (2004b) Learning in BDI multiagent systems. In: Dix, J. and Leite, J. (eds.) CLIMA IV. *Computational Logic in Multi-Agent Systems: Fourth International Workshop*, Fort Lauderdale, FL, January 6–7, 2004. Selected and Invited Papers. *LNAI* 325:218–233, Springer Verlag, Berlin and Heidelberg.

Guerra-Hernández, A., El-Fallah-Seghrouchni, A., and Soldano, H. (2005). On Learning Intentionally. *Inteligencia Artificial, Revista Iberoamericana de Inteligencia Artificial*, 9(25):9–18.

d'Inverno, M., Kinny, D., Luck, M., and Wooldridge, M. (1997). A formal specification of Dmars. In: Singh, M., Rao, A. and Wooldridge, M. (eds.), *Intelligent Agents IV:* Proceedings of the Fourth International Workshop on Agent Theories, Architectures, and Languages. *LNAI* 1365:155–176, Springer Verlag, Berlin and Heidelberg.

Lightfoot, D. (1991). *Formal Specification Using Z. Macmillan Computer Science Series*. Macmillan, London.

Moreira, Á. F., and Bordini, R. (2003). An operational semantics for a BDI agent-oriented programming language. In: Omicini, A., Sterling, L., and Torroni, P. (eds.), *Declarative Agent Languages and Technologies*, First International Workshop, DALT 2003, Melbourne, Australia, July 15, 2003, Revised Selected and Invited Papers. *LNCS* 2990:135–154, Springer Verlag, Berlin and Heidelberg.

Muggleton, S., and de Raedt, L. (1994) Inductive logic programming: Theory and methods. *Journal of Logic Programming*, 19:629–679.

Otterlo, M. van, Wiering, M., Dastani, M., and Meyer, J.-J. (2003). A characterization of sapient agents. In: *IEEE International Conference on Integration of Knowledge Intensive Multi-Agent Systems*, KIMAS, Boston.

Quinlan, J. (1986). Induction of decision trees. *Machine Learning*, 1(1):81–106.

Rao, A. (1996). AgentSpeak(L): BDI agents speak out in a logical computable language. In: van Hoe, R. (ed.), Seventh European Workshop on Modelling Autonomous Agents in a Multi-Agent World, Eindhoven, The Netherlands.

Rao, A. and Georgeff, M. (1998) Decision procedures of BDI logics. *Journal of Logic and Computation*, 8(3):293–344.

Russell, S. and Norvig, P. (1995). *Artificial Intelligence: A Modern Approach*. Prentice-Hall, New Jersey.

Singh, M., Rao, A., Georgeff, M. (1999) Formal Methods in DAI: Logic-based representations and reasoning. In: Weiss, G (ed.), *Multiagent Systems: A Modern Approach to Distributed Artificial Intelligence*. MIT Press, Cambridge MA.

Wooldridge, M. (2000). *Reasoning about Rational Agents*. MIT Press, Cambridge MA.

Toward Wisdom in Procedural Reasoning: DBI, not BDI

Kirk A. Weigand

Abstract Belief, Desire, Intention (BDI) procedural reasoning agent systems are founded on philosophic presuppositions that may be reassessed to aid the construction of sapient (wise) agents. This paper proposes a fundamental shift in order from BDI to DBI such that desire precedes belief and intention. This re-ordering may improve the ability of agent systems to wisely utilize procedural reasoning. This re-ordering to DBI is driven by interdisciplinary integration including the process philosophy of Alfred North Whitehead and philosophy of embodiment of George Lakoff and Mark Johnson. Their philosophic shift aids the re-definition of desire as the perception of affordances in the world. This new degree of freedom in the operation of procedural reasoning enables the use of human-in-the-loop evaluation qualities of aesthetic, affective, and emotional value structures or cue saliency constellations. These affective symbolisms may support dynamic re-structuring necessary for wisely adapting procedures to unknowable futures.

1 Introduction

Wisdom is the glory of man, not ignorance; light, not darkness! (Abdu'l-Bahá 1972)

And of wisdom is the regard of place and the utterance of discourse according to measure and state. And of wisdom is decision; for man should not accept whatsoever anyone sayeth. ('Abdu-'l-Bahá 1990)

Our hope of building sapient or wise information systems may require a fundamental integration of human and information systems. The Belief, Desire, Intention (BDI) procedural reasoning agent system can be re-framed to make this shift from an information system with a human interface (with a programmer and/or user) to a human and information system. This requires an explication of the relationship

K.A. Weigand
Air Force Research Laboratory Information Directorate Wright-Patterson AFB, Ohio, USA
e-mail: Kirk.Weigand@WPAFB.AF.MIL

R.V. Mayorga, L.I. Perlovsky (eds.), *Toward Artificial Sapience,*   93
© Springer 2008

between humans and their information systems. Wisdom, knowledge, information and data must also be explained, disentangled and inter-related. The process philosophy of Alfred North Whitehead (1978) and the philosophy of embodiment of George Lakoff and Mark Johnson (Lakoff 1987; Lakoff and Johnson 1999) suggest a novel integration of perception, consciousness, emotion and reasoning to yield an important re-ordering from BDI to a new order of Desire, Belief and Intention (DBI). This apparently subtle change in order goes to the heart of tacit assumptions about the procedural reasoning methodology. Foremost among these assumptions is the implicit notion that beliefs – conscious reasons – precede and thereby serve to define subsequent desires and intentions.

This preliminary re-ordering and redefinition of BDI to DBI is accomplished by a method of interdisciplinary integration. Through support from various disciplines, a preponderance of theoretical support and empirical evidence enables this inductive synthesis of a preliminary, new and interdisciplinary conceptualization of procedural reasoning theory. This interdisciplinary approach challenges presuppositions that at first seem intuitive, i.e. that thoughts (beliefs) generate emotions (desires), but this notion stems from a tacit, culturally-widespread premise from psychology that feeling is an epiphenomenon of rational thought. Significantly, this assumption implicates and impedes the development of sapient systems by placing feeling in a subservient rather than an orthogonal role with respect to conscious reasoning. Notice that procedural reasoning systems are not explicitly named reasoning *and* valuing systems, yet they depend fundamentally on the value structures implicitly ascribed by their authors, coders and users. These value structures manifest in the priority schema and organization of objects in the code. If wisdom requires dynamic evaluation to adapt to unknowable future states of the world as they arise, having explicit control over the re-structurization of the code may enable this re-evaluation. This paper argues for a fundamental re-thinking of the BDI paradigm toward sapient multi-agent DBI systems. By exploring tacit or reduced presuppositions, the emergent property of a wise system may be discovered.

To theorize the existence of a wise, multi-agent system, first this paper will take a pragmatic, selective look at the existing BDI paradigm to help reveal the tacit assumption that the emotional value state of the system is produced by the rule set describing beliefs. With this emancipation of a new degree of freedom in the design of multi-agent systems, an alternative, complementary and orthogonal relationship is established between emotionally-based value structures and rational beliefs. The orthogonality of emotional, affective value structures with respect to rational logic has been supported from cross-cultural anthropology, process philosophy, cross-cultural psychology, group dynamics and sociology (Weigand 2002), so this will not be covered in detail here. A rework of all the semantics, propositions and lemmas from BDI to DBI may be a difficult job and is left for future work. With the plausibility of the orthogonality of affective value structures to rational logic supported philosophically, this new degree of freedom is used to posit a sapient, dynamic process as the continual realization of internal logic, objective context, affective evaluation and human-in-the-loop grounding from salient cues and expectations.

2 Why Re-order BDI?

Of course, this proposal to re-order BDI to DBI may meet many, significant objections. This new theory may re-open a host of solved problems, may be impractical or require extensive re-work before a mature system is available. A new DBI theory must elegantly solve not just an anomaly in the existing BDI approach, but some crisis (Kuhn 1996). This crisis is now apparent as we attempt to move beyond intelligent and knowledgeable systems toward wise systems. The sapient system must not only deliver – as in a knowledge system – the more relevant data given the context of the system and user(s), but also employ a causally efficacious induction that rolls-up this relevant data into information that matches the expectations of subject matter experts and that guides the untoward expectations of the typical novice. For example, a wise human is a subject matter expert who chooses the appropriate cues to satisfactorily and sufficiently (to satisfice per Herbert Simon) recommend a causally efficacious course of action. The causal efficacy of this expert's decision produces a fortunate and satisfactory effect as grounded by reality (Alfred North Whitehead 1978). Conversely, an expert or novice can misread cues or mistakenly focus on irrelevant stimuli and, consequently, produce an erroneous or ill-advised decision with an increased probability of an unfortunate outcome. Whether an outcome is fortunate or not depends on how fortune is defined and evaluated. So, a means for this evaluation becomes central to the crisis in the ability of multi-agent systems to consistently present the expected cues to wisely describe a dynamically unfolding situation.

BDI contains a means for evaluation of causal efficacy, but the evaluation schema appears to be buried in the code and therefore not accessible for adapting to unpredictable contexts. Systems exist that attempt to resolve contradictions through rule-based schemes, but they have yet to exploit emotions as a means of evaluation. If the sapient system is viewed as a cognitive prosthesis (Hayes and Hoffman 2003) for causally efficacious decisions, the sapient system should enhance the sensitivity to what is key to making good decisions. Historically, what is good and appropriate was the sole purview of the human. The human chose the appropriate application for the given context, but with the advent of sapient systems, the system must dynamically assess goodness, relevance, and appropriateness toward the accomplishment of some efficacious purpose across diverse situations. This tie to prosthetic functional enhancement and affordances fits with the intentional stance of Daniel Dennett, where BDI attributes are ascribed to predict behavior (Long and Esterline 2000). The sapient system may be able to find the appropriate intentional stance, if the evaluation schema can be accessible as a kind data used to guide the structure and prioritization of the code. The novel introduction of a cue saliency structure (Warwick et al. 2002) as an affective constellation of values (Crandall et al. 2003; Weigand and Mitta 2002) may provide a sapient system with this other degree of freedom to adjust and restructure the priority and attention of the agents in the system. If these agents can work sympathetically (Weigand 2002) in pursuit of the satisfaction of causal efficacy and adjust their priorities accordingly, the system may be said to be wise.

Some may argue that the order of BDI versus DBI is somewhat arbitrary in their actual applications. If true, this may indicate the trivial role of desires in the current BDI implementations where desires are simply second-order beliefs. Rao and Georgeff's application of BDI and naming as a procedural reasoning system suggests a subservient role for desire. In their applications, desires appear to be abstractions of beliefs. At the heart of BDI is Michael Bratman's construction of Gricean creatures via thought experiments about simple imaginary creatures (Bratman 2000). Bratman begins with Gricean Creature 1 – an imaginary creature with beliefs but driven incessantly by desire. From Creature 1, a more robust Creature 2 is imagined with the added complexity of considered desires. Considered desires are desires as accorded with beliefs. This suggests an introspective agent that attempts to integrate its desires with its beliefs. Here, Bratman leaves open the independence of desires from beliefs. Rao and Georgeff seem to have taken considered (rational) desires as the definition of desires, thus setting the order in BDI. As discussed below, interdisciplinary work supports a revolutionary notion that desires are a non-rational and independent dimension of human awareness. Lakoff and Johnson's extensive work supports this thesis (Lakoff and Johnson 1999).

If the order of BDI is critical to its architecture and application, then this leads to an impasse as a wise agent system. If the system can only reason in an analytic deductive sense, it can never induce other interpretations of the data that may have other potentially valuable kinds of causal efficacy. If BDI is attempting to wisely reason inductively as well as deductively, it must explicitly deal with other value structures that are not in accord with its current belief set. Different criteria may result in different fortunate evaluations of a phenomenon. But if BDI's considered desires are derived from and consistent with its current set of beliefs, it logically cannot propose desires that do not accord with its current beliefs. Yet, if its current beliefs turn out to be unfortunate (not causally efficacious by the current evaluation scheme), the system is stuck with no way to change its evaluation criteria. This conclusion is supported by the 1992 call by Georgeff for significant advances in dynamic machine interpretation for intelligent decision systems, yet he describes this as a need to improve the process of analysis and reasoning rather than synthesis and valuing (Georgeff 1992). Therefore, if the order of BDI is fixed, this may imply a philosophic dead end for BDI as a sapient system. By positing the independence of desire from belief and from considered desire, this new DBI approach suggests that desire is a complement and an equal partner to belief.

3 DBI as a Human and Information System

3.1 Knowledge as Inherently Human

Implicit so far in this discussion of the re-ordering of BDI to DBI is the debatable attempt to mimic human consciousness and awareness in the agent system, yet since wisdom appears to be deeply entangled in human conscious and unconscious avenues of awareness – including tacit knowledge and intuition (Klein 2003) – this DBI agent framework needs to have tight coupling to humans to even begin to approximate wisdom. This tight coupling may be achieved by mimicking our current, ever-expanding understanding of the human mind as embodied in the brain and the rest of the body. The explicit premise of this re-ordering is that a sapient DBI system must be a human-in-the-loop integrated system. Some of the attraction to BDI may be the ease with which designers and programmers can translate notions of beliefs, desires and intentions and map them to real-world applications. In this way BDI provides some proficiency for including humans-in-the-loop *a priori* to establish the appropriate value structures during design and coding, which results in subsequent, run-time evaluation by the multi-agent application. In DBI, this may be enhanced by run-time, human-in-the-loop, and dynamic re-evaluation with the goal of adaptive re-structurization of the code aided by human expectations through *in-situ* knowledge elicitation.

Fasli notes that BDI is useful because of its flexibility to model different degrees of realism (Fasli 2003). Once an application is built in BDI, the degree of realism becomes fixed in the implementation. As an advance over this fixed realism, a new sapient DBI system might dynamically determine which kind of realism is better suited and wiser to employ given a dynamic context.

A sapient system, from this perspective, requires humans in the loop to establish knowledge. McQuay's review of tacit knowledge research finds that knowledge does not seem to exist except in the mind of humans (McQuay 2000). Information and databases may provide elements of knowledge, but without coupling to human purpose and context, the relevance of this information cannot be ascertained, organized, presented and used. For example, a model of the physical structure of a chair might at first appear to be knowledge, yet unless some agent cares about the structural affordances of chairs, this may be extraneous information, e.g. the material composition of the chair does not directly contribute to the agents functional needs for the chair to support weight. Some additional information must be integrated with this information to yield usefulness via load analysis data. A human may "know" that chairs made of wood are strong enough to sit on. This integration of humans with computer agents leads to the discussions of autonomy and agency that are beyond the scope of this paper, yet as an explicit premise, humans are ultimately responsible for any agency granted to software agents. Therefore, the evaluation criteria used in sapient systems must entail human tacit knowledge and intuitive understanding. This dictates a close coupling and coordination between the human and information system, which is supported by Woods' claim that more complex autonomous operation demands higher coordination (Woods 2003).

3.2 The Crisis in BDI: The Wake that Steers the Boat

Below, the metaphor of a boat and its wake is used to demonstrate the crisis in the BDI framework if it is to be used as a sapient system. In the attempt to move BDI from a procedural reasoning system to one that chooses procedures wisely, a logical circularity becomes apparent, as the structure for evaluation requires it to question its own structure. By what meta-structure can the system evaluate its evaluation? A re-ordering of BDI to DBI is much more than a change of workflow in the code. Instead, DBI seeks to tie the human intuitive genius of evaluation with the computational brilliance of traditional procedural reasoning algorithms and processes.

Where BDI has gone astray of being a human analog is in its linkage of sensing to belief, because cognitive psychology suggests that sensing is more directly driven by desire, but cognitive psychology appears conflicted because it also says that desire results from belief. BDI associates belief with sensing the environment (Ingrand et al. 1992). These founders of BDI built knowledge areas (KAs) out of beliefs, goals and intentions, but their notion of desires as goals seems to reduce desires to behavioral objectives, which are difficult to distinguish from intentions. Fasli suggests from Searle that pro-attitudes such as desires and wishes have a "world-to-mind" mapping (Fasli 2003). This supports a tie between desires and sensation, which in turn suggests a tie to an aesthetic sensitivity to the world. Intuitively, we seem to feel the world before we are able to contemplate it. Unfortunately, BDI's assumption of three cognitive states – information, motivation, and deliberation – associates desire with the motivational state as a pro-attitude, which disconnects it from the "world-to-mind" sensory inputs and places belief as the information gathering intermediary between the world and motivation (Fasli 2003). Below the cognitive psychology research of Lakoff and others is used to resolve the conflict in the primacy of belief and desire.

The perceptual sub-system in BDI is linked to the beliefs about the world and this appears to be consistent with Carbo, Morlina and Davia's definition of beliefs as assumptions about the world as perceived (Carbo et al. 2001). However, this is not supported by cognitive psychology studies of naturalistic decision making of experts in complex situations. For example Klein's Recognition-Primed Decision (RPD) model has empirically verified that expert's subconscious perceptions of cues determines their attention and expectancies (Klein 2001). Conscious beliefs can arguably set the stage for this subconscious experience and in this way past beliefs seem to precede this experience of current desires, which is the basis of psychotherapies such as Rational Emotive Therapy (Hunt 1993). This argument, while apparently true, becomes mute when we define desires as the emotional experience of reality and *considered desires* as the rational introspection over current desires in the wake of past beliefs and intentions.

The metaphor of a boat plowing the water of experience may help show how evaluation and perception bring the unknown world into consciousness. The prow is emotional subconscious awareness (desire). Its attitude on the world is determined by beliefs represented by the current settings of throttle and rudder in the cockpit. This nautical trim or balancing of the boat establishes its attack through the water. Intentions are represented by the actual thrust and vector of the propeller and rudder. Intentions like the rudder make contact with the water of reality at the stern. In this metaphor, conscious awareness grows from fore to aft, from bow to stern. As the prow's direction is established by the history of interactions of the rudder and propeller with the water, so too are present desires vectored by past conscious beliefs and intentions. Still at any moment the boat is led by the prow of subconscious expectations as set by past states of the system. This metaphor implies an on-going cycle of feeling, thinking and acting as supported by the process philosophy of Alfred North Whitehead (1978). Lakoff empirically validates this aspect of Whitehead's speculative philosophy via cross-cultural linguistic research (Lakoff 1987).

If this metaphorical boat experiences the world in a changing context according to Klein's RPD model, it can only respond to the world at that instant by its current configuration, speed, orientation and trim. The expert, according to Klein, seems to perceive what is relevant while excluding what is irrelevant and thereby rapidly converges on a causally efficacious perception of reality. Initially, all the expert can do is set the speed, trim and attitude of her perceptual system. For example, a fire-fighter can only be "ready" as she steps through the door of a burning building. All the years of training and experience boil down to that single step. Her prior beliefs, intentions and rationally considered desires shape that readiness, yet as she advances into the unknowable reality of a burning building, her perceptual state aesthetically values the plethora of sensory inputs in a way that maximizes survival and goal accomplishment – her definition of causal efficacy. As the metaphorical prow of the boat of awareness moves into the unknown, the expert pilot has trimmed her craft to just the right cues to steer the boat through unknowable water ahead. While the wake of awareness enables reflection, introspection and learning, it can only serve to set the stage for future perception of the unknown.

The current definition of desire in BDI may still be tenable, however its institution as lemmas, semantics and propositions may require significant changes. The above interpretation of desire as jointly an aesthetic sensitivity to causally efficacious cues and as subconscious emotional attitude toward the unknown world, may be viewed as the more general case of the more specific definition of desire now in use in BDI. Currently, Carbo, Molina and Davila define desire in BDI as preferences over future states of the world (Carbo et al. 2001). Preferences can be thought of as manifested in the current trim of our metaphorical boat and desires can be seen as sub-conscious embodiment of preferred reality (Lakoff and Johnson 1999). Cue saliency constellations may then be said to be the perceptual, aesthetic sensitivity that guides attention toward salient patterns in the world. What is salient at any given instant is dependent on the last vector of purpose. Our firefighter must have the right attitude to survive the burning building.

To summarize this claim, desire is not only a preference for future states, but is more generally a cue expectancy constellation of valuations that manifest as perceptual states of attention to certain cue patterns in the environment. These patterns may be physical low-level sensory perceptions from the senses or multi-modal, highly abstract patterns. Regardless of the level of abstraction, these patterns are felt as emotional states and as an aesthetic sense of the world that is a subconscious prehension preceding conscious awareness (Alfred North Whitehead 1978). At the instant of belief or disbelief, this prehension becomes available for rational understanding and subsequently drives intention as the rudder of the boat. Intention then can be defined as a process that is the outcome of subconscious cue expectancy constellations aesthetically filtering external states of the world according to a goal of survival in the world as constrained against the history of beliefs about that world. The pilot trims the attitude of the craft. Introspection about this attitude of the intentional state may be defined as the current role of the agent. Introspection about past beliefs in the wake of current beliefs defines learning. Introspection about the current cue expectancy constellation defines an awareness of the emotional state of the agent. Regardless of whether or not the agent introspects on its current emotional state and records it as a belief (considered desire) for future use, it still must have an emotional state. An agent that is never introspective about its current cue expectancy constellation, is oblivious of its emotional state, yet is nonetheless beholden to aesthetic perception by it.

3.3 Whitehead's Process Philosophy

Process philosophy supports a re-ordering of BDI to DBI as well as the subsequent re-definition of desire in emotional, affective, subjective and vaguely associative terms such as cue saliency constellations. In the search for sapient wise systems Whitehead provides a bridging philosophy between the logical and the emotional as an advance beyond Kantian dualism. Wise systems need to judge well. According to Whitehead, "Judgment is the decision admitting a proposition into intellectual belief" (Alfred North Whitehead 1978). "A proposition is an element in the objective lure proposed for feeling, and when admitted into feeling it constitutes what is felt" (Alfred North Whitehead 1978). This may be equivalent to desire being considered and thereby becoming a considered desire. "The word 'decision' does not here imply conscious judgment, though in some 'decisions' consciousness will be a factor. The word is used in its root sense of 'cutting off' " (Alfred North Whitehead 1978). A feel, think and act cycle cuts off the world as it is perceived and judges it as a decision in that moment. Carriers of intelligence may be equivalent to Whitehead's propositions as considered desires, and therefore, judgment is the admission into intellectual belief of these carriers of intelligence.

From a Whiteheadian perspective, desire, appetition or more specifically, prehension is the most primitive element of unconscious experience by which higher abstraction beliefs and intentions are produced. If desire becomes the primary component in a DBI framework, sensory input becomes an aesthetic and felt experience that creates patterns of relevance. "The primitive form of physical experience is emotional – blind emotion...[in other words this] primitive element is *sympathy*, that is, feeling the feeling *in* another and feeling conformally *with* another (Alfred North Whitehead 1978). This primitive pre-conscious kind of sympathy describes an aesthetic sense by which impinging sensory signals are converted into contrasts of pattern. Relevance, thereby, establishes feelings of attraction or repulsion to various cues and patterns in the world while ignoring less useful patterns.

This kind of primary shaping of sensed patterns suggests that desires may fundamentally constrain subsequent adaptation of beliefs by shielding evidence contrary to desire, perhaps, in spite of beliefs. Here, seeing is believing, unless higher abstractions of belief intervene in subsequent feel-think-act cycles to feel differently and, henceforth, see the world anew. Intentions follow as a satisfactory decision – in the moment – according to congruence of desire and belief.

3.4 Sympathetic Communication of Desire via Intent

If sympathy is considered a primitive aesthetic feeling of desire in a DBI conceptual model, then intent is the product of an aesthetic feeling of an entity for other entities, which defines the relevance of contextual data by which beliefs are confirmed and actions intended. A sympathetic communicative action model (Habermas 1987) suggests that a third channel of media richness is used in human communication to communicate the aesthetic sense of what is important or meaningful during speech actions. This third channel of "sincerity" supplements logical content and normative role-based aspects of speech. According to Habermas speech acts can fail if any of these three channels of information are not delivered. A speech act can fail if it doesn't make logical sense, if it is inappropriate according to the role of the speaker and if the speaker is not sincere. This third dimension of sincerity relates to a proper sympathetic mapping from speaker to listener (Weigand and Mitta 2002). Behavioral components of speech such as tone, inflection and facial gestures, describe an affective or emotional dimension to speech that adds value structures to the logic and illocutionary aspects of the spoken language. This affective behavior appears to tap the primitive aesthetic sense of relevance and maps the previous intent to communicate the speaker's ideas to the next cycle of desire, belief and intent in sympathy with the listener.

3.5 Cue Saliency Constellations

The definition of desire as a complement to belief accords with Modeling Field Theory's neural architecture (Perlovsky 2001) where a fuzzy association subsystem works with a fuzzy object modeling subsystem to jointly and dynamically adapt to the changing world and converge on an object model and a conceptual model that are mutually constrained. In the language of the proposed DBI theory, desire, and more generally, a cue expectancy constellation, form the association subsystem of MFT neural architecture while belief represents its object modeling subsystem. Desire drives perception toward relevant cues, which expects certain objects with certain purposes. As objects are seen they confirm the associative frame of reference. A chair becomes a chair in conscious awareness in the context of an affordance for sit-ability, if you intend to sit on it. Cazeaux makes the tie between the ecological theory of perception via affordances of Gibson, Maurice Merleau-

Ponty's body schema and Lakoff and Johnson's embodiment (Cazeaux 2002). By way of Cazeaux, wisdom in humans must be embodiment as causally efficacious metaphors. Therefore, cue saliency constellations may be posited to be the symbolization representing metaphor as embodied in a human. Given the link of desire and emotion to this embodiment, cue saliency constellations may well be affective symbolic representations of metaphor encoded in the human perceptual system. This has fascinating implications for the design of an integrated sensor, information and human system.

4 Conclusion

The principal result of this work is the potential plausibility of the notion that BDI may be adaptable for use as sapient systems. This may offer the advantage of leveraging on the vast effort already expended on this system. The main disadvantage is that the re-ordering of BDI to Desire, Belief and Intent (DBI) may invalidate some of this work. The advantage of DBI is the new degree of freedom from the disentanglement of emotional value structures as desires from the logical reasons as belief sets. Further research in this area may include a formalization of DBI semantics, propositions and lemmas. This would enable a comparative study of the strengths and weaknesses between the two approaches. Another avenue of future research is linking cue saliency constellations to the human as an *in situ* knowledge elicitation human-computer interface. The symbolization needed to elicit cue saliency constellations might help define the communication necessary for sympathetic agents to wisely share scarce resources including the scarce attention of humans in the loop.

References

Abdu'l-Bahá, *Paris Talks*, London: National Spiritual Assembly of the Bahá'ís of the United Kingdom, 1972.

'Abdu-'l-Bahá, *A Traveler's Narrative*, Wilmette: Bahá'í Publishing Trust, 1990.

Michael E. Bratman, "Valuing and the Will," *Philosophical Perspectives, Action and Freedom*, **14**, 2000.

Javier Carbo, Jose M. Molina and Jorge Davila, "A BDI Agent Architecture for Reasoning about Reputation," *IEEE*, 2001.

Clive Cazeaux, "Metaphor and the Categorization of the Senses," *Metaphor and Symbol*, **17**, 1, 2002.

Vaughn Crandall, Keith W. Jones and Kirk A. Weigand, "Virtual Sandplay Action Evaluation of Key Performance Parameters Relevant To Operational Requirements Documents," *Proceedings of Fourth International Symposium on Collaborative Technologies and Systems, Society for Modeling and Simulation International*, **35**, 1, 2003.

Maria Fasli, "Interrelations between the BDI primitives: Towards heterogeneous agents," *Cognitive Systems Research*, **4**, 2003.

Michael Georgeff, "CIDS – Australia's Intelligent Future," *Search*, **23**, 2, 1992 Mar.

Jürgen Habermas, The Theory of Communicative Action, Volume Two, Lifeworld and System: A Critique of Functionalist Reason, Boston, Massachusetts: Beacon Press, 1987.

Patrick Hayes and Robert Hoffman, Available at http://www.coginst.uwf.edu/LearnMore.html, (Accessed 2003).

Morton Hunt, *The Story of Psychology*, New York, New York: Bantam Doubleday Dell Publishing Group, Inc., 1993.

Francois F. Ingrand, Michael P. Georgeff and Anand S Rao, "An Architecture for Real-Time Reasoning and System Control," *IEEE Expert*, 1992 Dec.

Gary Klein, *Sources of Power: How People Make Decisions*, Cambridge MA: The MIT Press, 2001.

Gary A. Klein, Intuition at Work: Why Developing Your Gut Instincts Will Make You Better at What You Do, New York: Doubleday, 2003.

Thomas S. Kuhn, *The Structure of Scientific Revolutions*, Chicago, Illinois: The University of Chicago Press, 1996.

George Lakoff, *Women, Fire, and Dangerous Things; What Categories Reveal about the Mind*, Chicago, Illinois: The University of Chicago Press, 1987.

George Lakoff and Mark Johnson, Philosophy of the Flesh: The Embodied Mind and Its Challenge to Western Thought, New York: Basic Books, 1999.

Stephen A. Long and Albert C. Esterline, "Fuzzy BDI Architecture for Social Agents," *IEEE, Proceedings of SouthEastCon2000*, 2000.

William K. McQuay, "Distributed Collaborative Environments for the 21st Century Engineer," *NAECON 2000*, 2000 Oct.

Leonid Perlovsky, *Neural Networks and Intellect: Using Model-Based Concepts*, New York: Oxford University Press, 2001.

Walter Warwick, Stacey McIlwaine and Rob Hutton, "Developing Computational Models of Recognition-Primed Decisions: Progress and Lessons Learned," *Proceedings of the 11th Conference on Computer Generated Forces & Behavioral Representation 2002*, 2002.

Kirk A. Weigand, Sympathetic Communicative Action: A Preliminary Theory and Conceptual Model of Human Collaboration, Cincinnati: The Union Institute, 2002.

Kirk A. Weigand and Deborah A. Mitta, "Enhancing Collaborative Communication: Defining Three Dimensions of Media Richness," *Collaborative Technologies Symposium (CTS)*, 2002.

Alfred North Whitehead, *Process and Reality: An Essay in Cosmology*, New York: The Free Press, 1978.

David D. Woods, "Modifying Plans in Progress: Plans as Preparation to be Surprised," Pensacola, Florida, Sixth International Conference on Naturalistic Decision Making, 2003.

Sapients in a Sandbox

Pablo Noriega

Abstract The purpose of this Chapter is to set concrete grounds for two arguments. The first in favor of approaching the notion of sapient systems from the unlikely perspective of stupidity. The second, in favor of paying serious attention to the environment where agents endowed with decision autonomy—be they sapient, human or otherwise—interact. Although the paper is ostensibly speculative, some concrete elements are advanced to substantiate both arguments.

1 Introduction

This is a position paper where I dare to propose a two-pronged strategy to approach sapient systems. The two research directions I advocate are summed up in the title of this paper and consist of working with individual sapient behavior, on one direction, and on the other, the collective, interaction environment. Both strategies have quite different concerns and conceptual realms, thus they may be appealing to quite different research communities. Each direction contributes its own scientific and technological background and brings, in particular, its own performance indicators to assess progress. These features are positive, I claim, because they may appeal to researchers with distant interests with the clear advantage that progress along either direction may be brought to bear upon the other.

To set the grounds for the topic I will advance, in the next section of this paper, a tentative characterization of sapient systems in terms of the space for innovation that internet and nanotechology are opening for the long-held traditions of AI. The characterization involves three dimensions of sapient behavior that I will use to build my argument upon: self-sufficiency, adaptability and coordination. In Sec. 3, I pursue the argument for the study of a few features of individual intelligence that, I believe, are intrinsic to sapient behavior. I claim these features are inherently bounded and therefore a sensible approach to their artificial realization is to design simple-minded (stupid) sapients. In Sec. 4 I shift my attention to the intelligent behaviors involved

P. Noriega
IIIA, CSIC. Artificial Intelligence Research Institute of the Spanish Scientific Research Council, Barcelona, Spain
e-mail: pablo@iiia.csic.es

R.V. Mayorga, L.I. Perlovsky (eds.), *Toward Artificial Sapience,*
© Springer 2008

in coordination and on the need for reifying a space where sapient action takes place. Taking advantage of what I did for individual features, I propose the components of an artificial environment that would provide a safe playing ground for low cardinality groups of stupid sapient agents.

2 Sapient systems in AI

2.1 Sapient systems

For the purpose of this paper I will adopt a simplified notion of a sapient system that shares the main features expressed in Mayorga (1999) which in my understanding are compatible with other characterizations of *sapient, smart* or *wise* systems (cf. Mayorga (2003), Negrete-Martinez (2003), Skolicki and Arciszewski (2005), Weigand (2005)). Thus:

Notion 1 A sapient sytem *is a computational entity that interacts with its environment, exhibits learning and adaptation behavior, is capable of creating knowledge and produces sound judgement.*

The vague terms I use in the characterization will become sharper as the discussion of the proposal proceeds but I will begin by pointing out some elements that shade my use of these terms. Note that in approaching the subject of smart systems Mayorga (for instance in Mayorga (1999)) draws from his background in AI, and softcomputing in particular, as well as the areas of control and operations research. My proposal, in turn, is biased by my own perspective from AI with a significant bias towards multi-agent systems and social psychology. In keeping with that bias, I am aware that my characterization sidesteps two aspects of sapiency that are fundamental in some of the other characterizations. Namely, the physical realization of a sapient system and the actual implementation of sapient behavior. I claim that neither are fundamental to the proposal which is the focus of this paper.

2.2 An AI turning point?

Classic AI is sometimes described as the discipline concerned with the computational simulation of *cognitive processes* and the creation of artifacts that are adequate stand-ins for intelligent behaviors. It is a convenient definition for it corresponds to the manifest programme of some of the founders of the field (in spite of the difference in emphasis and commitment that individual groups might have, McCorduck (1979)) and also with the outcomes of fifty years of activity in the field. For it may be argued that even if "general intelligence" has not been achieved, considerable progress has certainly been made in the understanding of specific cognitive processes like problem solving, natural language understanding or learning, and, significantly, in the engineering of artifacts that exhibit competent isolated cognitive behaviors. The success, we may note, has been in the plurality of those cognitive processes that have been synthesized.

Perhaps, though, we should also note that methodologically and conceptually the first fifty years of AI have focused, mostly, in the intelligent behavior of individuals. But as I will argue, that individualist focus is shifting towards a social view of intelligence. That change of focus has at least three significant drivers: internet, embodied and ubiquitous computing, and nanotechnology.

Internet brings forth the awareness of social intelligence. A digital reality in which transactions involve digital objects and are carried out in a digital –virtual– environment. But also a social reality in which interactions may involve participants who may be numerous, geographically distant, ever-present and may be digital entities themselves. A reality, hence, that finds ideal tools in classic AI technologies but also a reality that gives AI splendid opportunities to innovate.

Embodied and ubiquitous computing is already proving to be a good example of those opportunities for AI. It shares with internet the relevant features of a digital-intensive environment with numerous participants. It involves significant inter-device activity but, as internet, it also is human-intensive in as much as the activity involves human users as the main beneficiaries. While we are already witnessing the first applications of ad-hoc networks, wireless communications and mobile devices, we can bet on a rapid adoption of cutting edge AI as well as conventional AI technologies that will expand the number and types of uses of embedded and pervasive computing.

Nanotechnology moves the boundary of artificial interactions to the nano-scale, thus opening the path not only of minute processors, but also for the design of devices that act *collectively* at a micro or nano-scale.

These three drivers are creating a wide innovation space for AI. The challenge is to build on top of the mature constructs of AI artificial systems that are able to coordinate with other systems (natural or artificial) to achieve a collective task, to be able to adapt and continue to operate under adverse circumstances and within dynamic environments while at the same time being able to rely on their own resourcefulness to achieve their tasks within a social milieu. Consequently, those three drivers bring into focus the need to study cognitive behavior as it happens within a social environment: the need to study not only individual behavior but *collective behavior* as well. In particular, instead of just focusing on *individual cognitive processes* as its primitive task, AI is poised to explore the wider notions of *interaction* and *environment*.

Ideally, sapient systems would be an appropriate artifact for the new AI because, ideally, sapient systems would be able to contend with the type of rational behavior needed to interact in a social environment. They should be adaptive, self-reliable, socially-aware and we would expect them to be competent in the tasks involved in collective action: negotiation, team making or conforming to an organization. The conceptual and engineering task of developing them may prove formidable, but perhaps a modest approach like the one I suggest in this paper might prove fruitful.

3 In praise of foolishness

Notion 1 was a first approximation to what I understand a sapient system might be. I may now add more detail. First I take advantage of the agent paradigm and assume a sapient system will be somewhat like an autonomous agent. Second, I avoid solipsism and will assume sapients interact with other sapients in social tasks that are as complex as the ones mentioned in the previous section. Hence, the three features of social interaction that I mentioned above –self-reliability, adaptability and coordination– should be part of the behavioral capabilities of a sapient, and I just paraphrase them in terms of likely operational realizations of each feature. Third I need to give some substance to the vague requirement of "creating knowledge and produce sound judgement". For that I will invoke the notion of "insight" and make it extensionally clear by enumerating the type of insightful behavior expected from a sapient system. The result is the following characterization that is represented in Fig. 1. Note that in this characterization I intend to profit as much as needed from classical AI developments and techniques by making explicit some capabilities that might be implemented in different ways.

Notion 2 *A sapient system is an autonomous entity whose social behavior entails a combination of capabilities that may be classified along four dimensions: (i)* Competence: *stable, predictable, successful, . . . (ii)* Social: *coordinate, communicate, negotiate, commit, . . . (iii)* Survival: *adapt, repair, compensate, delegate and absorb, reproduce, . . . (iv)* Insight: *deliberate, innovate, validate, assume responsibility, . . .*

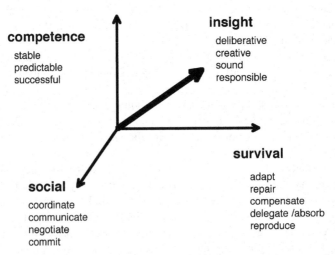

Fig. 1 A framework to describe the type of cognitive behaviors that a sapient agent should exhibit

I would like to make the notion of sapient system operational and for that purpose I will first propose a strategy by which we may approximate sapient proficiency in an "asymptotic" way.

Notion 3 *A* simple-minded *agent is a computational implementation of a sapient system that has defective capabilities or lacks some of them or fails in putting them properly into practice.*

In practice, stupid or simple-minded agents can be thought of as deliberative agents with distinct capabilities that are known to be defective to a certain degree. Capabilities that one would expect from a sapient system –like learning, planning, ontology matching or argumentation-based reasoning– may or may not be included by design in a given simple-minded agent and capabilities would be proficient up to a certain assessable degree. The intuition is that knowing in advance the composition and proficiency of primitive and compound capabilities would facilitate training and tailoring of simple-minded agents and be conducive to an overall behavior that is competent up to a certain objective degree. The same could be said about meta-capabilities –if we prefer to distinguish them from simpler more atomic capabilities for methodological or ontological reasons– like flexible goal attainment, achievement motivation, moral attitude, survival behavior. I should point out that dealing with meta-capabilities has two added advantages: it allows the design of control mechanisms that result or affect emergent behavior, like swarming or moral disposition, and also throws light on the possibility of task-dependent design of sapients by establishing competence measures –like the degree of docility of stupid agents towards other agents commands, or their stamina towards adverse outcomes– that are relevant for a given problem task.

I claim that simple-minded sapience, as just described, is a realistic project. Building deliberative agents with lacking or deficient cognitive capabilities is consistent with the tenant of bounded rationality, with the explicit advantage of setting the bounds at design time. It is conducive to incremental attainment of competence since intended degrees of accomplishment are made explicit at design time and validated at run-time. Ultimately, each capability would be stable and predictable. Moreover, building deliberative agents with lacking or defective meta-capabiliteis of the sort mentioned above is also advantageous from a methodological perspective since they facilitate addressing separately the tasks of designing tactic and strategical behaviors.

Since one can start building simple-minded agents from existing AI artifacts, this proposal would suggest an ideally monotonic process that approaches sapiency as the different behaviors are improved and more capabilities (and meta-capabiliteis) are modeled along the proposed four dimensions of sapient behavior.

The last element I need in order to give a characterization of a simple-minded sapient system is a device to control the actual behavior of the simple-minded agents. For that I rely on the notion of *regulated multi-agent system* (Fig. 2). A regulated MAS is a collection of agents whose interactions comply with a set

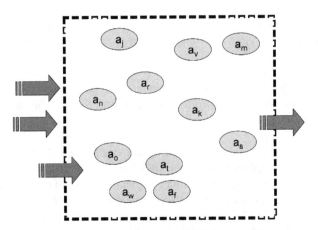

Fig. 2 A *simple-minded* sapient agent is a regulated MAS where conventional cognitive agents perform collective activities subject to explicit enforceable conventions

of conventions that "regulate" them. In a regulated MAS, there is some mechanism that makes participating agents held accountable for their actions. Depending on the type of mechanism and its implementation, the enforcement of conventions may be more or less strict, and unwanted outcomes restrained more or less effectively (cf. for example the COIN workshops proceedings Boissier et al. (2006) for a sample of alternatives).

In keeping with the idea of a monotonic approach to sapiency, I want to be able to impose a strict control over a simple-minded agent's behavior; hence choose a regulatory mechanism that is strict and effective. Even more, I want one that may be designed in advance and then adapted –or adapt itself– to become better suited to guarantee the ostensible behavior. In this manner the regulated MAS would be the *liable* outcome of an aggregation of "intelligent" capabilities and meta-cabalities orchestrated by the regulatory environment. If a simple-minded agent is built as a regulated MAS whose conventions are properly enforced, the only ostensible behavior of the MAS is that which is admissible by the conventions. Thus allowing an incremental "damage control" on individual simple-minded agents by tuning the regulations to the expected outcomes and tuning agent capabilities to the desired levels of proficiency.

I may now make my proposal for sapient systems explicit:

Proposal 4 (P_{MAS}) *Sapient systems are feasible as multiagent systems:*

P_{MAS_1} : *Sapience is a complex quality that results from a collection of interrelated capabilities whose proficiency within some objective thresholds may be assessed.*

P_{MAS_2} : *Sapient systems may be approximated by building simple-minded sapients as software agents –proficient in specific capabilities or meta-capabilities– in a regulated multiagent system.*

To clarify further what I take sapient systems to be, I may now make explicit the other assumptions I am making.

Notion 5 *Assumptions about sapient systems:*

Boundary. *I assume a given sapient system is an individual distinguishable from other sapient systems and its environment. Hence it has some permanence, even if it may vary or evolve over time. I do not commit to a physical presence for in some cases a sapient may be a virtual entity that may be present, acting, in two different situations simultaneously.*

Mental. *Behavior is determined by abstract processes that correspond to cognitive processes of the type living systems have.*

Composition. *In what follows I will assume that a sapient system is a system whose ostensible behavior is an aggregation of capabilities along the four dimensions included in Notion 2.*

Achievement. *Behavior is expressed in observable actions and these actions may be successful or not in achieving objective goals. The degree of achievement may be measured directly or through objective indicators that subsume the effects of combined or complex behaviors.*

Artifact. *In what follows I will assume that a sapient system is a computational system that may be situated in a, possibly, virtual environment and be able to interact with the environment which may include other sapient systems. That environment in some cases may also be engineered in advance as a regulated environment for autonomous agents (that will be the case for the sandboxes I discuss next).*

Confinement. *Ostensible behavior is mediated by a regulated interface –which is part of the sapient system, not of the environment– that determines the afferent and efferent information. That is, the regulated interface determines, in a strict way, what information from the environment may be received by the sapient system and what outcomes of the sapient system deliberations are eventually expressed into the environment.*

Implementation. *I assume simple-minded agents are feasible* in principle. *However, I am not concerned by the way actual capabilities and meta-cabalities are implemented, nor what the actual architecture of the MAS is, nor how the confinement is achieved. Second, I am also avoiding any commitment as to the physical realization of sapient systems, I adduce that the abstract problem is interesting enough and a software implementation would provide rich enough models for the theory of sapient systems and useful enough artifacts to be used in sapient applications.*

In consonance with what I suggested for capabilities, the design of the regulated environments may start from existing MAS technologies. In particular from the work on *electronic institutions* like the IIIA model and tools described in Arcos et al. (2005) and their extensions into autonomic ones as proposed in Bou et al. (2007).

4 Sapients in a sandbox

I will now turn to the second part of my proposal: environment engineering, or setting up a *sandbox* where simple-minded sapients are allowed to interact. I claim that this second element would make simple-minded sapients operational.

Proposal 6 (P_{env}) *Sapient systems are competent within a problem environment:*

P_{env_1} : *Sapient systems are* situated *in an dynamic environment whose state may be constantly changing but within a stable framework.*

P_{env_2} : *Sapient systems are* purpose-explicit *in the sense that their overall behavior is deemed competent with respect to that purpose and competence is measurable through explicit performance indicators.*

P_{env_3} : *A group of simple-minded agents may exhibit sapient behavior when interacting in a regulated structured multiagent environment.*

With the P_{MAS} proposal I argued that the notion of a stupid sapient agent is operational since it would involve modular deployment of simple minded components on the basis of available AI technologies and having explicit performance indicators would allow fine-tuning of the deployment. However, P_{MAS_2} introduced a design assumption that involves organizing many simple-minded components into an integrated MAS with the peculiarity of that MAS being *regulated*. What I am in fact assuming is that stupid sapient behavior is the social behavior achieved by the interactions of the agents that constitute the MAS with the specific proviso that those interactions are subject to the explicit conventions that regulate the MAS.

In this section I elaborate further the schema of a regulated environment so that a collectivity of simple-minded agents is set loose in another –ideally less strict– *regulated structured environment* that captures the problem domain where sapients are intended to work and reflects the environmental conditions that would ideally prevail in the problem domain.

Notion 7 *A* Regulated Structured Environment *involves two main components;*

Object-environment with a fixed ground ontology (agents, objects involved in actions, actions, . . .), fixed pragmatics of atomic actions (conditions, effects) and a collection of social, interaction, regulatory and achievement structures that constrain or articulate interactions. Agents interact in that environment, all their actions are observable and all environmental constraints and regulations are enforceable

Meta-environment that allows the observation of object environment interactions, and measure the outcomes of those interactions. Furthermore, the meta-environment permits the sapient designer (or supervisor) to act upon entities of the environment and in particular modify the population of agents in the environment or change conventions and structures if needed.

Thus, the notion of a regulated structured environment (RSE) involves an *object environment* where stupid sapients act. They interact among themselves but also with other entities that are part of the environment, like stoplights and highways, tumors and organs, mobile phones and medical devices, ...The environment is *structured* because, as part of the environment, there are coordination devices, regions, organizational structures, legal or normative resources that affect the way those interactions take place. For instance certain traffic regulations affect a sapient agent only when that agent is moving in a specific region, or a group of sapients may team-up to deal with a contingency invoking a particular type of contract that is available in the environment, or may choose to settle disagreements by voting according to specified protocols. This object environment involves elements and structures than were not available in the regulated MAS described above.

Regulated structured environments also have a *meta-environment* whose purpose is to observe the object environment and intervene on it. Thus it involves parameters that may be directly manipulated, behavioral and performance variables that may be observed, means to define observable indicators that synthesize outcomes of complex social interactions. In addition, the meta-environment includes different tools and mechanisms to set-up and register experiments and simulations, like deploying populations of sapient agents with specific features, automated generation of environmental conditions, ways of changing the structure of the environment or its regulatory aspects –adding more objects, changing rules and conventions, for example.

Thus, it is in that sense that a RSE is a "sandbox" where stupid agents are left on their own contending with an artificial world whose creator has control over all that is part of it and may see everything that happens in it.

The agent-based simulation community has been developing agent environments that may serve as a basis for such sandboxes (cf. Weyns et al. (2007) for a variety of examples).

Having regulated structured environment to deploy stupid sapients in them would be rather useful since RSE could be used as simulation environments to experiment, test and tune sapients. Stupid sapients would become competent in the problem and might be then deployed and left to their own resources. Analogously, RSE may evolve and adapt to the problem domain at run-time (Bou et al. (2007)) and constitute a model of a stable problem environment where sapient systems are intended to act (e.g. a RES to manage traffic control policies in a large metropolitan area; or a RES with simple minded agents injected in a high-risk patient as a nano device to deal with contingent blood clots).

5 Closing Remarks

I have presented a two-pronged strategy to address the design and development of sapient systems. On one dimension I suggested to build *simple-minded* agents whose cognitive capabilities and meta-capabilities are limited by design.

Sapient behavior, I postulated, would result from the *collective interaction* of conventional agents that interact within a a *regulated* social environment. The resulting regulated mulitagent system could be reified as a *stupid* sapient system and could in turn be immersed in a regulated environment so that many such sapient systems could interact within a confined environment –a *sand box*– whose features and properties are established at design time and may be enforced at run-time.

Sapient systems are asymptotically clever since each sapient MAS by changing the participating agents may involve as many and as varied cognitve capabilities as wanted, on one hand. On the other, the regulations that are imposed by the environment bind the activity of each simple-minded agent to admissible interactions, thus the collective outcomes are those that the conventions define and the conventions admit. Regulations themselves are object of design and consequently ostensible sapient behavior is tuned by tuning the simple-minded agents and the regulations. In particular, recent work on norm evolution and autonomic electronic institutions (e.g. Sierra et al. (2003), Bou et al. (2007, 2006)) indicate promising lines for future development.

I argue that stupid sapients, as I have proposed them, come close to the intuitive notion of sapiency discussed in literature (cf. Mayorga (1999, 2003), Negrete-Martinez (2003)) with two convenient properties: (1) Functionality is asymptotically proficient and (2) Resulting sapient behavior is restriction-compliant. In this way, simple-minded sapients would address the limitations of control and stability that Mayorga pointed out, and the social behavior of the MAS overcomes the AI-clumsiness outlined by Skolicki and Arciszewski (2005) while remaining independent from Weigand's DBI vs BDI propensities (Weigand (2005)).

I propose to embed simple-minded sapients in a (second order) regulated environment so that one can study their complex social interactions within a framework that facilitates observation, experimentation, and control of the social outcomes. The use of the sandbox is twofold: it can be used to test and deploy sapient agents that will eventually be left on their own resources in an open environment, say in web service deployment. Or for some applications, like for medical nano-therapies, the useful artifact would be the sandbox together with its sapients.

The intuition beneath this proposal is that one can approach the ideal of a general intelligence, that has remained elusive for AI, through social processes. Or, put in other words, once we bring into the AI agenda the notion of collective cognitive behavior and social intelligence we are again facing the challenges that were at the root of AI. I believe, therefore, that achieving even limited sapience is a worthy contemporary AI challenge.

Acknowledgments This work has been partly funded by project IEA (TIN2006-15662-C02-01). I would like to thank René V. Mayorga and José Negrete Martínez for their invitation to give a talk in the Workshop on Sapient Systems of the 2006 Mexican International Conference on AI, MICAI-2006, (November 13, 2006). This paper is a revision of that conference talk and benefits from their comments.

References

Arcos, J. L., Esteva, M., Noriega, P., Rodríguez-Aguilar, J. A., and Sierra, C. (2005). Environment engineering for multiagent systems. *Engineering Applications of Artificial Intelligence*, 18 (2): 191–204.

Boissier, O., Padget, J., Dignum, V., Lindemann, G., Matson, E., Ossowski, S., Sichman, J. S., and Vazquez-Salceda, J., editors (2006). *Coordination, Organizations, Institutions, and Norms in Multi-Agent Systems AAMAS 2005 International Workshops on Agents, Norms and Institutions for Regulated Multi-Agent Systems, ANIREM 2005, and Organizations in Multi-Agent Systems, OOOP 2005, Utrecht, The Netherlands, July 25–26, 2005, Revised Selected Papers*, volume 3913 of *Lecture notes in computer science*. Springer Verlag.

Bou, E., Lopez-Sanchez, M., and Rodriguez-Aguilar, J. A. (2006). Norm adaptation of autonomic electronic institutions with multiple goals. *International Transactions on Systems Science and Applications*, 1(3): 227–238.

Bou, E., Lopez-Sanchez, M., and Rodriguez-Aguilar, J. A. (2007). Towards self-configuration in autonomic electronic institutions. In Noriega, P., Vazquez-Salceda, J., Boella, G., Boissier, O., Dignum, V., Formara, N., and Matson, E., editors, *Coordination, Organizations, Institutions and Norms in Multi-Agent Systems II. Revised selected papers form the COIN workshops held in AAMAS 2006 (Hakodate, Japan) and in ECAI 2006, (Riva del Garda, Italy*, volume 4386 of *Lecture Notes in Computer Science*, Springer Verlag.

Mayorga, R. V. (2003). Towards Computational Sapience (Wisdom): A Paradigm for Sapient (Wise) Systems. *Proceedings IEEE International Conference on Integration of Knowledge Intensive Multi-Agent Systems KIMAS'03*, pages 158–165, Boston MA, USA. IEEE Press.

Mayorga, R. V. (1999). Towards Computational Wisdom: Intelligent / Wise Systems, Paradigms, and Metabots. In *Tutorial Notes. ANIROB, Congreso Nacional de Robotica, CONAR-99*, Cd. Juarez, Mexico, Dec. 13–15.

McCorduck, P. (1979). *Machines who Think*. W.H. Freeman and Company, Washington, DC.

Negrete-Martinez, J. (2003). Paradigms Behind a Discussion on Artificial Intelligent / Smart Systems. *Proceedings IEEE International Conference on Integration of Knowledge Intensive Multi-Agent Systems KIMAS'03*, pages 392–394, Boston MA, USA. IEEE Press.

Sierra, C., Sabater-Mir, J., Agusti-Cullell, J., and Garca, P. (2003). Integrating evolutionary computing and the sadde methodology. In Rosenschein, J. S., Sandholm, T., Wooldridge, M., and Yokoo, M., editors, *Second International Conference on Autonomous Agents and Multiagent systems (AAMAS-03) July-2003 Melbourne , Australia*, pages 1116–1117. ACM Press.

Skolicki, Z. and Arciszewski, T. (2005). Sapient Agents – Seven Approaches. In Mayorga, R. V. and Perlovsky, L. I., Eds. Sapient Systems Workhsop Monograph, *IEEE International Conference on Integration of Knowledge Intensive Multi-Agent Systems KIMAS'05*, Waltham MA, USA.

Weigand, K. A. (2005). Toward Wisdom in Procedural Reasoning: DBI, not BDI. In Mayorga, R. V. and Perlovsky, L. I., Eds. Sapient Systems Workhsop Monograph, *IEEE International Conference on Integration of Knowledge Intensive Multi-Agent Systems KIMAS'05*, Waltham MA, USA.

Weyns, D., Parunak, H., and Michel, F., editors (2007). *Environments for Multiagent Systems III*, volume 4389 of *Lecture Notes in Artificial Intelligence*. Springer-Verlag.

Sapient Agents – Seven Approaches

Zbigniew Skolicki, and Tomasz Arciszewski

Abstract In this Chapter seven approaches are proposed to distinguish Sapient Agents (SAs) from the entire class of Intelligent Agents (IAs). These approaches, taken both from engineering and computer science, are proposed mostly in the context of IAs for engineering design, but the results should have more general implications. First, we propose a distinction with regard to knowledge representation and domain knowledge, depending on how much general and multi-level they are. Then we compare tactical decisions with global strategies, in the context of planning, exploration of new representations in engineering, and evolutionary computation. Finally, we show how an SA should be able to "understand" the dynamics of search/reasoning by identifying emerging patterns and attractors.

1 Introduction

Engineering is undergoing a transformation, mostly driven by the ongoing Information Technology Revolution, which is understood here as a complex process of interrelated changes in the areas of Computer Science and Computer Engineering. In particular, the progress in AI has a tremendous impact on engineering practice, including design and manufacturing. During the last several years, a large class of computer programs, called "Intelligent Agents" (IAs), has emerged as a result of intensive research efforts in many countries. There is a significant diversity of IAs and the name has become fuzzy and poorly understood. Moreover, the ongoing research on complex agents gradually expands the boundaries of the IAs class.

In this paper, an IA is understood as an autonomous system situated within an environment, which senses its environment, maintains some knowledge and learns upon obtaining new data and, finally, which acts in pursuit of its own agenda to achieve its goals, possibly influencing the environment (Skolicki and Arciszewski 2003). However, this descriptive definition covers an entire spectrum of agents of various complexities, behavior, and intelligence. At one end of this spectrum are simple homogeneous agents (like in swarms (Kennedy and Eberhart 2001)), while

Z. Skolicki
Department of Computer Science, George Mason University, Fairfax, VA, USA
e-mail: zskolick@gmu.edu

R.V. Mayorga, L.I. Perlovsky (eds.), *Toward Artificial Sapience,*
© Springer 2008

at the other end such sophisticated agents like Disciple (Tecuci 1998) can be found. When engineering applications of IAs are concerned, there is confusion about the nature of intelligent agents and their usefulness for various engineering tasks. Also, it is obvious that a function of an agent that performs recording and classification of highway traffic is much different than a function of a complex agent conducting complete engineering design, including both conceptual and detailed design stages.

For all these reasons, a subclass of IAs, called "Sapient Agents" (SAs) has been proposed as IAs with "insight" and the ability of "sound judgment". Unfortunately, again it is difficult to formally discern between IAs and SAs, and this division is often subjective and based on the researcher's background and interests. SAs' complex and difficult to predict behavior could be attributed to their "wisdom," which is different from knowledge usually understood as a simple collection of decision rules, which drive other, less sophisticated agents. However, a vague definition describing sapient agent in terms of abstract knowledge, or wisdom, may be insufficient.

The class of SAs is defined in this paper using a classical approach called "a definition by coverings." In this case, a concept, here a class of SAs, is defined by a number of descriptors representing (covering) various aspects (features) of a given concept. Seven major aspects of SAs, or their behavior, are discussed and proposed to identify (define) the concept of an SA. The presented approaches can be used separately, or eventually jointly, when our understanding of sapient agents is sufficiently improved.

This paper reflects the authors' view that SAs should be able to see a "big picture" of the problem and sometimes to make tactically unjustified, or even incorrect, decisions, which would be strategically optimal. In other words, an SA should control its own behavior in the context of its wisdom and the general direction of the process. Such meta-control would be a far resemblance of an agent's consciousness, which term may also be connected with the term "sapience".

2 Seven Approaches

2.1 Knowledge Representation

A distinction between a general class of IAs and SAs can be made considering knowledge representation. This can be done for the most popular forms of knowledge representation, i.e. for knowledge in the form of decision rules and knowledge represented as a graph. In the first case of decision rules, it can be assumed that an SA uses a knowledge system containing a collection of decision rules, meta-rules, models, heuristics, etc. By contrast, an "ordinary" IA has knowledge exclusively in the form of a collection of decision rules, which obviously is much more brittle and inflexible than in the case of an SA.

In the second case of graph knowledge representation, one can easily imagine an IA analyzing the detailed relations between entities. An agent may use an ontology (which is in the form of a graph) for the task of generalization/specialization of particular rules, as it is in (Tecuci 1998). However, a wise agent should probably understand the whole structure of a graph, abstracting from particular, single connections. The argument can be made that intelligent behavior would consider nodes representing detailed solutions, by analyzing their interrelation, whereas sapient behavior would rather look at interconnections between different parts of the graph. An SA could use the topology of a meta-graph, where nodes are the sub-graphs of the knowledge graph, or use a separate structure representing the general features of the world modeled. In this context, **an SA can be defined as an IA capable of understanding the whole structure of a graph and capable of abstracting knowledge from this graph**.

2.2 Domain Dependence

Information coming from a given domain, after generalization, creates a body of knowledge about this domain. Unfortunately, all domain-specific information cannot be transferred into another domain. Only general behavioral patterns remain valid and create a body of meta-level knowledge about possible relationships among entities, which is applicable to a number of various domains. Ultimately, abstraction of knowledge from different domains may produce high-level knowledge, or wisdom, which will be a basis for sapient behavior.

Similarly, knowing the general knowledge classification rules may help in acquiring new knowledge. If the domains are of a similar nature, one can suppose that knowledge about any new domain can be at least partially acquired using the knowledge structures developed so far for similar domains (Michalski 1994). For example, human learning of foreign languages can be considered. Such "knowledge about knowledge" can be quite abstract, as shown in (Sowa 2000) using the example of three basic entities of object, supplement, and a relation (or Firstness, Secondness and Thirdness). Also, it is important to have proper intuition (or a collection of heuristics) when abstracting knowledge related to a particular domain. This knowledge should suggest which entities are more important and can later be expanded into many more detailed categories, and which entities are less important and will most probably remain unchanged. Specifically, such intuition (or meta-knowledge) may help to properly build ontologies and avoid their later restructuring. Currently only human experts are able to address this issue. However, one can hope that in the future SAs will be capable of making predictions about the nature of knowledge to be acquired. Finally, an SA should be able to adapt its own behavior in the knowledge acquisition process depending on the results of its own actions. Although this ability is to some extent a feature of all IAs — because they all actively search for new information — agents that modify the behavior at a very deep level, for example completely changing the way they store knowledge, should definitely be considered as SAs.

In the context of the above remarks, **an SA can be defined as an intelligent agent capable of abstracting knowledge and of adapting its behavior to drive further knowledge acquisition**.

2.3 Planning

Although local decisions based on simple rules and utilizing available information may lead to temporary correct moves, the strategic moves are usually driven by long-term, general rules or plans. Such plans may not necessarily rely on actual, tactical knowledge, but rather on a higher-level wisdom (strategic knowledge) about how the environment behaves over long time.

Short term vs. long term goals contradiction is especially visible in the area of planning (Rusell et al 1995). To facilitate the task of finding the proper order for a large set of actions, one utilizes the concept of hierarchical planning. In this approach, a general plan is constructed first and then the detailed plan is searched within the search space defined by the general plan. This mechanism, although it may miss some of possible solutions, discourages the system from expanding the local search too much in order to avoid the risk of loosing the global perspective and ultimately of missing the global optimum.

Heuristics implemented in computers playing different games, like chess (Campbell 1999), may be seen as another example of a long term, wise behavior. Although a local game tree search may suggest a different move, it seems sensible to implement some higher-level analysis of the game, which would establish a general plan of the game. Maybe that is why the game of Go was not mastered by computers yet (Richards et al 1998) computers still lack the holistic understanding (or feeling) of the game, which human players possess. It is interesting how often wisdom is related to intuition a seemingly non-deductive knowledge, based on experience. In this context, **an SA can be defined as an IA capable of making long-term decisions**.

2.4 Design Representation Space

In design science (Gero 2000), there is a clear distinction between exploitation and exploration in the context of conceptual design and searching a design representation space. If we assume that in the future the conceptual design process will be conducted by intelligent agents (Gero 2002), as it is expected, then this distinction can be used to distinguish an SA from an IA.

In the case of exploitation, design concepts are sought within a known design representation space, which remains unchanged during the entire design process. However, when design exploration is conducted, an entirely different paradigm is used. In this case, the design representation space is supposed to be modified and expanded to allow the designer to find novel design concepts. There is no question that exploration is much more challenging than exploitation and that it requires an entirely different set of methods and tools. In this context, **an SA can be defined as an IA capable of conducting exploration while an "ordinary" IA is capable only of performing exploitation**.

2.5 Evolutionary Computation

Evolutionary Computation (EC) may be seen as a guided search mechanism, in which we make decisions based on the outcome of the previous decisions. In this way, EC finds the solutions much faster, because it is able to climb up a hill in the search space. However, the price paid for that ability is a danger of ending up in the wrong region of the search space and without any means for escaping from there.

EC may be seen as a compromise between exploration and exploitation (De Jong 2006) (within a given representation). High level of exploration makes EC closer to a Monte Carlo (random search) method. In this case, a high probability of finding the best solution is associated with an uncertainty about the time required to find it. Random search would finally find the optimal solution, given an unlimited time. Unfortunately, when engineering applications are concerned, usually only a limited amount of time is available, and thus only a limited number of points in the solution space can be analyzed. A high level of exploitation makes the algorithm climb up local hills and "zoom in" on the optimal solution. In addition, making the algorithm utilize local information increases the probability that it will find only a local optimum, a solution that may be much worse than the global optimum.

Several decades of research in EC have demonstrated that an algorithm looking only at current individuals in a given population, which are all uniformly driven toward a solution, may have significant difficulties in finding the optimal solution in complex domains. Researchers have learned that although the current situation considered on a local, or tactical level, would suggest going directly to a particular optimal solution, it is much wiser "not to hurry" and let the algorithm slowly drift toward the optima. The local evaluation, conducted at every generation, may not justify this approach. However, a general knowledge about the domain and the behavior of evolutionary algorithms suggests that locally unjustified steps, like choosing an individual with a worse fitness may produce a better outcome in the long term. Some counterintuitive (at least at first sight) actions are thus taken. It is very important to maintain the proper diversity of a population. It occurs that once we lose a wide spectrum of genomes, it is difficult to recover the genetic diversity. There are many approaches developed that slow down the convergence. They include multi-population EAs, Pareto optimization, sentinels, fitness sharing, niches and demes, tags, and others (Baeck et al 2000). Other approaches involve meta-algorithms adjusting evolutionary algorithm parameters. Self-adaptation is another possibility.

It is the authors opinion that the methods mentioned above represent a wise (sapient) approach to EC. They are based on experience with many evolutionary algorithms and provide long-term benefits. The behavior they dictate is not based on any locally available information, and in some case may even seem unintelligent. In this context, **an SA can be defined as an IA capable of making strategic decisions, which may not be entirely justified by local results**.

2.6 Emergence

The phenomenon of emergence is understood as a sudden and unexpected occurrence of a new engineering pattern during an evolutionary process (Arciszewski et al 1995). As an example, an evolutionary conceptual structural design process is used, first controlled by a human designer and next by an IA. During such a process, an entire line of evolution of structural design concepts is generated. At a certain stage the human designer may observe that the generated structural configuration is unknown, but feasible, better than known configurations, and even potentially patentable. In such a case, a new structural shaping pattern has emerged.

When, hypothetically, an IA controls the same process, an "ordinary agent" will be able to make the decisions regarding its continuation or termination, based on a set of assumed criteria being used in a mechanistic way. However, when an SA controls the process, it will be able to recognize the emergent pattern and stop the process, if desired. In this context, **an SA can be defined as an IA capable of recognizing emergent patterns**.

2.7 Chaos Approach

One of the most important goals in the analysis of chaotic systems is the identification of their attractors. When a given representation space contains feasible design solutions, attractors represent locally best solutions (Arciszewski et al 2003). In this case, two very similar starting design solutions (points in the representation space) may lead to completely different final solutions, although they are both obtained by deterministic, algorithmic means. This observation may suggest that a proper selection of initial solutions could lead to a better final solution. Alternatively, after converging to a solution situated on a particular attractor, one could try to restart the search process to see if there is another attractor representing a much better solution.

A design process can be considered as traversing one large search space. Then attractors correspond to various final solutions and other points in the space represent solutions obtained in the earlier stages of the design process. In such a case, it is obvious that two similar initial conceptual designs, located close to each other in the space, may in the search process result in two different final solutions, having entirely different final features. Therefore, an SA should probably not focus on a single particular design from the very beginning, but "keep in mind" other possibilities.

Such an approach would prevent big changes later in the design process, allowing for a proper adjustment early enough. Of course, it may not be clear, or even it may be impossible at the conceptual stage of a project, to predict which particular way of solving the problem is better. It may be that the later, detailed analysis reveals some constraints impossible to foresee by the designer. Therefore, again, some kind of general knowledge about domains, some "engineering intuition," is needed to choose the right path, or to restrict thousands of possibilities to the very few important ones.

Chaotic dynamical systems, except of having the property of producing different results from nearly the same starting conditions, similarly may bring two very distant points to the same attractor. This means that the same results may be sometimes achieved using various search methods. An "intelligent enough" agent would probably be able to choose theoretically the best method. However, an SA should probably also look at how robust a given method is, considering previous experience. In this context, **an SA can be defined as an IA capable of avoiding undesired attractors in a representation space, or, if necessary, of using various search methods to reach a given attractor**.

3 Conclusions

The seven approaches to the definition of an SA proposed in Section 2, are summarized in Table 1. This result is only preliminary, and much more work is recommended to improve our present, still incomplete understanding of the concept of an SA.

Table 1 A comparison of simple IAs and SAs

No.	Def. Name	Intelligent Agent (IA)	Sapient Agent (SA)
1	Knowledge Representation	Only decision rules	A knowledge system
2	Domain Dependence	Limited adaptive behavior	Capable of abstracting knowledge and of adaptive behavior
3	Planning	Capable of making only short-term decisions	Capable of making long-term decisions
4	Design Repr. Space	Conducts only exploitation	Capable of conducting exploration
5	Evolutionary Computation	Classic Evolutionary Algorithm (tactical decisions driven by current population)	Algorithm maintaining diversity, long-term benefits (self-)adaptation (strategic decisions driven by global understanding)
6	Emergence	No recognition of emerging patterns	Recognition of emerging patterns
7	Chaos	Unaware of attractors	Capable of avoiding or finding attractors

The behavior of an IA results from an analysis of a given situation and from using acquired knowledge necessary for selecting the most promising strategy. It seems that an SA would follow some counter-intuitive steps, not necessarily justified by local observations. For example, an SA would suggest some seemingly illogical and inappropriate steps, under the assumption that knowledge of a certain kind will be acquired in the future and the steps will turn out beneficial.

If an IA is applied to a real world problem, it may happen that under specific circumstances, not predicted or incorporated in the model, the IA will fail because of its relative brittleness. An SA is supposed to be much more flexible, mostly because it uses experience, and some built-in general rules about adaptation and about acquiring new data. Possessing more knowledge (preferably more abstract) than needed for solving a given problem would help in adapting to the changes in requirements.

Last decades saw significant progress in computing. However, most computer programs still must be run under a strict supervision of humans, who must assure that all assumptions are satisfied and that the selected problem solving method is appropriate in a given case. In other words, it is still the experience of humans and their wisdom that make it possible to control complex processes.

Acknowledgments The authors gratefully acknowledge support for their research from the NASA Langley Research Center under the grant NAG-1-01030 and from George Mason University that provided the Graduate Interdisciplinary Research Scholarship for the first author during the academic years 2002–2004.

References

Arciszewski, T., Sauer, T. and Schum, D. (2003) Conceptual Design: Chaos-Based Approach. Journal of Intelligent and Fuzzy Systems, No. 13, IOS Press, 45–60.

Arciszewski, T., Michalski, R.S., and Wnek, J. (1995) Constructive Induction: the Key to Design Creativity Preprints of Computational Models of Creative Design. Third International Round-Table Conference, Heron Island, Australia, 397–426.

Baeck, T., Fogel, D.B., and Michalewicz, Z. (2000) Evolutionary Computation: Advanced Algorithms and Operators. Institute of Physics, London.

Campbell, M. (1999) Knowledge discovery in deep blue. Communications of the ACM, vol. 42, No. 11.

De Jong, K. (2006) Evolutionary Computation: A Unified Approach. MIT Press.

Gero J. S. and Brazier F. M. T., (eds.) (2002) Agents in Design. Preprints of the First International Workshop on Agents in Design, University of Sydney.

Gero, J. (2000) Computational Models of Innovative and Creative Design Processes In: Arciszewski, T. (ed.) Technological Forecasting & Social Change, Special Issue: Innovation: The Key to Progress in Technology and Society. Vol. 64, No. 2 & 3.

Kennedy, J. and Eberhart, R. C. (2001) Swarm Intelligence. Morgan Kaufmann Publishers.

Michalski, R.S. (1994) Inferential Theory of Learning: Developing Foundations for Multistrategy Learning, In: Machine Learning: A Multistrategy Approach. Volume IV, Morgan Kaufmann Publishers.

Richards, N., Moriarty, D. E. and Miikkulainen, R.(1998) Evolving neural networks to play Go. Applied Intelligence, vol. 8, no. 1, 85–96.

Russell, S. J., and Norvig, P. (1995) Artificial Intelligence: A Modern Approach Prentice Hall, New Jersey.

Skolicki, Z., Arciszewski, T. (2003) Intelligent Agents in Design. Proceedings of ASME 2003 Design Engineering Technical Conferences and Computers and Information in Engineering Conference.

Sowa, J.F. (2000) Knowledge Representation: Logical, Philosophical and Computations Foundations. Brooks/Cole.

Tecuci, G. (1998) Building Intelligent Agents: An Apprenticeship Multistrategy Learning Theory, Methodology, Tool, and Case Studies. Academic Press.

Part III
Paradigms for Sapient Systems/Agents

A Characterization of Sapient Agents

Martijn van Otterlo, Marco Wiering, Mehdi Dastani, and John-Jules Meyer

Abstract This chapter presents a proposal to characterize *sapient agents* in terms of cognitive concepts and abilities. In particular, a sapient agent is considered a cognitive agent that learns its cognitive state and capabilities through experience. This characterization is based on formal concepts such as beliefs, goals, plans and reasoning rules, and formal techniques such as relational reinforcement learning. We identify several aspects of cognitive agents that can be evolved through learning and indicate how these aspects can be learned. Other important features such as the social environment, interaction with other agents or humans, and the ability to deal with emotions are also discussed. The chapter ends with directions for further research on sapient agents.

1 Introduction

Intelligent agents have already found their way to the public, and during the last decades many intelligent agents have been shown to be effective in solving particular tasks. However, an intelligent agent is often used for a single task only, e.g., think about a chess-playing program that is only used to play chess. If an agent has to fulfill multiple tasks, more complicated issues arise, such as a decision method for choosing the current goals based on current information about the environment and refining the decision method based on learning capabilities. Making the transition from intelligent agent to agents that decide autonomously and learn to refine their decision-making capabilities, requires some new type of agent. This type of agent is referred to as a *sapient agent.*

We look upon sapient agents from the starting perspective of cognitive agents extended with (relational reinforcement) learning capabilities. A cognitive agent is assumed to have some internal state consisting of mental attitudes such as beliefs, goals, and plans; receives inputs through its sensors; and performs actions. The actions are determined based on its mental state in such a way that its effort to attain a goal will be minimal. Many reasoning mechanisms could be useful for this,

M. van Otterlo

Human Media Interaction, Department of Computer Science, University of Twente, The Netherlands

e-mail: otterlo@cs.utwente.nl

R.V. Mayorga, L.I. Perlovsky (eds.), *Toward Artificial Sapience,*
© Springer 2008

such as logical deduction, neural networks, fuzzy logic, Bayesian networks, etc. We consider an agent in which all of these mechanisms may run in parallel. For example, pattern recognition may be accomplished using neural networks, whereas communication is best done using logical languages.

In this chapter we first characterize sapient agents and then describe how we can use learning methods for them. In Section 2 we define sapient agents starting from the notion of a cognitive agent. In Section 3 we discuss a general cognitive architecture, the deliberation cycle, and possible influences stemming from emotions. In Section 4 we describe the reinforcement learning paradigm, as well as recent extensions important for sapient agents. Section 5 discusses the learning opportunities in the cognitive architecture defined in Section 3.1 and proposes some solutions in the framework of reinforcement learning. Section 6 deals with the broader context of sapient agents: the interaction with other agents and communication and social issues with both humans and agents. In Section 5 we reflect on the characterization given in the chapter and suggest directions for further research.

2 Defining Sapient Agents

Sapient agents are assumed to have accumulated learning skills and knowledge, the ability to discern inner qualities and relationships, often called the agent's *insight*, and good sense or *judgments*. These concepts and properties are, however, not intuitive and are informal, without explicit formal semantics. In this chapter, we consider sapient agents as a specific type of cognitive agent for which many formalizations are proposed. In particular, we believe that properties such as knowledge, insight, and judgments of sapient agents are related to, and should be defined in terms of, mentalistic concepts such as beliefs, goals, and plans as used for cognitive agents. Therefore, we propose an interpretation of properties of sapient agent based on mentalistic concepts of cognitive agents and identify certain problems such as the integration of learning and decision-making processes that together influence the behavior of these agents.

We assume that insight and judgment properties of sapient agents determine their course of action. For cognitive agents the course of action can be specified in terms of their mental attitudes, which contain at least beliefs, goals, and norms, capabilities such as actions and plans, reasoning rules that can be used in connection with mental attitudes, communication, and sensing. Given the above-mentioned entities, the decision-making ability of agents can be considered as consisting of reasoning about mentalistic attitudes, selecting goals, planning goals, selecting and executing plans, etc. (Dastani et al. 2003a).

In our view, the judgment of an agent can be considered at the lowest level as making choices about how to reason regarding its mental attitudes at each moment in time. For example, an agent's judgment can be established by reasoning about its goals or by reasoning about its goals only when they are not reachable using any possible plan. Some more moderate alternatives are also possible. For example, the agent can create a plan for a goal and execute the plan. If this leads to a stage where the plan cannot be executed any further, then the agent can start reasoning about the plan and revise it if necessary. If the goal still cannot be reached, then the agent can revise the goal. This leads to a strategy where one plan is tried completely and if it fails the goal is revised or even abandoned. In general, an agent with judgment ability should be able to control the relation between plans and goals. For example, an agent should control whether a goal still exists during the execution of the plan to reach that goal. If the corresponding goal of a plan is reached (or dropped), the agent can allow or avoid continuing with the plan.

We consider the insight of agents to be directly related to their ability to evaluate their mental states and mental capabilities. We therefore assume that the insight ability is the ability to learn how to reason about mental attitudes and thus how to make decisions. The reasoning capability determines the agent's decision-making behavior and the learning capability determines the evolution of the reasoning capability through experiences. The focus of this chapter with respect to the agent's insight is on the aspects of the agent's mental state and mental capabilities that are influenced by the learning process. These could be the goals, beliefs, desires, or reasoning rules of even basic capabilities (the agent can learn new actions).

3 Cognitive Agents

In this section, we consider various aspects of the mental states and mental abilities of cognitive agents that may evolve through learning and from experiences resulting in properties associated with the sapient agents. In general, cognitive agents are assumed to have mental states consisting of mental attitudes such as beliefs, goals, plans, and reasoning rules (Rao and Georgeff 1995,1991,Rao 1996, d'Inverno et al. 1997, Hindriks et al. 1999, Broersen et al. 2002). For example, a cognitive agent may believe there is no coffee available, want to drink coffee, and desire to have tea if there is no coffee. Moreover, the behavior of cognitive agents, i.e., the actions they choose and perform, is assumed to be determined by deliberating on the mental attitudes (Rao and Georgeff 1995, Dastani et al. 2003a,b). The deliberation process is a continuous and iterative process that involves many choices and decisions through which actions are selected and performed. For example, a deliberation process may select one goal, plan the goal, and execute the plan. If the goal cannot be planned, it may either drop the goal or revise it. The revised goal may be planned. It is also possible that a plan cannot be executed since some of its constituent actions are blocked. In such a case, the agent may either decide to drop the plan or revise it. The existing proposals of cognitive agents (Rao 1996, d'Inverno et al. 1997, Dastani et al. 2003a, Hindriks et al. 1999, Broersen et al. 2002) assume that many of these choices and decisions are fixed. These choices and decisions are based on predefined criteria and remain unchanged during an agent's lifetime. In this section, we introduce a general architecture for cognitive agents and discuss possible choices and decisions that are involved in the deliberation process.

3.1 Cognitive Agent Architecture

In what follows, we consider a general architecture for cognitive agents consisting of the representation of mental attitudes and the deliberation process. This agent architecture is illustrated in Fig. 1. According to this architecture, an agent observes the environment and communicates with other agents. The observation of an agent provides the facts that the agent recognizes from its sensory information. These facts can be used to update the agent's mental state. The communication provides information that an agent receives from other agents. The information received consists of messages that are stored in the agent's message box (Mesg.). These messages can be represented in terms of the identifier of the sender and receiver, a logical sentence that determines the content of the message, and a performative that indicates the modality of the message, i.e., whether the content is meant to inform the receiver, contains requests for the receiver, etc.

The beliefs of an agent represent its general world knowledge as well as its knowledge about the surrounding environment. The beliefs are usually represented by sentences of a logical language, e.g., sentences of a first-order predicate language. The goals represent the states that the agent desires to reach. Like beliefs, goals are also represented by sentences of a logical language. Actions represent basic capabilities that an agent can perform. These actions can be cognitive such as belief updates or external (physical) such as communication or movement actions. The actions are usually specified by pre- and postconditions, which are belief formulas. The plans represent structured patterns of actions that agents can perform together.

3.2 Acting, Planning, and Deliberating

A planning rule expresses that a goal can be achieved by performing a plan under a certain belief condition. A planning rule has the form $\phi \leftarrow \beta \mid \pi$, which indicates that goal ϕ can be achieved by plan π if belief condition β holds. A goal rule

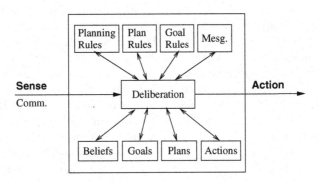

Fig. 1 A general architecture for cognitive agents

determines how to modify a goal under a certain belief condition. A goal rule has the form $\phi \leftarrow \beta \mid \psi$, which indicates that goal ϕ can be revised as goal ψ if belief condition β holds. Likewise, a plan rule determines how to modify a plan under a certain belief condition. A plan rule has the form $\pi \leftarrow \beta \mid \pi'$, which indicates that plan π can be revised as plan π' if belief condition β holds.

Cognitive agents deliberate on these concepts to decide which actions to perform at each moment in time (Dastani et al. 2003c). The deliberation process involves many activities, such as applying a reasoning rule for the above-mentioned purposes, selecting a goal to achieve, selecting a plan to execute, generating a plan to achieve a goal, etc. In particular, a cognitive agent decides at each moment in time which activity to perform. It should be noted that different applications require different deliberation processes and that there is not one single such process. An example of a deliberation process is the following iterative procedure:

```
repeat
      Find and apply goal rules that are applicable
      Find and apply plan rules that are applicable
      Find a goal and a planning rule which is applicable to it
      Apply the selected planning rule to the selected goal
      Find and execute a plan
end repeat
```

In order to specify, design, and implement a cognitive agent one needs to initialize its cognitive state and specify, design, and implement various decisions and choices involved in the deliberation process beforehand. For example, the agent designer should develop beforehand various selection functions to select goals, plans, and various types of rules at various stages of the deliberation process. The agent designer should also indicate beforehand how goals and plan are generated and dropped. For many types of agents, especially sapient ones, it is not possible, or even desirable, to specify all these concepts at design time. Therefore, sapient agents should be capable of learning.

3.3 Emotions

Emotions will also be important for truly sapient agents. Emotional attitudes toward agents, objects, events, etc. can become important in the process of acting, planning, and deliberation. Emotions motivate and bias behavior, but they do not completely determine it. They play a *reflective* role in decision making and learning (Picard 1997), may monitor planning, and may be *prospect based* (Ortony et al. 1988). By focusing on *emotion-inducing* events, the agent can decide more effectively. Basic emotions such as fear can trigger an agent to act fast or to quickly change plans. Emotions such as happiness can influence choices for certain goals or plans. In some sense, emotions complement *ratio* so that the agent becomes wiser, more sapient.

It is acknowledged that, at least in humans, emotions are not a separate process from cognition; but rather that they are inextricably intertwined. It can even be stated that without emotions, decision making and acting are hardly possible and that reason itself uses emotions to guide its decision-making processes (Damasio 1994). Even though some may argue that it is not important for machines (agents) to actually *have* emotions, it surely is important to be able to *reason about* emotions. Especially in situations in which natural language understanding and cooperative problem solving are important. When interaction with humans is involved, a capability to deal with emotions, whether to express or to understand them, becomes highly desirable or even needed (Picard 1997).

4 Learning

There is general agreement nowadays that intelligent agents should be *adaptive*, i.e., capable of learning. For learning to work, agents should be able to make the proper generalizations to reuse learned knowledge to apply it to new situations similar to encountered ones. For sapient agents, learning as a capability should be extended to learning how to organize the deliberation cycle. Sapient agents can learn how to solve multiple tasks in parallel, how to deal with multiple goals, and how to set the right priorities. They can use their own experiences as well as the social context to do so.

There are roughly three learning paradigms. *Unsupervised* and *supervised* learning are used mainly for isolated *clustering* and *classification* tasks, respectively. However, for agents, the *reinforcement learning* paradigm is dominant, given the fact that it deals with *behavior* learning. In this section we describe its main features and discuss extensions useful for learning within (cognitive) sapient agents.

4.1 Reinforcement Learning

In reinforcement learning (RL) (Sutton and Barto 1998), an agent learns how to behave by interacting with its environment (including other agents) using a trial-and-error process. The agent has to learn a policy to decide on actions based on its mental state in such a way that its cumulative intake of rewards will be maximized. In general, RL methods are used to estimate utility values for certain belief states and certain actions. These values can be used to determine optimal actions for the agent's current state. We can see an agent with RL capabilities as an agent that tries to find out which goal to select and how to achieve the selected goal with minimal effort. RL has already been successfully applied to learn to play the game of backgammon at the human world class level (Tesauro 1992).

4.2 Abstraction in Reinforcement Learning

Although RL is a general method for behavior learning, standard RL is not powerful enough for the rich knowledge structures and capabilities of sapient agents. Recently a number of extensions to the RL framework have been developed that deal with various kinds of higher-order *abstractions*. Abstractions *over actions* (or time, i.e., *temporal* abstraction) can be used to abstract over different ways an abstract action can be instantiated. For example, an action $moveTo(room1)$ can abstract over a number of motor actions actually needed for a robot to move to $room1$. Whole action sequences can be abstracted into a *plan* or a *macroaction*. Methods that use abstraction over time or action sequences are termed *hierarchical* RL methods (Dietterich 2000, Sutton et al. 1999; Parr and Russell 1997). Hierarchies of actions and behaviors can be defined or even learned.

Another recent direction in RL involves abstraction by using more powerful representation languages. Quite naturally, cognitive concepts like beliefs about the world and goals are expressed in terms of *objects* and *relations*. Traditionally, RL has used feature-based and propositional representations for representing cognitive concepts and actions, although for logic-based agents, richer representational formalisms are needed. Recently progress has been made in closing the gap between logic-based agent formalisms and methods for learning behavior such as RL.

On the one hand, formalisms such as the situation calculus (Reiter 2001) have been extended with means to calculate values for actions and mental states (Boutilier et al. 2001). These values enable the agent to choose rationally between goals and actions. On the other hand, progress has been made in upgrading RL methods toward richer representational formalisms. Relational reinforcement learning (Dzeroski 2002, van Otterlo 2002, 2003) methods learn values for relational expressions over mental concepts and actions. By means of logical induction, useful concepts that are important for optimal behavior of the agent can be learned from experience. These concepts are expressed in terms of knowledge the agent has and are based on actual experience gained in performing different actions.

By integrating value-based behavior learning methods such as RL, the notion of a logic-based cognitive agent and concept induction methods, behavior learning of an agent can be directly connected to cognitive notions, represented in terms of *objects* and *relations* (Kaelbling et al. 2001).

5 Learning in Cognitive Agents

In Section 3.2 we mentioned the fact that in cognitive agent architectures, many aspects are specified beforehand. However, for a sapient agent we believe that various choices and decisions involved in the deliberation process should be learned through experience instead of being fixed and defined beforehand.

5.1 Adapting the Deliberation Cycle

There are many opportunities for learning in cognitive agents. In particular, the agent should learn various concepts $(car(x))$, facts $(car(p))$, and rules (e.g.,

$bird(x) \rightarrow fly(x))$ that constitute its beliefs at runtime. Moreover, given goal formulas ϕ and ψ, plan expressions π and π', and belief formula β, the following can be the subject of learning with regard to the agent's goals and plans:

- Which goal to select in order to plan, and which plan to select in order to execute? Two types of selection functions can be learned. The goal selection functions should be learned based on the agent's beliefs and the plan selection functions should be learned based on the agent's beliefs and goals.
- Which goal or plan to generate in certain situations? This can be achieved by learning goal or plan rules of the form $\top \leftarrow \beta \mid \phi$ and $\top \leftarrow \beta \mid \pi$, respectively.
- Which goal or plan to drop in a certain situation? This can be achieved by learning goal or plan rules of the form $\phi \leftarrow \beta \mid \top$ and $\pi \leftarrow \beta \mid \epsilon$ (where ϵ is the empty plan), respectively.
- Which goal or plan to modify in a certain situation? This can be achieved by learning goal or plan rules of the form $\phi \leftarrow \beta \mid \psi$ and $\pi \leftarrow \beta \mid \pi'$, respectively.
- How to plan a goal in a certain situation? This can be achieved by learning planning rules of the form $\phi \leftarrow \beta \mid \pi$.

Finally, for each type of rule a selection function should be learned that selects a rule to apply at each moment in time. These selection functions should be learned based on agents' mental state and differ for each type of rule. In particular, the selection function for planning rules should be learned based on agents' beliefs, goals, and plans, the selection function for plan rules should be learned based on agents' beliefs and goals, and the selection function for goal rules should be learned based on agents' beliefs. In the following section we discuss how these aspects can be learned by various techniques.

5.2 Learning goals, Plans, and Concepts

In order to cope with the demands of a sapient agent we can use hierarchical RL (using relational representations). We consider goal selection and plan selection first.

For goal selection, the agent has to map its beliefs to a particular goal that it will adopt. The agent can change its mind about the goal at each time step, but in order to allow the agent to continue with one particular goal, we can use a mapping from beliefs and the previous goal to a newly selected goal. Reinforcement learning algorithms learn value functions for this by trial and error using, e.g., Q-learning (Watkins 1989). The goal is to learn to select goals leading to the maximal average reward intake per time step. By trying out goals, and using plans or actions to achieve these goals, the agent gets estimates about the quality value (Q-value) of selecting each of its goals given some mental state. Since the agent can change its goal at any time, it can drop previous goals and continue with new ones. It can also learn that committing to some goal is good until some mental state tells the agent to adopt another one. Thus, with the hierarchical RL framework, selecting and revising goals may be learned just as learning action sequences.

For learning to select plans, the agent has to map a goal and beliefs to a plan. There can be multiple plans, some plans may even consist of single actions. Although some plans take longer than single actions, this is not a problem if hierarchical RL is being used. The agent can even choose to invoke a planner that will plan at a specific time step. If this planner returns useful plans given some mental state, it will be invoked more often in that context. Plans can be dropped or revised at any time, since the agent selects a plan or action at each time step. Thus, again, with the hierarchical RL framework, selecting and revising plans can be learned just as learning action sequences.

Finally, the agent has to learn to map sensory information obtained by, e.g., cameras to concepts. This can be done by using pattern recognition methods such as neural networks or support vector machines. Each time the agent receives sensory information and does not understand what it sees, it should get feedback about the concept it is looking at. This can only be done in a social setting in which humans communicate with the agent, and the agent is also able to communicate with other agents. We examine this issue further in Section 6.

5.3 Emotions in Learning

Emotions may influence behavior, as was explained in Section 2. Emotions may also influence learning. For example, a negative emotion that produces a bad feeling may trigger reassessment of what causes the bad feeling, followed by learning how to avoid it in the future. A sapient agent can also predict that by not doing an action, it will feel even worse, and by feeling this, it can interrupt its current behavior to do that action. Emotions can also help focus on a goal or trigger to reassess a situation (e.g., by *insight*, *reflection*) and look for a way to improve it, thus adapting its behavior.

6 The Social Environment

Agents, especially sapient ones, will usually be *situated* in complex, multiagent, social environments in which they have to interact with other agents and humans. Such complex environments create difficulties, but also opportunities, especially in learning. We discuss some of these in this section.

Reinforcement learning has already been applied successfully for solving particular multiagent problems such as network routing (Littman and Boyan 1993), elevator control (Crites and Barto 1996), and traffic light control (Wiering 2000). For all these problems, the agent still has to solve a particular task, such as controlling a specific traffic light, and therefore these agents are not sapient at all. We can, however, use multiagent systems to make it easier for agents to learn to become sapient agents.

If the agent has to learn to achieve a goal and it can choose which task to learn, there are several complicated issues. In some sense, the agent has to devote its time to learning something useful. But what if the agent is unable to learn to solve a particular task? When should it stop trying to learn the task? Furthermore, how much reward can it expect if it would be able to learn to perform the task? A solution is to let the agent learn from other agents. For example, the agent can estimate its learning time by looking at other agents or by communicating with them. The agent can also ask the reward functions of other agents, it can estimate the learning time by asking or looking at the other agent, and can even ask another agent about the decision skill to solve a particular task. Thus, some issues seem complicated, but may become easier when the agent is not alone in the world. Although the whole system would become much more complex, particular subproblems would be easier to solve. Some problems would even be impossible if the agent could not learn by imitating other agents. For example, suppose one agent, a robot, approaches a deep canyon and just near the edge, it slips and falls into the canyon. Because of the fall, the agent is destroyed and it no longer exists. The only way of learning that one should not come too close to the edge of the canyon is to look at the results of other agents approaching it. Since it is easy to see that coming too close to the edge of the canyon was bad for the other agent, a sapient agent can learn that this is a wrong action in this context.

In multiagent settings we have to distinguish among competitive, cooperative, and semicompetitive settings. Although we would like all agents to be cooperative, this is not realistic since each agent tries to maximize its own average reward intake per time step. However, even in (semi)competitive settings it makes sense to let agents communicate (e.g., if two agents try to walk through the same corridor and bump against each other, they can signal to which side they will go). By communicating knowledge, agents can share experiences, concepts, and procedural knowledge of how to solve tasks. Using communication, possibly with humans, is also a good way to get a lot of examples for learning to classify sensory information into concepts. These are examples of *learning by communicating*. Classical experiments show that in many cases, communication between agents can have a positive influence on learning behavior, provided that communicated information is useful and not superfluous (Tan 1993). On the other hand, agents can also *learn how to communicate* (Weiss 1999). This involves learning *what, when, with whom*, and *how* to communicate. Social laws, protocols, and shared *ontologies* are important factors in communication.

Agents can learn to judge just like other agents, and agents can reward each other using ethical or social laws that have existed for a long time and therefore can be evolved or preprogrammed. Thus, in multiagent systems judgment and insight can also be learned, obtained, and refined using communication. For communication between agents some issues such as trust (insight in relationships) play an important role and have to be learned based on the experiences of the agent. If another agent provides wrong estimates about the learning time or reward for solving a particular task or gives a wrong decision skill for solving the task, the agent can learn that this other agent cannot be trusted. The agent can also ask other trusted agents whether they trust another agent. In this way social relationships among agents can evolve.

The problem of using reward functions is that it is difficult to say how much reward one should get for task A relative to task B. The agent's decision will be to do the task leading to maximal average reward per time step. However, if these relative reward values are incorrect, the agent could always do one single task at which it is good. Therefore the reward function should also be dynamic, where a reward is given only under particular circumstances. The reward could be made dependent on the agent's emotions such as boredom, pride, pity, disappointment, satisfaction, anger, etc. In this way, an agent that is angry with another agent may learn not to communicate interesting information. Also, if the agent is bored with its current task, it will get less reward for doing it, and therefore may switch to another goal.

7 Conclusions

In this chapter we have given a characterization of *sapient agents*. By starting from the notion of a *cognitive* agent, for which many formalizations exist, we place cognitive notions such as *beliefs*, *desires*, *goals*, and *plans* at the core of the deliberation cycle of a sapient agent. Furthermore, with this as a starting point, we have a firm basis for a model of true *sapience* as well as being able to take advantage of existing knowledge and formalizations concerning the modeling of cognitive notions, logic-based systems, and agent programming languages such as 3APL.

Furthermore, we have emphasized the need for managing control over different tasks that can be performed in parallel, by choosing constantly among actions, goals, and plans in the deliberation cycle. Various tasks can also be run in parallel on different cognitive levels. On the perceptual level, pattern recognition can transform visual images to (logical) concepts, while planning and acting can be performed on a higher cognitive level.

We have also stressed the importance of *emotions* as a possible factor in both behaving and learning. In a single agent, emotions may influence decision making and planning. In a multiagent social context, emotions may play an important role in the interaction, especially when humans are involved.

A very important feature of sapient agents that we discussed is *learning*. We discussed reasons, opportunities, and solutions for learning. For sapient agents, learning transcends the idea of single-task learning by focusing on the whole deliberation cycle, emotional attitudes, and the social context. Of much importance will be the integration of RL methods and logic-based, cognitive agents. Relational languages and hierarchical learning methods in RL may function as a bridge between cognition and learning.

One line of further research should focus first on formal definitions of the various elements discussed in this chapter. Notions present in formalizations of cognitive agents and agent programming languages should be extended with learning mechanisms and emotional attitudes.

A second line of research should aim at *experimenting* with and *developing* concrete applications of increasingly sapient agents. By integrating learning mechanisms such as relational RL into agent programming languages such as 3APL, ideas can be put to a test in order to develop truly sapient agents.

Acknowledgments This chapter originally appeared as a paper in: M. van Otterlo, M. Wiering, M. Dastani, and J-J. Meyer. A, Characterization of Sapient Agents, *Proceedings of the First International Conference on Integration of Knowledge Intensive Multi-Agent Systems* (KIMAS-03), edited by H. Hexmoor, IEEE Press, Boston, MA, pages 172–177, 2003. A survey of recent developments in relational reinforcement learning can be found in van Otterlo (2005).

References

Boutilier, C., Reiter, R., and Price B. (2001). Symbolic dynamic programming for first-order MDP's. In Bernhard Nebel, editor, *Proc. of the 17th Int. Joint Conference on Artificial Intelligence (IJCAI-01)*, pages 690–697, San Francisco, CA, August 4–10 2001. Morgan Kaufmann.

Broersen, J., Dastani, M., Hulstijn, J., and van der Torre, L. (2002) and. Goal generation in the BOID architecture. *Cognitive Science Quarterly*, 2(3-4):428–447.

Crites, R. H., and Barto, A.G., Improving elevator performance using reinforcement learning. In Touretzky, D.S., Mozer, M.C., and Hasselmo, M.E., editors, *Advances in Neural Information Processing Systems 8*, pages 1017–1023, Cambridge MA, 1996. MIT Press.

Damasio, A.R., *Descartes' Error: Emotion, Reason and the Human Brain*. Gosset/Putnam, New York, NY, 1994.

Dastani, M., de Boer, F., Dignum, F., and Meyer, J-J.Ch. Programming agent deliberation: An approach illustrated using the 3apl language. In *Proc. of the Second Int. Conference on Autonomous Agents and Multiagent Systems (AAMAS'03)*. ACM Press, 2003a.

Dastani, M., Dignum, F., and Meyer, J-J.Ch. Autonomy and agent deliberation. In *Proc. of The First Int. Workshop on Computatinal Autonomy - Potential, Risks, Solutions (Autonomous 2003)*, 2003b.

Dastani, M., van Riemsdijk, B., Dignum, F., and Meyer, J-J.Ch. A programming language for cognitive agents: Goal-directed 3APL. In *Proc. the ProMAS 2003 Workshop at AAMAS'03*, 2003c.

Dietterich, T.G. Hierarchical reinforcement learning with the MAXQ value function decomposition. *Journal of Artificial Intelligence Research*, 13:227–303, 2000.

d'Inverno, M., Kinny, D., Luck, M., and Wooldridge, M. A formal specification of dMARS. In *Agent Theories, Architectures, and Languages*, pages 155–176, 1997.

Dzeroski, S. Relational reinforcement learning for agents in worlds with objects. In *Proc. of the Symposium on Adaptive Agents and Multi-Agent Systems (AISB'02)*, pages 1–8, 2002.

Koen V. Hindriks, Frank S. De Boer, Wiebe Van der Hoek, and John-Jules Ch. Meyer. Agent programming in 3apl. *Autonomous Agents and Multi-Agent Systems*, 2(4):357–401, 1999.

Kaelbling, L. P., Oates, T., Hernandez, N., and Finney, S. Learning in worlds with objects. In *The AAAI Spring Symposium*, March 2001.

Littman, M. L., and Boyan, J. A. A distributed reinforcement learning scheme for network routing. In J. Alspector, R. Goodman, and T.X. Brown, editors, *Proc. of the First Int. Workshop on Applications of Neural Networks to Telecommunication*, pages 45–51, Hillsdale, New Jersey, 1993.

Ortony, A., Clore, G. L., and Collins, A. *The cognitive structure of emotions*. Cambridge University Press, Cambridge, MA, 1988.

Parr, R. and Russell, S. Reinforcement learning with hierarchies of machines. In *Advances in Neural Information Processing Systems 11*, 1997.

Picard, R. W. *Affective Computing*. MIT Press, Cambridge, MA, 1997.

Rao, A. S. AgentSpeak(L): BDI agents speak out in a logical computable language. In Rudy van Hoe, editor, *Seventh European Workshop on Modelling Autonomous Agents in a Multi-Agent World*, Eindhoven, The Netherlands, 1996.

Rao, A.S. and Georgeff, M. P. Modeling rational agents within a BDI architecture. In *Proc. of Second Int. Conference on Knowledge Representation and Reasoning (KR'91)*, pages 473–484. Morgan Kaufmann, 1991.

Rao, A. S. and Georgeff, M. P. BDI agents: from theory to practice. In *Proc. of the Int. Conference on Multi-Agent Systems (ICMAS'95)*, pages 312–319, 1995.

Reiter, R. *Knowledge in Action: Logical Foundations for Specifying and Implementing Dynamical Systems*. The MIT Press, Cambridge, Massachusetts, 2001.

Sutton, R.S. and Barto, A.G. *Reinforcement Learning: an Introduction*. The MIT Press, Cambridge, 1998.

Sutton, R.S. Precup, D. and Singh, S. Between MDPs and semi-MDPs: A framework for temporal abstraction in reinforcement learning. *Artificial Intelligence*, 112(1–2):181–211, 1999.

Tan, M. Multi-agent reinforcement learning: Independent vs. cooperative agents. In *Proc. of the Tenth Int. Conference on Machine Learning*, pages 330–337, June 1993.

Tesauro, G. Practical issues in temporal difference learning. In D. S. Lippman, J. E. Moody, and D. S. Touretzky, editors, *Advances in Neural Information Processing Systems 4*, pages 259–266. San Mateo, CA: Morgan Kaufmann, 1992.

van Otterlo, M. Relational expressions in reinforcement learning: Review and open problems. In E. de Jong and T. Oates, editors, *Proc. of the ICML'02 Workshop on Development of Representations*, 2002.

van Otterlo, M. Efficient reinforcement learning using relational aggregation. In *Proc. of the Sixth European Workshop on Reinforcement Learning, Nancy, France (EWRL-6)*, 2003.

van Otterlo, M. A survey of reinforcement learning in relational domains. Technical Report TR-CTIT-05-31, July 2005, 70 pp, CTIT Technical Report Series, ISSN 1381-3625, Department of Computer Science, University of Twente, 2005.

Watkins, C. J. C. H. *Learning from Delayed Rewards*. PhD thesis, King's College, Cambridge, England, 1989.

Weiss, G. *Multiagent Systems: A Modern Approach to Distributed Artificial Intelligence*. The MIT Press, Cambridge, Massachusets, 1999.

Wiering, M. A. Multi-agent reinforcement learning for traffic light control. In P. Langley, editor, *Proc. of the Seventeenth Int. Conference on Machine Learning*, pages 1151–1158, 2000.

A Paradigm for Sapient (Wise) Systems: Implementations, Design & Operation

René V. Mayorga

Abstract This Chapter presents a Paradigm, from a Cybernetics point of view, that can contribute with some essential aspects to establish a baseline for the development of *Artificial / Computational Sapience (Wisdom)* as new disciplines. It is demonstrated here that, under the proposed Paradigm, *Artificial / Computational Sapience (Wisdom)* methodologies can be developed as a natural extension of some non-conventional (Soft Computing and Computational Intelligence) approaches. It is also also shown here that the proposed Paradigm serves as a general framework for the development of Intelligent / *Sapient (Wise)* Systems and *MetaBots*.

It is also demonstrated here that under the proposed Paradigm, it is possible to establish some performance criteria for the proper Design and Operation of Intelligent and *Sapient (Wise) Systems*. These criteria are based on establishing proper bounds on some characterizing matrices having a prominent role on the performance of Intelligent and *Sapient (Wise) Systems*.

1 Introduction

In a recent article (Mayorga 1998a) the author presented a Paradigm for Intelligent Systems Design/Operation, and outlined its implementation by some non-conventional (Artificial Intelligence, Soft Computing, Computational Intelligence) techniques. The article (Mayorga 1998a) also introduced the novel concept *MetaBot* intended as a generalization of the term *robot* to encompass software agents, hardware units, or hybrid combination of both; performing systematically and automatically some tasks, in an *"intelligent"* and *"stable"* manner. It is shown in (Mayorga 2000a), (Mayorga 1999), and (Mayorga 1998a), that the Paradigm can also lead to a unified framework for the study of *MetaBots*.

In this Chapter a similar approach and concepts as in (Mayorga 2000a), (Mayorga 1999), and (Mayorga 1998a) are followed. Here, it is shown that the Paradigm can contribute with some essential aspects to establish a baseline for the

R.V. Mayorga
Faculty of Engineering, University of Regina, Regina, Saskatchewan, Canada
e-mail: Rene.Mayorga@uregina.ca

R.V. Mayorga, L.I. Perlovsky (eds.), *Toward Artificial Sapience*,   143
© Springer 2008

development of *Artificial / Computational Sapience (Wisdom)* as new disciplines (Mayorga 1999). It is demonstrated here that, under the proposed Paradigm, the development of Artificial / Computational Sapience (Wisdom) methodologies can be accomplished as a natural extension of some non-conventional (Soft Computing and Computational Intelligence) approaches. Furthermore, it is also demonstrated here that the Paradigm serves as a general framework for the development of Intelligent/ *Sapient (Wise)* Systems and *MetaBots*, (Mayorga 1999).

First, here a brief discussion on the evolution of some Artificial Intelligence areas towards Soft Computing and Computational Intelligence is provided. It is noticed that over the years these areas have been influencing the field of Robotics; however, the reverse effect has not been significant (Mayorga 1999). In this Chapter it is shown that under the proposed Paradigm some concepts mainly developed for the Robotics field can actually have a favorable impact on some Soft Computing and Computational Intelligence methodologies (Mayorga 1999).

Next, the terms "Intelligence", and "Wisdom" are properly addressed highlighting their similar and differential aspects. This leads to briefly discuss the terms "Intelligent Systems" and "Agents". It is pointed out that the various and diverse current definitions of the term Agent do not explicitly take into account a "stability" (that is so essential to deal effectively with dynamic systems) criterion. More significantly, here also some learning, adaptation, and cognition aspects are considered, that lead to postulate a "formal" concept of *Artificial / Computational Sapience (Wisdom)* as in (Mayorga 2003), (Mayorga 2000a), (Mayorga 2000b), (Mayorga 1999).

Following the ideas (to characterize the field of Intelligent Control) presented in (Saridis 1977) and (Fu 1971); it is proposed here to characterize the *Sapient (Wise)* Decision/Control field as the intersection of Automatic Control, Operations Research, A.I., Artificial / Computational *Sapience (Wisdom)*, and Robotics. Then, the discussion naturally leads to the proper formulation of the terms *Sapient (Wise)* Systems and *MetaBots* (Mayorga 1999).

Next, a Paradigm appropriate for hierarchical multi-layer and/or distributed structures, which can include aspects of a global or local nature is presented. In particular, some learning, adaptation, and knowledge (essential for cognition (Perlovsky 2001)) principles are properly addressed. However, here also the concepts of "stability", "discerning", and "inference" (here, as a condition for judgment) are considered. Furthermore, here it is postulated that under this Paradigm, inferential capabilities and the ability to determine direct and inverse relationships and to include globals aspects, can contribute to built up knowledge with capacity for cognition and sound judgment; and leading to Artificial / Computational Sapience (Wisdom).

Here as in (Mayorga 2000a), (Mayorga 1999), (Mayorga 1998a), under the proposed Paradigm an effect/cause relationship between the outputs to the inputs of a system is formulated, for a general class of differentiable functions, at an inverse functional and a rate of change setting. The Paradigm, appropriate for hierarchical or distributed structures, can be considered of a local nature and is based on the "stability" principle, (Mayorga 2000a), (Mayorga 1999), (Mayorga 1998a), that for small changes in the inputs, there should correspond small changes in the outputs.

Here, also some theoretical results on the difference between exact inverse functional evaluations and inexact approximations, and a criterion for optimal system design are presented (Mayorga 2000a), (Mayorga 1999), (Mayorga 1998a). Next, some necessary conditions for the implementation of general (Adaptive) Inference Systems under the proposed Paradigm are established. It is demonstrated that the proposed Paradigm permits to develop simple but efficient Learning strategies for some Classes of (Adaptive) Inference Systems: for the case in which there is knowledge of an input/output system relationship, and also when there is no knowledge of this relationship (Mayorga 1999), (Mayorga 1998a). Furthermore, it is also shown that these Classes can effectively used to approximate the corresponding inverse functions characterizing this relationship (Mayorga 1999), (Mayorga 1998a).

Thence, under the Proposed Paradigm, the aspects of learning, and adaptation (essential for cognition (Perlovsky 2001)) are properly addressed. In addition, since the Proposed Paradigm enables the ability to estimate (via adaptive inference systems) direct and inverse relationships (sequentially, concurrently, or a combination of both, in hierarchical multi-layer and/or distributed structures) in a stable manner, and to include global aspects; it can contribute to the construction of knowledge and the capacity for delivering sound judgment. Consequently, the Paradigm can lead to cognition and Artificial / Computational Sapience (Wisdom).

Here it is pointed out that the generality character of the Paradigm permits its implementation in many and diverse fields. Here, in particular the application of (ordinary and adaptive) Fuzzy and Neuro-Fuzzy Inference Systems for Intelligent/*Wise* Decision making/resolution, and Systems Design is amply discussed.

In this Chapter it is also demonstrated that, under the proposed Paradigm, it is possible to establish some performance criteria for the proper design and operation of Intelligent and *Sapient (Wise)* Systems. These criteria are based on establishing proper bounds on some characterizing matrices having a prominent role on the performance of Intelligent and *Sapient (Wise)* Systems. In particular, here it is shown that from these characterizing matrices it is possible to establish:

(a) an upper bound on a homogenized condition number;

(b) a generalization of an isotropy condition;

(c) a proper bound on the rate of change of a generalized isotropy condition; and,

(d) a proper bound on the rate of change of the Jacobian matrix.

As discussed here, these criteria can be easily used for proper system design analysis. Moreover, as shown here some of these criteria can be expressed in explicit form; thus, they can be easily utilized for the design optimization and operation of Intelligent and *Sapient (Wise)* systems.

2 Preliminary Concepts

It is well known that the field of Artificial Intelligence has gone through many changes and transformations over the past three decades. In fact, it went through a "slump" period in the late seventies and early eighties; but some of its areas (Artificial Neural Networks, and Fuzzy Inference Systems) began to have a wide acceptance since the mid eighties. The resurgence was in part the result of the great interest on these areas by the Control Engineering community. This interest has focused at the *Applications level* - The capability of some A.I. techniques to provide real time solutions to some complicated problems; and more recently at the *Theoretical level* - The capability of some A.I. techniques to approximate non-linear functions.

But, perhaps the A. I. discipline by trying to encompass many areas has unnecessarily extended itself; and it would be more appropriate that it focuses on some limited fields/areas. This may be evidenced by the recent evolution and migration of some A. I. techniques, such as Artificial Neural Networks and Fuzzy Inference Systems, towards the fields of Soft Computing and Computational Intelligence. In fact, some areas that could be normally covered by the A.I. discipline can each one of them be considered on its own as a separate discipline. One could easily think of considering disciplines such as: Computational Consciousness, Computational Wisdom, Computational Intelligence, and Computational Creativity.

Another fact to observe is the influence and impact that non-conventional (A.I., Soft Computing, and Computational Intelligence) disciplines have had on the Robotics field over the years. However, it is worth to notice that the reverse (the impact of Robotics on the A.I., Soft Computing, and Computational Intelligence) has not been significant (Mayorga 1999). A more desirable (from the Intelligent Systems and Intelligent Robotics point of view) state of affairs should be a bottom to top approach. That is, the fields of Intelligent Systems and Intelligent Robotics having a favorable impact to A.I.. Soft Computing and Computational Intelligence. This is not a proposition too simplistic; since Systems Theory can contribute with proper architectures, structures, and valuable concepts (such as adaptability and stability concepts) to those disciplines.

Also, a non-conventional concept that has impacted greatly many (i.e. Robotics) fields is the term *Agent*. These facts are clearly illustrated in Fig. 1.

A more desirable (from the Robotics point of view) state of affairs is depicted in Fig. 2.

There are many definitions for the term *Agent*, (Franklin and Graesser 1996); but in general, they implicitly encompass an "Intelligent" software program based on: Expert Systems, and/or other A.I. techniques, (Mayorga 1999). Notice that other Agent definitions incorporate explicitly an "Intelligence" attribute.

In recent years, Agents have been widely utilized in many and diverse fields; and in many cases they are implicitly used to mean "Intelligent Systems". Also in many cases they have proved to be practical and effective for some complex problems. However, as pointed out in (Mayorga 1999), there is an important and unfavorable fact about current Agents. For *decision making/resolution* problems,

Fig. 1 Impact of
non-conventional
methodologies

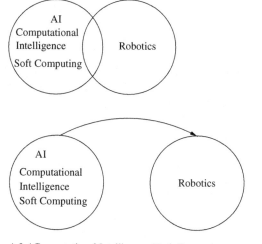

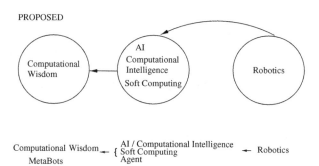

A.I. / Computational Intelligence / Soft Computing
Agents

} → Robotics

PROPOSED

Computational Wisdom ← { AI / Computational Intelligence
MetaBots   Soft Computing   ← Robotics
        Agent

Fig. 2 Impact of Robotics on affine disciplines

characterized by *dynamical* systems. In general, Agents can exhibit the following
drawbacks:

- It is difficult to justify *formally* the Agents application from a *theoretical* point
  of view.
- It is difficult to claim that the solution provided by a particular Agent is "better"
  than the one provided by other Agents, and/or the one obtained by the use of
  other techniques.
- It is difficult to ensure *formally* system stability.

That is, currently Agents usually only provide feasible, but not optimal, solutions.
Those drawbacks are relevant in view of the fact that Agents are supposed to handle
properly knowledge leading to good judgment. Consequently, it is necessary to:

- Conceptualize a better term than Agent.
- Set the alternative novel concept(s) in an appropriate Framework.

This can lead to:

- Establish new Frameworks/Paradigms.
- Foundation/Development of new disciplines/fields and areas.

Here, it is shown that the proposed Paradigm can serve to attain the desirable situation depicted in Fig. 2. That is, the Robotics field can have a desirable effect on affine disciplines (such as A.I., Soft Computing and Computational Intelligence). This can be accomplished by properly extending and generalizing some usual Robotics concepts such as Inverse Kinematics, Pseudoinverse Robustness/Perturbation, Local Motion Planning (Singularities/Obstacle avoidance), and Sensor Fusion/Integration; then, deal in a non-conventional fashion with Inverse Functions, Robust Solutions, and Constraint Compliance (Mayorga 1999). as shown below:

- Inverse Functions $\Longleftarrow$ Inverse Kinematics
- Robust Solutions $\Longleftarrow$ Pseudoinverse Robustness
- Constraint Compliance $\Longleftarrow$ Local Motion Planning

Now, let's examine in detail some (Webster's) dictionary definitions:

Intelligence:

- The ability to learn or understand or deal with new or trying situations: *Reason*; also: the skilled use of reason.
- The ability to apply knowledge to manipulate one's environment or to think abstractly as measured by objective criteria (as tests).
- Mental acuteness: *Shrewdness*.
- the act of understanding: *Comprehension*.

Intelligent:

- Having or indicating a high or satisfactory degree of intelligence and mental capacity.
- Revealing or reflecting good judgment or sound thought: *Skillful*.
- Possessing intelligence.
- Guided or directed by intellect: *Rational*.

Wisdom:

- Accumulated philosophic or scientific learning: *Knowledge*.
- The ability to discern inner qualities and relationships: *Insight*.
- Good sense: *Judgement*.
- A wise attitude or course of action.

Wise:

- Characterized by wisdom: marked by deep understanding, keen discernment, and a capacity for sound judgment.

- Exercising sound judgment: *Prudent.*
- Evidencing or hinting at the possession of inside information: *Knowing.*
- Crafty, shrewd: marked by clever discerning awareness and hardheaded acumen.

Insight/Discernment:

- The power or act of seeing into a situation.
- The act or result of apprehending the inner nature of things or of seeing intuitively.
- Mental or spiritual perception.
- the quality of being able to grasp and comprehend what is obscure: skill in discerning.

From the previous definitions the similarities and differences between Intelligence, Intelligent, Wisdom, and Wise are evident. From the definitions of Wisdom, and Wise; it is easy to observe (Mayorga 1999) that two attributes that stand out are:

(a) the ability to discern inner qualities and relationships;
(b) the exercise of good judgment/knowledge.

From a Cybernetics point of view, in some way "Intelligence" is related to an "Analysis" → "Action" process, to attain local goals; whereas, "Wisdom" is related to "Analysis", "Reflection", → "Synthesis" → "Action" process to attain global objectives. It should be mentioned that this point of view implicitly considers a Hegelian (dialect) process.

There are several ways to interpret the above to postulate a suitable formulation for *Computational Sapience (Wisdom)*. In particular, the attributes regarding the ability to discern inner qualities and relationships, and a capacity for exercising good judgment should be properly addressed.

Now, as previously mentioned, some areas of A.I. have evolved and migrated to constitute the field of Computational Intelligence. In fact, the term Computational Intelligence has been used loosely by the Computer Science and the Robotics community. An attempt to provide a formal definition is given in (Bezdek 1994):

Computational Intelligence – J.C. Bezdek – 1994

- Discipline dealing with (low-level) data
- It includes a pattern recognition component
- Does not use knowledge in the A.I. sense
- Additionally, it also deals with:

  - Computational Adaptivity
  - Computational Fault Tolerance
  - Speed approaching human-like turnaround - Error rates that approximate human performance

Based on this definition the author recently proposed (Mayorga 1999) a definition for Computational Wisdom as follows:

Computational Wisdom (Sapience) – R. V. Mayorga – 1999

- Discipline dealing with (low, medium, – level) data
- It can include an identification (pattern recognition) component for direct and/or inverse relationships
- It can use knowledge in the A.I. sense; but in any case, acts upon it

    - to discern inner qualities and relationships; and
    - to yield good judgment

- Additionally, it also deals with:

    - Computational Stability
    - Computational Adaptability
    - Computational Fault Tolerance
    - Speed approaching human-like turnaround

- Error rates that approximate human performance

Notice that this definition can be easily extended to an *Artificial Sapience (Wisdom)* definition; for example, by allowing to deal with high level data and using knowledge in the A.I. sense to act upon it as described above. From the previous definitions, it is clear the role of the Wisdom/Wise attributes. However, the Artificial / Computational Wisdom (Sapience) definitions, unlike the one in (Bezdek 1994), also contain important explicit provisions to:

- deal with direct and/or inverse relationships;
- act upon knowledge;
- to yield good judgment;
- include the previously forgotten concept of stability.

Also, notice that the proposed formulation (Mayorga 2003), (Mayorga 2000a), (Mayorga 2000b), (Mayorga 1999), includes learning, and adaptation, and explicitly addresses a "judgment" attribute. Consequently, it complies with a concept of cognition. Furthermore, it also permits to consider "Analysis", and "Reflection" processes, as well as a "Synthesis" process. All of these processes can be concurrent, sequential, or a combination of concurrent/sequential, leading to attaining global objectives.

Now, here it becomes pertinent to address closely the concepts of Intelligent Control and Intelligent Systems. An early suggestion for the concept of Intelligent Control was provided in (Fu 1971), as:

Intelligent Control - K. S. Fu, 1971
Intersection between:

- Automatic Control Systems
- Artificial Intelligence

Afterwards, Operations Research was included to constitute Intelligent Control (Saridis 1977), as:

Intelligent Control – G. N. Saridis, 1977
Intersection between:

- Automatic Control Systems
- Operations Research
- Artificial Intelligence

There are also many definitions on Intelligent Systems. A recent one is provided by the author (Mayorga 2000b):

Intelligent Systems:

- Capable to Incorporate-Reflect Experts Knowledge
- Able to deal with Linguistic inputs
- Possess Learning abilities
- Show Inference abilities
- Can cope with diverse and changing environments
- Yield a solution better than feasible

Furthermore, following the concepts in (Fu   1971), and (Saridis   1977), the author also recently proposed that Intelligent/*Wise* Decision and Control be constituted (Mayorga 2000a), (Mayorga 2000b), (Mayorga 1999), (Mayorga 1998a), as:

Intelligent/*Wise* Decision/Control – R. V. Mayorga, 1998, 1999
Intersection between:

- Automatic Control Systems
- Operations Research
- A.I., Soft Computing, Computational Intelligence
- Computational Wisdom
- Robotics

This framework facilitates to establish a definition for Wise (Sapient) Systems as provided by the author in (Mayorga 1999), (Mayorga 1998a):

Wise (Sapient) Systems – R. V. Mayorga, 1998, 1999

- Capable to Incorporate-Reflect Experts Knowledge
- Able to deal with Linguistic inputs
- Possess Learning abilities
- Show Inference abilities
- Can perceive and cope with diverse and changing environments
- Exhibit insight capabilities
- Able to discern inner qualities and relationships
- Capable for sound judgment

It is (becoming) accepted by the scientific community that learning, adaptation, and judgment, conduce to "cognition" (Perlovsky 2001). It is also clear that it is plausible to construct Agents or Intelligent Systems with (modular) structure/architectures such that the learning, adaptation, and judgment functions are concretely realized (Perlovsky 2001).

From the above formulation of Sapient (Wise) Systems it can be easily observed that it is necessary to have a structure and architecture with capabilities for learning, adaptation, judgment, (as in an "Intelligent System"); but additionally the (hierarchical multi-layer and/or distributed) structure/architecture should also be capable, from input/output data:

- To discern inner qualities and relationships (sequentially, concurrently, or in combination); and
- To yield good judgment.

Furthermore, here it is considered that the enabling capabilities of a general system to properly infer from general inputs plausible general outputs, and such that for any particular input it permits to infer a "reasonably good" (to attain a specific goal) output; constitute a key element to construct knowledge and exercise "*wise and sound judgment*".

The above approach permits to deal properly with the subject of "cognition" in terms of learning, adaptation, and judgment. In a very concise and simple manner several important concepts can be properly addressed. Furthermore, the approach can lead to the realization of Sapient (Wise) Systems in a concrete manner in terms of a (modular) structure and architecture and corresponding functionalities.

Consequently, here some Adaptive Inference Systems methodologies that properly achieve the above under the proposed Paradigm are considered. Here, in particular some efforts are directed to the implementation of Adaptive Inference Systems based on non-crisp Logics (Fuzzy Logic).

Based on the previous discussion and concepts, an early definition for MetaBot, to generalize the concept of Agent / Robot as a Sapient System, is provided by the author in (Mayorga 1999) – (Mayorga 1998a):

MetaBot – R. V. Mayorga, 1998, 1999

- General (Intelligent/*Wise*) System, composed of:

  - Software modules, or
  - Hardware units; or an
  - Hybrid combination of both

- Possessing a high level of *autonomy*
- Performing tasks in an intelligent/*wise* and *stable* manner
- Can interact *dynamically* with unstructured environments

The above definition can easily extended to include Bionic units in the composition of the Intelligent / Sapient (Wise) System. It is worth to notice that the above definition for *MetaBot*, unlike the Agent concept, provides provisions to encompass:

– Intelligent/*Wise* systems of a diverse nature;
– A stability criterion.

3 Sapient (Wise) Decision & Control

In 1971 K. S. Fu (Fu 1971) proposed *Intelligent Control* as a field of interaction between the Artificial Intelligence and the Automatic Control Systems disciplines. Over the years numerous studies were attempted to formalize the field into a unified and comprehensive discipline. However, in most studies either Artificial Intelligence, or Automatic Control tended to dominate; as a result, the intended discipline generality was only partially achieved.

A wider approach was proposed by G. N. Saridis in (Saridis 1977), and (Saridis 1979), considering Operations Research, Artificial Intelligence and Automatic Control Systems, to constitute the field of Intelligent Control. In these early works it was suggested that the theoretical foundations of Intelligent Controls should be pursued in the intersection of these disciplines, and should be structured according to the hierarchical principle of "increasing precision with decreasing intelligence". In subsequent and recent works (Saridis 1990) – (Saridis 1983) some theoretical foundations for Intelligent Controls and Machines have been established as analytical methods based on the use (minimization) of entropy as a performance metric on all levels of a hierarchical control structure (Mayorga 1998a).

In (Saridis 1990) – (Saridis 1983) the entropy based techniques were developed for both high-level planning and low level control in an intelligent machine. This formulation has the advantage that it provides a consistent performance measure for a wide diversity of tasks. However, it can only deal with uncertainties in the state variables that describe the intelligent machine. Since no task information is considered, it is not easy to generalize the entropy measure for overall system performance. More recently another metric for performance measure of intelligent machines has been presented in (Musto and Saridis 1997). It fuses some earlier concepts on Intelligent Machines (Saridis 1990) – (Saridis 1983), with traditional reliability analysis. This measure reflects both the uncertainty inherent in the intelligent machine as well as the uncertainties from the task description.

The approaches developed in (Musto and Saridis 1997) and (Saridis 1990) - (Saridis 1983), are of a stochastic and global nature (Saridis 1977). Although they have been developed conceptually to serve as a bridge between Automatic Control Systems, Artificial Intelligence, and Operations Research disciplines; their foundations still rely mainly on the traditional techniques of Automatic Control, Optimization, and Probability Theory. Furthermore, their use and implementation in conjunction with Artificial Intelligence techniques has been limited (Mayorga 1998a).

Recently a Paradigm for *Intelligent Decision and Control* has been presented by the author (Mayorga 1998b), (Mayorga 1997). This Paradigm is somewhat similar in principle to the approaches presented in (Saridis 1990), and (Saridis and Valavanis 1988a). However, in (Mayorga 1997) the problem is formulated locally as a deterministic relationship in the time domain between (as in Automatic Control Systems) outputs and inputs; for which (as in Operations Research) a high level damped Levenberg-Marquardt type solution is developed; and which can be implemented easily and effectively using non-conventional (A.I., Soft Computing, Computational Intelligence) techniques such as: Neural Networks, Fuzzy Inference Systems, or Coactive Neuro-Fuzzy Inference Systems. Furthermore, as recently observed by the author (Mayorga 1999), the Paradigm also facilitates to discern direct/inverse relationships and to act on the given knowledge (as in Computational Wisdom); and by considering inverse functions it allows to encompass a stability criterion (as in Robotics).

The proposed Paradigm (Mayorga 1997) is based on the bounded control principle that for small changes in the system inputs, there should correspond small changes in the outputs. Its deterministic and local nature it is not a detriment; rather, it allows to derive simple approaches that can be easily and effectively implemented with non-conventional techniques.

Under the Paradigm the relationship between a given system outputs to its inputs is formulated in the time domain at an *inverse functional* and a *rate of change* level. In (Mayorga 1997) some finite bounds on an *homogenized* norm on the difference between exact and inexact solutions are established. It is shown (Mayorga 1997) that under this formulation: Neural Networks; Fuzzy Inference Systems (FIS); and Coactive Neuro-Fuzzy Inference Systems (CANFIS) (Jang et al 1997), (Mizutani and Jang 1995); can be effectively used to approximate a general class of *inverse functions*.

It is also demonstrated that the proposed Paradigm permits to develop simple but efficient (Learning) strategies for the updating/tuning of antecedent/consequent and scaling parameters for a general class of FIS (Jang et al 1997) (becoming in fact Adaptive Inference Systems (AFIS)); and also for Co-Active Neuro Fuzzy Inference Systems (CANFIS) (Jang et al 1997), (Jang 1993), (Mizutani and Jang 1995). Moreover, as shown in (Mayorga 1997), under the proposed Paradigm FIS, AFIS, and CANFIS can deal also effectively with those cases in which there is no knowledge of a direct (or inverse) function between some (input-output) systems variables.

The proposed Paradigm (Mayorga 1998a), (Mayorga 1997) has been conceived for Intelligent Control or Decision problems (Mayorga 1998b). However, from the previous discussion, and as observed by the author in (Mayorga 1999) the Paradigm is based on an expression that permits to deal with and act upon a direct-inverse relationship in a bounded and stable manner. Furthermore, if implemented in a non-conventional fashion, the Paradigm can be used for *Sapient (Wise)* Decision/Control; and it can also serve as a baseline for the development of *Artificial / Computational Sapience (Wisdom)* as new disciplines (Mayorga 2003), (Mayorga 2000a), (Mayorga 2000b), (Mayorga 1999). Here, also some important aspects/issues on its application to decision making/resolution, and systems design problems are amply discussed. It is shown in (Mayorga 2000c), and (Mayorga 2000d), that this Paradigm exhibits some inherent characteristics that make it suitable for its application (in fact serving as a baseline for novel Paradigms) on diverse fields such as:

- The Intelligent / Sapient (Wise) Design and Operation of a Human-Computer Interface (Mayorga 2000c);
- The Intelligent / Sapient (Wise) Design and Motion Planning of Robot Manipulators (Mayorga 2000d).

4 Paradigm

First, it is worth to notice that the proposed Paradigm (Mayorga 1999) it is:

- Based on an effect-cause relationship;
- A behavioural approach of a deterministic nature;
- Based on a Control System framework;
- Based on a stability (bounded control) principle;
- An approach that facilitates concurrent Systems Modeling and Operation.

Furthermore, it is important to point out some attributes of the Paradigm (Mayorga 1999):

- It is a simple *Local* Approach;
- Considered at the *Rate of Change* Level;
- Based on an *Inverse Functional* conceptualization;
- Based on an Optimization Problem Formulation;
- Solution can be implemented by non-conventional (A.I., Soft Computing, Computational Intelligence) techniques.

It is also important to mention that the proposed formulation is based on the development of an inverse *effect-causal* time-variant relationship. For a given system, at any instant of time, a set of variables in the Plant (*causal state*) space establishes a unique set of variables in the Task/Performance (*effect state*) space. Formally, consider a system with n Plant variables as shown in the Figure 3.

At any instant of time, denote the plant variables by $\psi_i \equiv \psi_i(t); i = 1, 2, \cdots, n$. Also, define the Task/Performance variables describing system tasks by a vector of m variables $y_j \equiv y_j(t); j = 1, 2, \cdots, m$. Also, let $t \epsilon [t_o, t_f]$ where t_o and t_f are the initial and final time of the task interval; and let $\Re^m$ and $\Re^n$ be the m-dimensional and the n-dimensional Euclidean spaces respectively. Assume that $y \equiv y(t) = [y_1, y_2, \cdots, y_m]^T \epsilon \Re^m$ and $\psi \equiv \psi(t) = [\psi_1, \psi_2, \cdots, \psi_n]^T \epsilon \Re^n$ can be related by a

Fig. 3 A general System relating Plant variables to Task variables

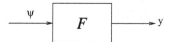

twice continuously differentiable function (Mayorga):

$$y(t) = \mathcal{F}(\psi(t)). \tag{1}$$

In many applications it is more convenient to set the task variables (*effect state*) to follow a desired state transition, and try to calculate the corresponding Plant variables (*causal state*). This implies establishing an inverse relationship from Eq. (1). In general, this relation is nonlinear; hence an analytical inverse relationship cannot be easily obtained. Under a local approach the problem can be treated at the inverse functional and rate of change level. That is, the problem can be addressed in the following indirect fashion. By differentiating Eq. (1) with respect to time, the next equation is obtained:

$$\dot{y}(t) = J(\psi(t))\dot{\psi}(t); \tag{2}$$

where $\dot{y} \equiv \dot{y}(t) = dy(t)/dt$, $\dot{\psi} \equiv \dot{\psi}(t) = d\psi(t)/dt$, and

$$J(\psi) \equiv J(\psi(t)) = \frac{\partial}{\partial \psi}\mathcal{F}(\psi(t)), \tag{3}$$

is the $(m \times n)$ Jacobian Plant matrix.

From the Eq. (2), it is possible to compute a $\psi(t)$ plan in terms of a prescribed state transition y (t). As shown in (Mayorga 1997), a solution in an inexact context is given by, (Mayorga and Carrera 2004):

$$\dot{\psi} = J_{wz\delta}^{+}(\psi)\dot{y} + [I - J_{wz\delta}^{+}(\psi)J(\psi)]v; \tag{4}$$

where, v is an arbitrary vector, and $\delta > 0$; and the weighted-augmented pseudoinverse $J_{wz\delta}^{+}(\psi)$ is given by:

$$J_{wz\delta}^{+}(\psi) = W^{-1}J^{T}(\psi)[J(\psi)W^{-1}J^{T}(\psi) + \delta Z^{-1}]^{-1} \tag{5}$$

$$= [J^{T}(\psi)ZJ(\psi) + \delta W]^{-1}J^{T}(\psi)Z; \tag{6}$$

where, the positive definite symmetric matrices W, Z, act as metrics to allow invariance to frame reference and scaling (homogenize dimensions). Also let

$$J_{wz} \equiv Z^{1/2}J(\psi)W^{-1/2}. \tag{7}$$

Notice that if $\delta = 0$, the expression given by Eq. (4) reduces to the exact solution. Also, as shown in Fig. 4, notice that the procedure to approximate a solution can be represented by considering as inputs to the system the Task variables, a "feedforward block" consisting of the computation of and approximated solution (via the augmented-weighted pseudoinverse), and an "external block" containing the Jacobian matrix.

Fig. 4 Inverse Function
Approximation

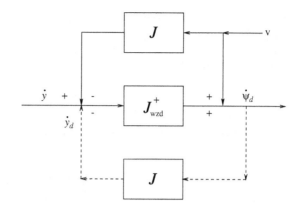

The process for approximating the Jacobian matrix, the null space vector v (direct functions);, and the augmented-weighted pseudoinverse matrix (inverse function) can be performed sequentially, and/or concurrently. Furthermore, it is this approximating process of both the direct and inverse functions, and the means to include global aspects (in the above equations, via the computation of the null space vector and the parameter δ), that characterize a Sapient (Wise) system.

Now, let $\| \ . \ \|_s$ represent an homogenized norm (Mayorga and Carrera 2004), (Mayorga 1998b). Consider $m < n$, notice that for $\delta = 0$ in Eq. (5), the Eq. (4) turns out to be the exact solution. The next Theorem properly establishes a finite bound on the norm of the difference between the exact and inexact solution (Mayorga and Carrera 2004), (Mayorga 1997).

Theorem 1. *Let $m < n$; and also let $\dot{\psi}$ be generated according to an exact solution; and $\dot{\psi}_\delta$ be generated according to an inexact solution given by Eq. (4). Also let $\dot{y} = J(\psi)\dot{\psi}$, and $\dot{y}_\delta = J(\psi)\dot{\psi}_\delta$. Then, for all $\delta > 0$,*

$$\|\dot{\psi} - \dot{\psi}_\delta\|_s \leq [\delta/(\tilde{\sigma}_m^2 + \delta)]\|\dot{\psi} - v\|_s; \tag{8}$$

$$\|\dot{y} - \dot{y}_\delta\|_s \leq [\delta/(\tilde{\sigma}_m^2 + \delta)]\|\dot{y}\|_s + \tilde{\sigma}_1\|v\|_s; \tag{9}$$

where, $\tilde{\sigma}_1 \equiv \sigma_1\{J_{wz}\}$, and $\tilde{\sigma}_m \equiv \sigma_m\{J_{wz}\}$, are the J_{wz} largest and smallest singular values respectively.

Similar results can be shown for the case $m \geq n$ (Mayorga 1997). More relevantly, similar finite bounds can be established for the case in which there is no knowledge, or there is limited knowledge about the direct relationship between y and ψ; that is, the Jacobian matrix is unknown, or partially known (Mayorga 1997). For these cases the following development is considered. First, let the $(m \times n)\Delta(\psi)$ matrix be an approximation to the Jacobian matrix $J(\psi)$ expressed as:

$$\Delta(\psi) = J(\psi) + \rho E(\psi); \tag{10}$$

where, $\rho \geq 0$ is a small scalar; and $E(\psi)$ is an $(m \times n)$ matrix. Now, let's drop the index ψ in the subsequent expressions; and let W be an $(n \times n)$ positive definite matrix. Now, let Z_m be a $m \times m$ positive definite matrix, and (Mayorga 1997):

$$Y = \rho J W^{-1} E^T + \rho E W^{-1} J^T + \rho^2 E W^{-2} E^T + \delta Z_m^{-1}; \qquad (11)$$

$Z^{-1} = (1/\delta)Y$, in Eq. (7). Also, let

$$\Delta_{wz\delta}^+ = W^{-1} \Delta^T [\Delta W^{-1} \Delta^T + \delta Z_m^{-1}]^{-1}. \qquad (12)$$

Now, an approximated solution ψ_{am} can be given as follows

$$\dot{\psi}_m = \Delta_{wz\delta}^+ \dot{y} + [I - \Delta_{wz\delta}^+ \Delta]v; \qquad (13)$$

where, $\dot{y}$ is the exact task/performance vector. In the next Theorem a bound on the difference between a conceptual exact solution and an approximated solution is established, (Mayorga 1998b), (Mayorga 1997).

Theorem 2. *Let $m < n$; and also let $\dot{\psi}$ be generated according to an exact solution (with $\delta = 0$ in Eq. (4)); and $\dot{\psi}_m$ be generated according to an approximated solution given by Eq. (13). Also let $\dot{y} = J(\psi)\dot{\psi}$ and $\dot{y}_m = J(\psi)\dot{\psi}_m$. Then, for all $\delta > 0$,*

$$\|\dot{\psi} - \dot{\psi}_m\|_s \leq [1/(\tilde{\sigma}_m^2 + \delta)][(\delta + \gamma_1)\|\dot{\psi} - v\|_s + \gamma_2\|v\|_s]; \qquad (14)$$

$$\|\dot{y} - \dot{y}_m\|_s \leq [1/(\tilde{\sigma}_m^2 + \delta)][(\delta + \gamma_1)(\|\dot{y}\|_s + \tilde{\sigma}_1\|v\|_s) + \gamma_3\|v\|_s]; \qquad (15)$$

where, $\tilde{\sigma}_1 \equiv \sigma_1\{J_{wz}\}$, $\tilde{\sigma}_m \equiv \sigma_m\{J_{wz}\}$; $\gamma_1 = \tilde{\sigma}_1\|E\|_s$, $\gamma_2 = \|\Delta\|_s\|E\|_s$, and $\gamma_3 = \tilde{\sigma}_1\gamma_2$. Again, similar results can be obtained, (Mayorga 1998b), (Mayorga 1997), for $m \geq n$, or for $v = 0$.

From the Eqs. (4), and (13), it can be easily observed that the solutions depend heavily on the computation (approximation) of the pseudoinverse matrices. This computation can be performed in a conventional (numerical) manner; or as postulated here, it can also be approximated, as shown in Fig. 5, via non-conventional techniques (N-C.T.) such as (but not limited to) ANNs, and Adaptive Inference Systems.

The above Theorems provide the foundation of the proposed Paradigm. In particular, the Theorems indicate that as long as the inverse (augmented-weighted pseudoinverse matrix) function approximation is done as above, it is possible to establish finite bounds on the error on the Task variables. Furthermore, it can be easily observed that here approximations for both direct (Jacobian matrix, null space vector) and inverse (augmented-weighted pseudoinverse) relationships are properly considered. These approximations can be realized (sequentially and/or

Fig. 5 Non-conventional
Inverse Approximation

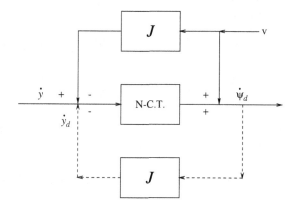

concurrently) utilizing conventional (numerical) techniques, and/or via non-conventional methodologies (Mayorga 2003), (Mayorga 2000a), (Mayorga 1999).

It is important to point out once more that the (sequential and/or concurrent) realization of the (direct and inverse) approximations constitutes a characteristic of *Sapient (Wise)* Systems. Furthermore, it is also important to notice that the use of non-conventional techniques (N-C.T.) such as ANNs and Adaptive Inference Systems, as shown in Fig. 5, has the additional feature that these techniques allow to incorporate adaptation, learning, and inference aspects. Consequently, the Paradigm implementation via these N-C.T. techniques, in fact constitutes a stepping stone towards the realization of *Sapient (Wise)* systems.

In the Fig. 5, an N-C.T. appears explicitly in the feedforward loop to indicate that it is mainly applied to the approximation of the (augmented-weighted) pseudoinverse matrix. However, also as easily an N-C.T. can utilized in the top feedback loop, for the computation of the Jacobian matrix J and (to incorporate global characteristics (Mayorga 2003), (Mayorga 2000a), (Mayorga 2000b), (Mayorga 1999)) the vector v, as shown in Figs. 6.

An example of a Sapient (Wise) System approach is the novel procedure for *global* optimization of non-linear functions using Artificial Neural Networks developed by the author (Mayorga 2002). The procedure has shown effective, for highly

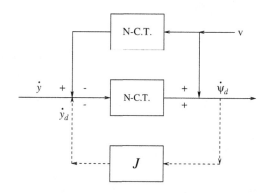

Fig. 6 Non-conventional
Direct-Inverse
Approximation

Fig. 7 Global Minimum of
the Peaks function

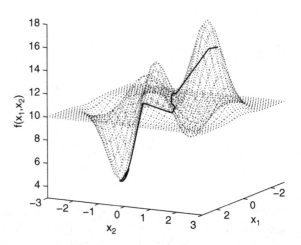

non-linear functions with many local minima, such as the Peaks function, and the
Griewank function, (Mayorga and Arriaga 2007), (Mayorga 2002). Notice that
current conventional optimization techniques normally fail to attain the global minimum. As shown in the Figs. 7, 8, the proposed technique (Mayorga 2002), is
capable to obtain the *global* minimum for these functions, (Mayorga and Arriaga

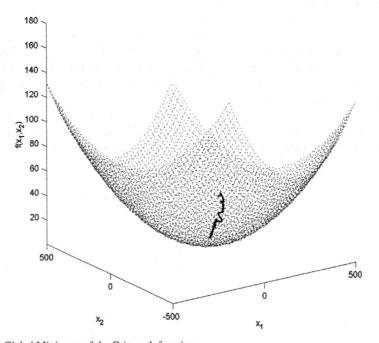

Fig. 8 Global Minimum of the Griewank function

2007), (Mayorga 2002). It is important to notice that in this procedure: the Jacobian matrix (a direct function) approximation, the inverse function approximation, and the null space vector (properly including a sufficiency condition for optimality) are done using ANNs. Furthermore, the null space vector and the δ parameter in Eq. (5) are utilized to make a sound decision on attaining a global optimum. That is, the null space vector and the δ parameter facilitate the consideration of important aspects to reach a global objective.

Notice that in this case the aspects of learning, adaptation, and sound judgment, have been complied with. Consequently, this approach complies with the proposed Paradigm that is illustrated in Fig. 6. Finally, it should be mentioned that this ANN optimization technique (Mayorga 2002), compares favorably with other non-conventional global optimization methods such as genetic algorithms and simulated annealing techniques (Mayorga and Arriaga 2007), (Mayorga 2002).

5 Implementations

Notice that the Eq. (4) could be implemented numerically. However, the large amount of computation required for the calculation of the pseudoinverse matrix may be cumbersome. A simple approach, also numerical, is as follows (Mayorga 1997). Let $m < n$, and suppose that at iteration i the damping factor δ_i, as given by a proper scheme and the vector v, intended for constraint compliance (Mayorga 1998b), are available. Then, solve for ϕ the following system

$$[J(\psi)W^{-1}J(\psi)^T + \delta_i Z^{-1}]\phi = \dot{y} - J(\psi)v, \tag{16}$$

by a Gaussian elimination process that takes into account the symmetry of the matrix as described in (Mayorga 1998b). Next, just compute $\dot{\psi}$ by

$$\dot{\psi} = W^{-1}J(\psi)^T\phi + v. \tag{17}$$

This simpler approach may not yet conduce to real-time implementations. In many applications real-time solutions are required; and/or only an estimation of the direct function is available; and/or dedicated custom built microprocessors are desired. For these cases, some A.I. techniques are appropriate. In particular, it is convenient to consider (ordinary, adaptive) Fuzzy, and Neuro-Fuzzy Inference Systems that possess the additional advantages that can incorporate experts knowledge and deal with linguistic attributes.

5.1 Artificial Neural Networks Implementation

First notice that the null space vector v can be easily computed conventionally or by using a properly trained ANN. In this case, the $\psi_1, \ldots, \psi_n$ are the inputs to the ANN, and the $v_1, \ldots, v_n$ are the ANN outputs. Now, let the $m < n$. A direct approach to implement the Eq. (4) is to solve for ϕ the Eq. (16) utilizing a recurrent neural network that solves linear matrix equations such as discussed in (Mayorga 1998b). Then, just set $\dot{\psi}$ as in Eq. (17). An indirect approach consists as follows. Let an $(m \times m)$ symmetric positive definite matrix A be defined as follows

$$A \equiv [J(\psi)W^{-1}J(\psi)^T + \delta_i Z^{-1}]. \tag{18}$$

Then, train a neural net (such as a multilayered feedforward with backpropagation) with inputs $\dot{y}$, ψ, and v; such that

$$A^{-1}[\dot{y} - J(\psi)v] = \phi. \tag{19}$$

Then set, $\dot{\psi}$ as in Eq. (17). A step by step procedure is as follows (Mayorga 1997):

(a) Specify an initial set of Plant variables $\psi(t_o)$;
(b) Consider a specified task $\dot{y}(t_i)$;
(c) Apply $\psi(t_i)$; and $y(t_i)$; to a trained neural network to obtain $\phi(t_i)$;
(d) Set $\dot{\psi}(t_i)$ as in Eq. (17);
(e) Apply a fourth-order Runge-Kutta numerical integration method to get $\psi(t_{i+1})$;
(f) Set $t_{i+1} = t_i + \Delta t$;
(g) If $t_{i+1} = t_f$ stop; otherwise set $i = i + 1$ and return to step (b).

Recently, a particular case of this approach has been successfully implemented for the computation of the inverse kinematics of a redundant planar manipulator (Mayorga and Sanongboon 2005a), (Mayorga 1998b). In this case in order to achieve reasonable accurate results; the training data set has to be limited to fit the desired range so that within the required range the neural net performs better. However, given the right number of training data sets and a longer training time; a well-trained network can be developed which exhibits generalizing ability over the entire range (Mayorga 1998b), (Mayorga 1997).

Notice that a similar approach can be followed for the case in which $m \geq n$. For the case that there is no knowledge of the Jacobian matrix J, the implementation of a neural network to approximate an inverse function is not that straight forward. A simple approach is to obtain an approximate estimation of the direct relationship given by

$$\dot{y} = J(\psi)\dot{\psi}, \tag{20}$$

by conventional methods; or by the use of other A.I. techniques. Once this estimation is proved satisfactory; then it can be set as Δ, and used to train a neural net (such as a multilayered feedforward with backpropagation) with inputs $\dot{y}$, ψ, and v.

Consider $m < n$, and also

$$A^{-1}[\dot{y} - \Delta(\psi)v] = \phi. \tag{21}$$

Then set, $\dot{\psi}$ as

$$\dot{\psi} = W^{-1}\Delta^T(\psi)\phi + v. \tag{22}$$

Then, the previous approach for J known can be easily followed.

5.2 Fuzzy, and Neuro-Fuzzy Inference Systems Implementations

Notice that for a general class of ordinary FIS the system output can be expressed as (Mayorga 1997)

$$\Omega = \mathcal{F}_2(\alpha, c, u, d) = \Psi_o(\alpha, c, u)u + \bar{d}; \tag{23}$$

where, Ψ_o is an $(n \times m)$ matrix; c and $\bar{d}$ are the consequent parameters; α are the antecedent/premise and scaling parameters; and u are the system inputs. This class use the Eq. (23) with fixed parameters and have been successful for some Control Problems (Jang et al 1997). However, the corresponding AFIS and CANFIS have demonstrated a superior/better performance (Jang et al 1997).

For Control problems generally there is available a desired/reference (optimal) solution, and an error measure is usually defined in terms of the difference between the desired/reference output and the actual system output. This error measure is normally used by AFIS and CANFIS for Learning purposes by properly optimizing the measure according to some parameter tuning/updating (resulting in an appropriate shifting/shaping of the membership functions) Schemes.

However, the FIS application for Decision making/resolution problems is not that simple, since it is not easy to justify *a priori* a desired nor optimal output vector. Moreover, it is also difficult to establish *a priori* an output reference and an error measure to devise schemes for proper parameter tuning/updating. Therefore, the application of AFIS or CANFIS becomes more complicated, mainly due to the additional trouble on defining an error measure.

For a general class of FIS a possible way to deal with the difficulty is to establish as a target for optimization a Performance criterion, rather than an error measure. However, this criterion should represent truly Plant performance subject to a wide range of constraints. Thence, it is convenient to establish a performance criterion in terms of the outputs as follows (Mayorga 1998b), (Mayorga 1997):

$$\mathcal{P}(\Omega(\alpha, c, u, \bar{d})) = \mathcal{P}(\alpha, c, u, \bar{d}). \tag{24}$$

Tuning/Updating Schemes

A typical *Learning* (parameter tuning/updating) Scheme, can be devised as follows (Mayorga 1998b):

Scheme I - General Tuning/Updating

- Establish a Performance Criterion $\mathcal{P}$ as in Eq. (24).
- Set an input u.
- Optimize the Performance Criterion, to obtain the optimal set of antecedent/premise, scaling, and consequent parameters.
- Repeat the optimization process for a wide range of inputs u.

Another approach (Mayorga 1998b), a variant of the procedure normally used by adaptive neural-fuzzy inference systems (Jang et al 1997), can be as follows

Scheme II - General Tuning/Updating

- Set the Performance criterion as an error measure representing the difference between a desired/reference and the actual output expressed explicitly in terms of the scaling, and antecedent/premise parameters.
- Fix the scaling, antecedent/premise (non-linear) parameters, and for a wide range of inputs u get the corresponding outputs Ω. Then, get the consequent (linear) parameters using a least squares method.
- With the obtained consequent parameters fixed, for a sequential range of inputs optimize the Performance criterion to obtain the optimal scaling antecedent/premise parameters.

Several other efficient Learning Schemes are derived in (Mayorga 1998b), and (Mayorga 1997). Thus, in fact turning this FIS class into an AFIS class. In particular, some Schemes appropriate for AFIS, and CANFIS are derived by establishing the Performance criterion in terms of truly *internal* states. Notice that from Eq. (23), it immediately follows that

$$\dot{\Omega} = J_2(\alpha, c, d, u)\dot{u} = \Psi(\alpha, c, u)\dot{u}; \tag{25}$$

where, $J_2 = \partial \mathcal{F}_2/\partial u$. Now, let $\dot{\Omega} \equiv \dot{\omega} - v$; and $\dot{u} \equiv \dot{y} - Jv$; thence,

$$\dot{\omega} - v = \Psi(\alpha, c, u)[\dot{y} - Jv]. \tag{26}$$

Also, let $\dot{u}_\omega = J\dot{\omega}$; then the next Theorem immediately follows (Mayorga 1998b), (Mayorga 1997).

Theorem 3. *Consider $\dot{\psi}_\delta$ be generated according to an inexact solution given by Eq. (4) for $m < n$; and let $\dot{y}_\delta = J\dot{\psi}_\delta$. Also, let the output of a fuzzy inference system be given by Eq. (23). Also assume that*

$$\|\Psi - J^+_{wz\delta}\|_s \leq \varepsilon. \tag{27}$$

Then, for   m < n,

$$\|\dot{\psi}_\delta - \dot{\omega}\|_s \le \varepsilon \tilde{\sigma}_1 \|\dot{\psi} - v\|_s; \qquad (28)$$

$$\|\dot{y}_\delta - \dot{u}_\omega\|_s \le \varepsilon \tilde{\sigma}_1 [\|\dot{y}_\delta\|_s + \tilde{\sigma}_1 \|v\|_s]. \qquad (29)$$

Where $\dot{\psi}$ is an exact solution. Notice that in this Theorem there are no assumptions on the nature of the matrix Ψ in Eq. (23). This matrix can be linear or nonlinear in the parameters α, and or c. As long as one can establish a relationship as in Eq. (23), the results of the Theorem remain valid for Fuzzy Inference systems other that the Sugeno class (Jang et al 1997).

Thus, if $\Psi \approx J_{wz\delta}^+$; the Eq. (25) can approximate the Eq. (4). From the matrix difference $[\Psi(\alpha, c, u) - J_{wz\delta}^+(\psi)]$ a Performance criterion $\mathcal{P}(\alpha, c, u, \bar{d})$ can be easily established (Mayorga 1998b), (Mayorga 1997). This allows the development of several efficient schemes/strategies for tuning/updating parameters, and also for scaling the rules and membership functions with a validity factor and/or importance measure (Mayorga 1998a), (Mayorga 1998b), (Mayorga 1997). It is important to mention that similar results can be developed for $m \ge n$, and for the case that the Jacobian matrix is unknown, or partially known (Mayorga 1998a), (Mayorga 1998b), (Mayorga 1997). Consequently, the proposed Paradigm is suitable for the development of effective approaches for Intelligent/Decision Control; and particularly it is appropriate for the development of Intelligent/Wise Decision making/resolution approaches (Mayorga 1997).

6 Performance Criteria for Systems Design/Operation

From the Eqs. (4), and (13), it can also be easily observed, (Mayorga 2005c), that the solutions to generate plans depend heavily on the norm of the pseudoinverse matrices expressions, which in turn depends on the rank preservation of J_{wz}. Furthermore, as pointed out in (Mayorga 1997), the condition number of a matrix it is also an appropriate criterion for measuring system performance.

As discused in (Mayorga 1997) it is relatively easy to define a matrix norm and a homogenized condition number on the Plant Space. This homogenized condition number can be utilized to measure task/performance invariant to frame reference selection and/or scaling; and also to deal with non-homogeneous Plant dimensions. Therefore, as shown in the next development it can also serve for optimal Plant design.

First, recall that the $(m \times n)$ matrix $J_{wz}(\psi(t))$ is the weighted Jacobian matrix at any $t \epsilon [t_o, t_f]$ given by Eq. (7). Now, notice that it is relatively easy to show that

$$\|J\|_s \equiv \|J_{wz}\|_2 \equiv \|Z^{1/2} J(\psi) W^{-1/2}\|_2. \qquad (30)$$

Then, the next Proposition easily follows (Mayorga 1997).

Proposition 1 *Let* $\tilde{\sigma}_1 \equiv \sigma_1\{J_{wz}\}$, *and* $\tilde{\sigma}_m \equiv \sigma_m\{J_{wz}\}$, *be the largest and smallest singular values of the matrix* $[J_{wz}]$ *respectively. Then, a* homogenized *condition number can be given by:*

$$\kappa_s \equiv \|J\|_s \|J^+\|_s = \tilde{\sigma}_1/\tilde{\sigma}_m. \tag{31}$$

Notice that in general it is quite difficult to express explicitly the condition number; then, its direct use for systems design is limited. Still, it can be used for design analysis/optimization by considering the Eq. (31) and performing an extensive simulation on the entire Task space. A better performance index can be developed by considering instead an upper bound on the condition number. From Eq. (31) it is relatively easy to show the following Proposition.

Proposition 2 *Let* $\tilde{\sigma}_1$, *and* $\tilde{\sigma}_m$, *be as in Proposition 1; then, an upper bound for the condition number is given by:*

$$\kappa_s(\psi) \equiv \tilde{\sigma}_1(\psi)/\tilde{\sigma}_m(\psi) \leq \|J_{wz}(\psi)\|_F^m /\lambda^{1/2}(\psi); \tag{32}$$

where, $\lambda(\psi) = det[J_{wz}(\psi)J_{wz}^T(\psi)];$ *and* $\|.\|_F$ *stands for the Frobenius norm.*

Due to the difficulty on expressing explicitly $\lambda(\psi)$; for general cases this upper bound on the condition number can not be easily expressed explicitly either. However, it is useful for those cases ($m = 2, 3$) in which it is relatively easy to express explicitly $\lambda(\psi)$.

The above, illustrates the need to develop performance indices that can be easily expressed explicitly for general cases. For this purpose the following Proposition and Theorems have been developed. Notice that it can be easily shown that:

Proposition 3 *Let* $\tilde{\sigma}_1, \ldots, \tilde{\sigma}_m$, *be as above; and* $\sigma_{iso} > 0$. *Then, the singular values are equal to the same value; that is,* $\tilde{\sigma}_1 =, \ldots, = \tilde{\sigma}_m = \sigma_{iso};$ *if and only if*

$$J_{wz}J_{wz}^T = \sigma_{iso}^2 I. \tag{33}$$

Furthermore, in this case, $\kappa_s = 1$.

Notice that σ_{iso} is the isotropic value of the singular values; that σ_{iso} is in fact a function of ψ. and that the Eq. (33) represents the so-called isotropic condition of a matrix; Next, the following Theorem can be easily shown.

Theorem 4. *Consider the weighted matrix* J_{wz} *as given in Eq. (7). Then, an upper bound for the rate of change of its homogenized isotropic value is given by:*

$$\dot{\sigma}_{iso} \leq \beta \sum_{i=1}^{m} \sum_{j=1}^{n} |J_{wz(i,j)}| \ |\sum_{k=1}^{n} \partial J_{wz(i,j)}/\partial \psi_k|; \tag{34}$$

where $\beta = [l/\sqrt{m}\|J_{wz}\|_F]$; and $l = |\dot{\psi}|_{max}$, and $J_{wz(i,j)}$ are the elements (i, j) of the matrix J_{wz}.

The Proposition 3 and Theorem 4, permit to develop performances criteria that can be easily expressed on explicit form and used for systems design. Some other criteria that can be also expressed in explicit form can be developed as shown next. Now, let's define

$$\bar{J}(\psi(t_i), \dot{\psi}(t_i), \ddot{\psi}(t_i)) \equiv \dot{J}(\psi(t_i), \dot{\psi}(t_i))\Delta t \tag{35}$$
$$+ (1/2)\ddot{J}(\psi(t_i), \dot{\psi}(t_i), \ddot{\psi}(t_i))\Delta t^2$$
$$+ O(\Delta t^3);$$

where

$$\dot{J}(\psi(t_i), \dot{\psi}(t_i)) = d[J(\psi(t_i))]/dt; \tag{36}$$

and $O(\Delta t^3)$ is an $(m \times n)$ matrix of third order terms. Notice that for $t_i \epsilon [t_o, t_f]$

$$J(\psi(t_{i+1})) = J(\psi(t_i)) + \bar{J}(\psi(t_i), \dot{\psi}(t_i), \ddot{\psi}(t_i)). \tag{37}$$

Now for convenience, let's drop the index t_i in the subsequent expressions. It can be easily shown that an upper bound for $\bar{J}(\psi(t_i), \dot{\psi}(t_i), \ddot{\psi}(t_i))$ is given by:

$$\|\bar{J}(\psi, \dot{\psi}, \ddot{\psi})\|_s \leq \zeta(\eta + \xi); \tag{38}$$

where

$$\eta \equiv \Delta t \sum_{j=1}^{n} \{\|\hat{J}_j\|_s + \Delta t(\zeta_a/2\zeta)\|\hat{J}_j\|_s\}, \tag{39}$$

$$\xi \equiv (\zeta \Delta t^2/2) \sum_{j=1}^{n} \sum_{k=1}^{n} \|\check{J}_{jk}\|_s + \|O(\Delta t^3)\|_s. \tag{40}$$

where $\hat{J}_j \equiv \hat{J}_j(\psi) \equiv \partial J(\psi)/\partial \psi_j$; $\check{J}_{jk} \equiv \partial \hat{J}_j/\partial \psi_k$; $j, k, = 1, 2, \ldots, n$; and $\zeta = max |\dot{\psi}_j|_s$; $j = 1, 2, \ldots n$; and $\zeta_a = max |\ddot{\psi}_k|_s$; $k = 1, 2, \ldots, n$. Notice that ζ can be considered arbitrary, and that $\zeta \Delta t \approx \Delta \psi_{max} \equiv max |\Delta \psi_j|_s$; $j = 1, 2, \ldots, n$. Also notice that the η, and ξ are dimensionless.

Now, let's consider an upper bound (in terms of η, and ξ) for the condition number of the Jacobian matrix at a given Plant configuration $\psi(t_i)$ as follows:

$$\varpi(\psi(t_i)) \equiv \|J(\psi(t_i))\|_s /\zeta(\eta + \xi). \tag{41}$$

The next Theorem states that such an upper bound constitutes a sufficiency condition for the preservation of the rank of the Jacobian matrix at $\psi(t_{i+1})$ (Mayorga 1997).

Theorem 5. *Let $m \leq n$; η, and ξ as in Eqs. (39), and (40); and ϖ as in Eq. (41). Also, suppose that at $t_i \epsilon [t_o, t_f]$, $Rank\{J(\psi(t_i))\} = m$. If the condition number κ_s is bounded as follows*

$$\kappa_s(\psi(t_i)) < \varpi(\psi(t_i)). \tag{42}$$

Then, $Rank\{J(\psi(t_{i+1}))\} = m$.

Now, notice that $(\eta + \xi) \leq (\eta_F + \xi_F)$; where, η_F and ξ_F are similar to Eqs. (39), and (40) respectively, with $\| Z^{1/2} \hat{J}_j W^{-(1/2)} \|_F$, and $\| Z^{1/2} \check{J}_{jk} W^{-(1/2)} \|_F$ instead of their corresponding expressions $\|.\|_s$ The next Corollary states that such an upper bound in terms of η_F and ξ_F constitutes a sufficiency condition for the preservation of the rank of the Jacobian matrix at $\psi(t_{i+1})$.

Corollary 1 *Let $m \leq n$; η_F, and ξ_F, as above. Also, suppose that at $t_i \epsilon [t_o, t_f]$, $Rank\{J(\psi(t_i))\} = m$. If*

$$\zeta(\eta_F + \xi_F)\|J_{wz}^+(\psi(t_i))\|_F < 1. \tag{43}$$

Then, $Rank\{J(\psi(t_{i+1}))\} = m$.

Thence, according to Corollary 1, a sufficiency condition to preserve the Rank of the Jacobian matrix, is that the condition given by Ineq. (43) must hold. Therefore, a low value of $\eta_F + \xi_F$ will indicate some space neighborhoods where the Ineq. (43) can be satisfied in an easy manner to preserve the Rank of the Jacobian matrix. Now, notice that the Ineq. (43) can be expressed as

$$\zeta(\|J_{wz}^+(\psi(t_i))\|_F) < 1/(\eta_F + \xi_F). \tag{44}$$

Also, notice that for states *near* singularities, $\|J^+(\psi(t_i))\|_F$ and the variables $\dot{\psi}$ take very large values; whereas, *far* from singular states they take small values. Hence, the value $1/(\eta_F + \xi_F)$ sets a proper upper bound on $\zeta(\|J_{wz}^+(\psi(t_i))\|_F)$ and serves to monitor it and ensure the Rank preservation. Then, this upper bound can be used in some way (to indicate space neighborhoods far from singularities) to establish a proper criteria for system performance.

7 Sapient Systems Design & Operation

Notice that the main objective for Plant design is to ensure that the matrix J_{wz} preserves its rank and that is well conditioned on a specific region; that is, that $\|J_{wz\delta}^+\|_s$ (for $\delta \to 0$), remains bounded in that region, (Mayorga 2005c). One of the main obstacles on developing simple and general procedures for Plant design is the inherent difficulty to find an explicit expression for $J_{wz\delta}^+$. This explains the merit of a design procedure based on Ineq. (34), Ineq. (41), or Ineq (44), since the procedure relies on explicit expressions.

A conventional Plant Design procedure based on Ineq. (34), Ineq. (41), and Ineq. (44), involves a trial and error process consisting of solving a series of optimization problems. The optimization procedure normally involves formulating a constrained nonlinear programming problem which considers properly any of the above performance criteria as an objective function and subject to some parameter constraints.

7.1 Use of Proposition 3 and Theorem 4

The Proposition 3 and Theorem 4 can be the basis for systems design optimization. In particular, the isotropy condition given by Eq. (33), or the upper bound given by Ineq. (34) can be used alone or in conjunction. In this case, a proper objective function can be defined only in terms of $\| J_{wz}(\psi) J_{wx}^T(\psi) - \sigma_{iso}^2(\psi) I \|_F^2$, or on the upper bound given by Ineq. (34); or by properly combining both expressions.

7.2 Use of Theorem 5

Since the condition number $\kappa_s(\psi)$ is a continuous function, the minimum of the upper bound given by Ineq. (41) besides ensuring the rank preservation; implies a $\Delta\psi_{max}$ neighborhood, around the optimal set of Plant parameters, yielding a condition number with the *smallest* upper bound. Notice that this upper bound is a nonlinear function which may have several local minima. Consequently, a simple and sensible strategy to find this neighborhood, for an assigned $\Delta\psi_{max}$, is to minimize the upper bound given by Eq. (41) to obtain a set of optimal parameters and/or Plant variables values. Next, using these values the condition number of the Jacobian matrix is evaluated. If the resultant condition number satisfies Ineq. (42), then in a neighborhood the rank is preserved and the condition number is bounded. If the resultant condition number does not satisfy it, then the optimization process is repeated with a different set of initial values, until a satisfactory solution is found. Here, it has been implicitly assumed that the Plant parameters are invariant with respect to time. A similar overall development can also performed for the case that these parameters vary with respect to time. In this case, it will be also necessary to take into account in the Eqs. (17)–Eq. (41) the proper (rates of change) expressions corresponding to the parameter variations.

7.3 Use of Corollary 1

Now, from Ineq. (43) it is desirable to have a low value for $\eta_F + \xi_F$; whereas from Ineq. (44) the value $1/(\eta_F + \xi_F)$ sets an upper bound for Rank preservation which it is also desirable to be low. Thence, is quite reasonable to combine these two conditions to make up a simple performance criterion for rank preservation. This criterion (in terms of η_F and ξ_F) can considered as an objective function in the formulation of the constrained nonlinear programming problem.

7.4 Non-conventional Techniques Issues

It is important to notice that the above Propositions, Theorems, and Corollary have been developed assuming that the weighted Jacobian matrix J_{wz} is available. However, their use remains valid in the case that an approximation (by conventional or non-conventional -ANNs, AFIS, CANFIS- techniques) to the weighted Jacobian matrix is considered.

Moreover, as previously mentioned, for Inference Systems the Eq. (25) also provides the means to establish a simple explicit expression that can serve to develop a non-conventional approach for Plant design. Notice that in this case it is desired that $\Psi \approx J_{wz\delta}^{+}$; and that Ψ can be expressed explicitly in terms of antecedent/premise, scaling, and consequent parameters. Furthermore, in this case a proper norm of the matrix Ψ can be easily expressed explicitly in terms of the system parameters. That is, it is desired to optimize the norm (objective function) subject to some constraints in the antecedent/premise, scaling, and consequent parameters (Mayorga 2000a), (Mayorga 1997). Based on this observation the author (Mayorga 1998a), (Mayorga 1998b), (Mayorga 1997), has devised several strategies (optimization schemes) for Intelligent & *Sapient* (Mayorga 2000a), (Mayorga 2000b), Plant Design and Operation.

8 Pertinent Observations

The Paradigm presented here (Mayorga 2000a), (Mayorga 2000b), (Mayorga 1999), has been conceived for Intelligent/*Wise* Decision/Control (Mayorga 1998b), (Mayorga 1998b), (Mayorga 1997). Here, as in (Mayorga 2000c), (Mayorga 1998c), (Mayorga 1997), it is shown that this Paradigm constitutes a novel and general Framework and exhibits some inherent characteristics that make it suitable for its application to the Intelligent/*Wise* design and operation of a Human-Computer interface (Mayorga 2000c).

Some areas of System Design constitute an important class overlapping with the Decision making/resolution field. Therefore, the proposed Paradigm is also appropriate for the development of effective approaches for these areas. Normally, the optimal design of systems deals with a large number of aspects and issues of a diverse nature. Also, besides dealing with inherent technological aspects, it requires to consider some subjective aspects. Hence, the direct use of conventional techniques may conduce to ineffective design of systems.

It is well known that some non-conventional (A.I., Soft Computing, Computational Intelligence) techniques have the capability to deal with linguistic attributes, as well as to incorporate human expert knowledge, and perform high level reasoning and inference. These properties entail the capability to deal with subjective issues;

thence, they are of great relevance for the design of systems. These facts lead to consider these techniques, under the proposed Paradigm, as candidates to be used for the design of systems. In particular, to point out the versatility of the Paradigm, the author has proposed the application of these techniques for the Intelligent Design and Interaction of a Human-Computer Interface (Mayorga 2000c), (Mayorga 1998c), (Mayorga 1997).

9 Conclusions

In this Chapter a Paradigm that can contribute with some essential aspects to establish a baseline for the development of *Artificial / Computational Sapience (Wisdom)* as new disciplines has been presented. It is demonstrated here that, under the proposed Paradigm, the development of Artificial / Computational Sapience (Wisdom) methodologies can be accomplished as a natural extension of some non-conventional (Soft Computing and Artificial / Computational Intelligence) approaches. Furthermore, it is also demonstrated here that the Paradigm serves as a general framework for the development of *Sapient (Wise)* Systems and *MetaBots* (Mayorga 1999).

The proposed Paradigm constitutes (from a Cybernetics and Systems point of view) a Framework which conduces to results which are theoretically justifiable. It has been shown that under the proposed Paradigm:

- Artificial Neural Networks;
- Fuzzy Inference Systems; or
- Coactive Neuro-Fuzzy Inference Systems;

can be effectively used to approximate inverse functions at the rate of change level, in a bounded and stable manner. It is also demonstrated that the proposed Paradigm permits to develop simple but efficient Learning Schemes (updating/tuning of antecedent/consequent parameters) for a general class of Fuzzy Inference Systems (in fact becoming Adaptive); and also for Coactive Neuro-Fuzzy Inference Systems.

In this Chapter also several performance criteria for the proper Design and Operation of Intelligent and *Sapient (Wise) Systems* are presented. These criteria are based on establishing proper bounds on some characterizing matrices having a prominent role on the performance of Intelligent and *Sapient (Wise)* Systems. In particular, here it is shown that from these characterizing matrices it is possible to establish:

(a) an upper bound on a homogenized condition number;

(b) a generalization of an isotropy condition;

(c) a rate of change of a generalized isotropy condition; and,

(d) a proper bound on the rate of change of the Jacobian matrix.

As discussed here, these criteria can be used for design analysis and optimization as well for determining the best regions for systems operation.

Although the proposed Paradigm has been conceived mainly for Control or Decision problems; here, also some important aspects/issues on its application to decision making/resolution, and systems design and operation problems are amply discussed.

References

Albus J. S. and Meystel A. M. (2002) Engineering of Mind, and Introduction to the Science of Intelligent Systems, John Wiley & Sons, Inc.

Bezdek J. C. (1994) What is Computational Intelligence?, Computational Intelligence, Imitating Life. Eds. J. M. Zurada, R. J. Marks II, C. J. Robinson, IEEE Press.

Franklin S. and Graesser A. (1996). Is it an Agent, or just a Program?: A Taxonomy for Autonomous Agents. Proc. of the 3rd Intl. Workshop on Agent Theories, Architectures, and Languages, Springer-Verlag.

Fu K. S. (1971) Learning control systems and intelligent control systems: An intersection of artificial intelligence and automatic control. IEEE Trans. on Automatic Control, Vol. AC-16, No. 1.

Jang J.-S. R., Sun C.-T., and Mizutani E. (1997). Neuro-Fuzzy and Soft Computing: A Computational Approach to Learning and Machine Intelligence. Prentice Hall, Inc.

Jang J.-S. R. (1993) ANFIS: Adaptive-Network-based Fuzzy Inference Systems. IEEE Trans. on Systems, Man, and Cybernetics, 23 (3).

Mayorga R. V. and Arriaga M. (2007) Non-Linear Global Optimization Via Parametrization and Inverse Function Approximation: An ANN Approach. International Journal of Neural Systems, Vol. 17, 5.

Mayorga R. V. (2006) Sapient (Wise) Systems: Implementations, Design, and Operation. Proc. 2006 IEEE World Congress on Computational Intelligence, IEEE International Joint Conference on Neural Networks, Vancouver, BC, Canada, July 16–21.

Mayorga R. V. and Sanongboon P. (2005a) An Artificial Network Approach for Inverse Kinematics Computation and Singularities Prevention of Redundant Manipulators. Journal of Intelligent and Robotics Systems, Vol. 44, 2005, pp. 1–23.

Mayorga R. V. (2005b) Towards Computational Sapience (Wisdom): Sapient (Wise) Systems, Their Design & Operation. Monograph - Workshop on Sapient Systems, MICAI-2005, Monterrey, Mexico, November 14–18.

Mayorga R. V. (2005c). Performance Criteria for the Design of Sapient (Wise) Systems. Proc. International Conference of Knowledge Intensive Multi-Agent Systems, KIMAS-2005, Cambridge MA, USA, April 18–21.

Mayorga R. V. and Carrera J. (2004). "The Computation of Inverse Time Variant Functions Via Pseudoinverse Bounding: An RBFN Approach". Journal of Artificial Intelligence Tools, Vol. 13, No. 3.

Mayorga R. V. (2003) Towards Computational Sapience (Wisdom): A Paradigm for Sapient (Wise) Systems. Proc. International Conference of Knowledge Intensive Multi-Agent Systems, KIMAS-2003, Cambridge MA, USA, September 30-October 4.

Mayorga R. V. (2002) A Paradigm For Continuous Function Optimization: An Intelligent/Wise Systems Implementation. Proc. International Symposium on Robotics and Automation, ISRA'2002, Toluca, Mexico, Sept. 1–4.

Mayorga R. V. (2000a) Towards Computational Wisdom and MetaBotics: A Paradigm for Intelligent/Wise Systems, and MetaBots. Proc. International Symposium on Robotics and Automation ISRA'2000, Monterrey, Mexico, Nov. 10–12.

Mayorga R. V. (2000b) Towards Computational Wisdom and MetaBotics: Intelligent/Wise Decision/Control, Systems, and MetaBots. Tutorial Notes Monograph, International Symposium on Robotics and Automation ISRA'2000, Monterrey, Mexico, Nov. 10–12.

Mayorga R. V. (2000c) A MetaBotics Paradigm for Wise Design and Operation of a Human-Computer Interface. Proc. International Symposium on Robotics and Automation ISRA'2000, Monterrey, Mexico, Nov. 10–12.

Mayorga R. V. (2000d) A MetaBotics Paradigm for Intelligent/Wise Design and Local Motion Planning of Robot Manipulators. Proc. International Symposium on Robotics and Automation ISRA'2000, Monterrey, Mexico, Nov. 10–12.

Mayorga R. V. (1999) Towards Computational Wisdom: Intelligent/Wise Systems, Paradigms, and MetaBots. Tutorial Notes Monograph, ANIROB, Congreso Nacional de Robotica, CONAR'99, Cd. Juarez, Mexico, Dec. 13–15.

Mayorga R. V. (1998a) A Paradigm for Intelligent Systems Design/Operation. Proc.International Symposium on Robotics and Automation ISRA'98, Saltillo, Mexico, Dec. 12–14.

Mayorga R. V. (1998b) A Paradigm for Intelligent Decision and Control: Neural Nets, Fuzzy and Neuro-Fuzzy Implementations. Proc. IASTED Int. Conf. on Artificial Intelligence and Soft Computing, Cancún, México, May 27–30, 1998.

Mayorga R. V., (1998c) A Paradigm for Intelligent Design and Interaction of a Human-Computer Interface. Proc. IASTED Int. Conf. on Applied Informatics, Garmich-Partenkirchen, Germany, February 23–25.

Mayorga R. V. (1997) A Paradigm for Intelligent Decision and Control: An Application for the Intelligent Design of a Human-Computer Interface. Dept. of Systems Design Eng., U. of Waterloo, Tech./Res. Report, UFW-310797, July 31.

Meystel A. M. and Albus J. S. (2002) Intelligent Systems: Architecture, Design, and Control, J. Wiley & Sons.

Mizutani E. and Jang J.-S. R. (1995) Coactive Neural Fuzzy Modelling, Proc. Int. Conf. on Neural Networks, November.

Musto J. C. and Saridis G. N. (1997) Entropy-based reliability analysis for intelligent machines, IEEE Trans. on Systems, Man, and Cybernetics, Part B: Cybernetics, Vol. 27, No. 2, April.

Perlovsky L. I. (2001) Neural Networks and Intellect, Oxford University Press.

Saridis G. N. (1990) Theory of Intelligent Machines, Proc. IEEE Int. Workshop in Intelligent Motion Control, Istanbul, Turkey, August 20–22.

Saridis G. N. and Valavanis K. P. (1988a) Analytical Design of Intelligent Machines, Automatica, Vol. 24, No. 2.

Saridis G. N. (1988b) On the theory of intelligent machines: A survey, Proc. 27th. Conf. on Decision and Control, Austin, TX.

Saridis G. N. (1983) Intelligent Robot Control, IEEE Trans. on AC-29, No. 4.

Saridis G. N. (1979) Toward the realization of Intelligent Controls, IEEE Proceedings, Vol. 67, No. 8, 1979.

Saridis G. N. (1977) Self-organizing controls of stochastic systems, Marcel Dekker, New York, New York.

Bi-Sapient Structures for Intelligent Control

Ron Cottam, Willy Ranson, and Roger Vounckx

Abstract The control of autonomous systems requires provision of at least a synthetic form of intelligence or sapience. While descriptions of these are common, there is no current model which relates their definitions to the physical structure of an information-processing system. Sapience is a direct result of hierarchical structure. In this chapter we describe the self-consistent general model of a birational hierarchy, and associate data, information, understanding, sapience and wisdom with aspects of its constitution. In a birational hierarchy there are two sapiences, one associated with each hyperscalar correlation, and their interactions support the most general information-processing relationship – wisdom. One and the same general model applies both to material structure and information-processing structure: the brain is the unique example of material-structural and information-processing-structural correspondence. We attribute the stabilization of dynamic self-observation to anticipative stasis neglect, and propose that neuron mirroring provides a useful metaphor for all of the brain's information-processing, including the bi-sapient interactions which generate auto-empathy. We conclude that hyperscalar bi-sapience is responsible for Metzinger's 'illusory self', for Theory of Self, presence transfer, and Theory of Mind, and indicate how multiscalar access from within hyperscale provides a massive advantage in promoting survival.

1 Introduction

Sapience is a direct result of hierarchical structure.

Formal information-processing systems operate mono-rationally and presume temporal completion: living systems do not. Living systems are functionally hierarchical; formal information-processing systems are not, although they may often appear to be so (Cottam, Ranson, and Vounckx 2003a). Living systems can achieve sapience: others cannot. Formal processors consist of predictable elements at every

R. Cottam
The Evolutionary Processing Group, Department of Electronics & Informatics,
Vrije Universiteit Brussel, Brussels, Belgium
e-mail: evol@etro.vub.ac.be

R.V. Mayorga, L.I. Perlovsky (eds.), *Toward Artificial Sapience,*
© Springer 2008

level of their organization: living organisms most ably demonstrate that the most resilient stable systems can be constructed from nominally unstable elements. Formal information-processing systems may be able to provide enough processing power for an aware entity to survive in a restrictedly hostile unaware environment, but it will certainly not be sufficient to guarantee survival in the multiply aware environment of a biological ecosystem. Life is, and must be, the most relevant paradigm for sapience.

The biggest blockage in synthesizing high-level sapient processors is the formally mono-rational sequential nature of current hardware (Cottam, Ranson and Vounckx 1999a). Large processing systems run up against the capacitive and relativistic capping of communication speed. It is the spatial information-processing *density* which must be maximized, and not simply the *quantity* of processing (Cottam, Ranson, and Vounckx 1998). This is why the distinction between formal complication and natural complexity is so important. Rationally constructed and operating computational machines can exhibit extremely complicated behavior, but their information-processing density is irrevocably coupled to the physical size of their individual processing elements. Complex living systems are not automatically subject to the same limitation, and they can explore their phase spaces and generate new information in a manner which is more related to their characteristic Lyapounov exponents than to their characteristic elemental size (Cottam, Ranson and Vounckx 2004).

(Conventional) Boolean logic gates throw away the physical component of information and reformulate it from their power supply: this approach corresponds conceptually to the reductive destruction of information, whose re-use requires restitution from pre-established non-local memory: this does nothing to aid the rapid processing of large volumes of data. The extension of mono-rational sequential processing into its parallel counterpart does not change this – formal parallel processing systems are sequential in everything other than name. Formal parallel processing implements sequentially:

1. separation of a process into independent threads,
2. separate processing of those threads, and
3. formal reassembly of the thread outcomes.

True parallelism exploits continuous simultaneous interaction and separation of its different threads, in the manner of a quantum interaction rather than that of a linear superposition. In the world of computers, hardware/ software co-designed concur-rent processors are closing in on this ideal, but they fall far short because of their restriction to Boolean logic.

Formal information-processing systems are by their very nature and construction single-leveled: change in the bit output of a single (low-level) gate can of necessity influence directly a (high-level) decision output. Consequently, 'everyone has to wait until the smallest guy has done his job!' Thus – the imposition of maximal clock speeds for processors, which define how fast you can run them while still being absolutely certain that there is no discrepancy across organizational levels. Biological systems, however, have evolved to satisfy a major requirement of survival: it must not be necessary to wait for each and every bodily cell to react before jumping out of the way of a speeding train! (a classic case of this is the cortex-bypassing fear-learning pathway through the amygdala in our own brains – LeDoux 1992). This is the central meaning of hierarchy: massively complex systems are provided with multiply-scaled adaptable reactions and choice in the face of diverse stimuli, and in doing so they provide a substrate for multiply-leveled information-processing and integration – the basis for sapience.

2 Hierarchy and Birationality

Evolution demands that expanding systems split into functional sub-units in a sensibly integrated manner, if they are to persist. The materialization of a higher-level single organization from a lower-level multiply populated one is most popularly characterized as the *emergence of novelty* at the higher level. The vast majority of their relationships, however, depend on the cross-level transport of order, and not on novelty (Cottam et al. 2003a). Systems which are stable are precisely that – stable. The transport of order between system levels freezes a multilevel structure into a quasi-permanent form. Stability is not an 'added value' which can be obtained from multilevel structuring; it is its very nature.

An organism's information-processing structure is often described as a perception-action or sensori-motor loop, but natural hierarchical information-processing structures do not necessarily rely on loop-like architectures, although they may indeed use these at a motor control level. A more useful paradigm is that of an irreversible process, which may indeed be modeled to some (small) extent as a loop, but only by dropping out fundamental intimacy-of-interaction between the different operational directions. Simplistically, rather than 'sense → perceive → act', which is formulated from individually formally-modelable 'sense', 'perceive' and 'act' modules, somehow tied together, it makes far more sense to concentrate on the two tying-together '→' processes, whose interaction is principal. The question is not primarily one of 'constructing knowledge out of information', but one of 'propagating information through knowledge' (Langloh, Cottam, Vounckx and Cornelis 1993) as a way of modifying it.

The two most common hierarchical forms which are used in modeling natural and social systems are those of the 'scalar' hierarchy and the 'specification' hierarchy (Salthe 1993). A scalar hierarchy consists of recognizable levels of different sizes of elements, for example, atoms, through molecules, bio-molecules, cells, organs and organisms to societies. A specification hierarchy, on the other hand, consists of different overlaid levels of description of the same entity, for example we can simultaneously describe our environment at the physico-chemical level, at the biological level, and at the social level. Neither of these two hierarchical descriptions captures sufficiently the character of a natural system, however, and we believe that a better solution is to use a 'model' hierarchy (Langloh et al. 1993), where different hierarchical levels correspond to different scalar perceptions of the same entity. For example, we could imagine describing 'a tree as atoms', 'a tree as molecules', 'a tree as cells', 'a tree as branches' and 'a tree as itself'. This provides an extremely powerful representation for naturally self-coherent integrated systems, where the various levels must not only be independently self-sufficient, but each of them must be correlated with all the other levels: a 'tree as branches' must be consistent with the same 'tree as atoms'.

Figure 1 illustrates the most general form of a model hierarchy (Cottam, Ranson and Vounckx 2000). The various perceptional levels are those indicated as 'Newtonian potential wells', and they are coupled by regions of extreme complexity. The simplest representation (for example 'a tree as itself') is at the right hand side of the assembly; the most complicated representation is towards the left hand side (for example, 'a tree as atoms').

The appearance of nonlocality at the extreme left hand side of the figure corresponds to the nonlocal nature of the most complicated formal model of 'a tree', namely the (or a) quantum mechanical one. The reader should note, however, that the extension of conventional quantum mechanics to large systems leads to a breakdown in the logical completeness of the description (Antoniou 1995): this corresponds to the transit of at least one of the complex transition regions illustrated in Fig. 1).

Hierarchical systems, then, are assemblies of different levels of organization which are more-or-less tied together in ways which simultaneously promote level *isolation* and level *integration*: their overall correlation is one of context and temporally dependent negotiated compromise, and not one of formal relationships. However, this cross-scale correlation itself makes up the defining unity of the system: it is as much a system property as are the operational parameters of the smallest constructional element.

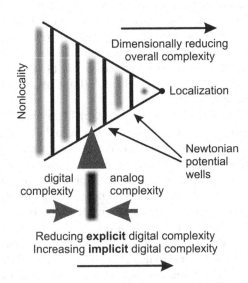

Fig. 1 A general model-hierarchical representation between nonlocality and localization

True hierarchical systems of the kind illustrated in Fig. 1 can be decomposed into two quasi-independent mono-rational hierarchies (Cottam et al. 2003a), one consisting of the more usually noticed scaled levels, the other consisting of the complex inter-level negotiation/transition regions (see Fig. 2). In a world where Newtonian physics provides a good approximation across a wide range of scales, the former consists of a set of Newtonian potential wells (Cottam et al. 1999a), which is reductive in terms of local level description towards the highest level. The latter then consists of the set of inter-Newtonian-level quantum-entanglement-like regions (Cottam, Ranson and Vounckx 2003b), each of which provides a rational ecosystem for its adjacent Newtonian level (Cottam, Ranson and Vounckx 1999b), and this set is reductive towards nonlocality (Cottam, Ranson, and Vounckx 1997). The complementarity of the two hierarchies is functionally symmetrical: the quantum-like system provides a rational ecosystem for the Newtonian one; the Newtonian system provides a rational ecosystem for the quantum-like one (see Fig. 3). Newtonian and quantum mechanical descriptions are *not* parallel scale-related physical models, they are *complementary* representations of our surroundings (Cottam et al. 2003b).

The cross-scale correlation of levels in the (more normal) Newtonian system is mirrored by a cross-scale correlation of levels in the complex quantum-like one (Cottam et al. 2003a), whose nature is again a fundamental system property. These two hyperscalar correlations each provide ultra-high level entity-ecosystemic exchanges, much as we ourselves use each of *logic* and *emotion* to resolve the others' decision-making dead-ends (Cottam et al. 2003a). As each of the hyperscalar systems builds from the bottom up it generates levels which are progressively more and more abstract and general. (see Fig. 4). The first, more concrete hyperscalar levels are extremely complex, as their characteristics relate to all the different scales of the system they represent, and they are closely coupled to their complementary partners.

As higher levels develop, the complementary hyperscales progressively separate to achieve two completely different characters. One of the two hyperscalar systems corresponds to 'information which is accessible at specific scales of the global system' (i.e. 'normal' system models); the other corresponds to 'information which is inaccessible at specific scales, but which complements that which is accessible' (Cottam et al. 2003b) (i.e. 'hidden variables' which promote transit between

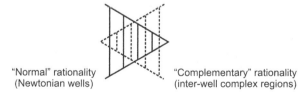

"Normal" rationality   "Complementary" rationality
(Newtonian wells)   (inter-well complex regions)

Fig. 2 Decomposition of the generalized model-hierarchical representation into two complementarily-rational representational assemblies. The 'normal' assembly is reductive towards localization; the 'complementary' system is reductive towards nonlocality

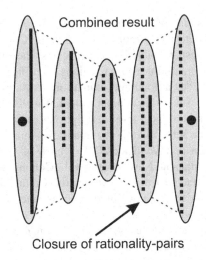

Fig. 3 Pairing of the scaled Newtonian-wells with their co-scaled complex precursor layers

different modeling levels). The hyperscalar complementarity may be crudely compared to the Freudian proposition of the 'conscious' and 'unconscious' parts of the human psyche. Segregation of them fuels the generation of fluctuating asymmetries in the inter-scalar negotiations, much as our desires fuel our own beliefs and actions through the generation of conscious-unconscious asymmetries.

Surprisingly, inorganic systems can develop very restricted materializations of hierarchical character: even single crystals of the electronics-important zinc blende structure materials (diamond, Ge, Si, GaAs, InSb, HgTe, ...) show cross-scale in-formation transport which does not precisely match the spatial symmetry of the lattice structure (Cottam et al. 2003a). However, the informational differences

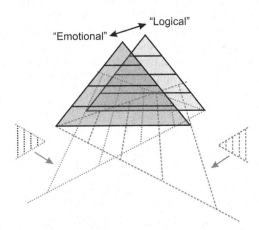

Fig. 4 Illustration of the progressive decoupling of the complementary hyperscale hierarchies with abstraction

between small and large scales of crystals remain minimal, and although higher organizational levels may be marginally different from lower ones there is a high degree of self-similarity across scales. Living systems, on the other hand, expand to far greater system complication, segregate into more numerous organizational levels, and the closure of a specific level with respect to its neighbors is characteristically more complete. A consequence is that living systems are capable of generating extraordinary richness in their highest levels of their organization. It is also notable that, while the higher levels of an inorganic system remain extremely 'physical' in Nature, those of a living system are far less tangible. Our own society of individuals is a case in point.

3 Data and Information – Understanding and Knowledge

Information may be described as "a difference which makes a difference" (Bateson 1972); that is to say it has some meaning within some context. Data, on the other hand, may be described as lacking a context within which to make a difference. We associate data with the individual levels of a hierarchy – whether Newtonian or quantal levels, whether entity or ecosystemic levels – and information with the coupling between a pair of levels (as illustrated in Fig. 3), where data (as the description of an 'entity') exchanges contextual meaning with its ecosystemic partner.

Knowledge is a difficult beast to get hold of. It, too, is certainly context-dependent, and more so than information. It is easier to begin by representing understanding, as an approach to knowledge, rather than tackling it head on. The commonly used sense of understanding something suggests that we are aware not only of how it is 'made up' from its constituents, whether physical or abstract, but also how it fits into a wider picture: it implies some degree of awareness of both sub-scale and super-scale. In its extreme form it corresponds to a state of hyperscalar awareness, or a process of arriving at that state (Cottam, Ranson, Vounckx 2007b). We deduce that understanding in a model-hierarchy may be simplistically associated at the very least with a combination of the relevantly-scaled representation with its nearest lower-scale and nearest higher-scale neighbors. Fig. 5 illustrates this. More realistically, we would expect understanding to involve at least the correlation of the three associated ecosystemic pairs, and not of just the Newtonian wells. Knowledge, then, is different from information in the extended nature of its contextual validity or relevance. As such, as many authors maintain, knowledge is a higher-level representation than information, but it cannot be simply 'extracted' from information *per se*, as its contextuality is birational.

Our main interest here is not particularly the nature of data, information and knowledge, but more specifically the manner in which they may be obtained. In a multiscalar system we must first of all focus on the way a collection of information at one scalar level can give rise to its compilation at another. This phenomenon, mysteriously described as 'emergence', and often wrongly referred to as 'self-organization', identifies *intelligence* (Cottam, Ranson and Vounckx 2003c).

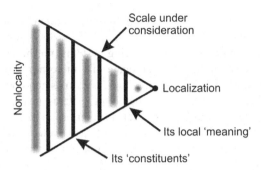

Fig. 5 Illustration of the simplistic representation of "understanding" in a model-hierarchy

Intelligence is the capacity for successful[1] scale change. If that were all there is, we would now be finished, but the reader should note that we did not here refer to a specific *kind* of multiscalar system. If we now restrict ourselves to natural hierarchical systems, and even more specifically to *living* systems, then further capacities appear. The capacity to cross-correlate *all* the scales of a natural multiscalar system characterizes *sapience* (Cottam et al. 2003c). These simplistic definitions of *intelligence* and *sapience*, therefore, correspond to the lowest and highest computational capabilities which may be required within a single natural multiscalar system, and they constitute the boundaries of a wide continuous range of processing styles.

The last line of a paragraph should never start a new page. Neither should a new paragraph start at the bottom of a page. Optimally, there should be at least three lines before a page break occurs or three lines of text on a new page before a new section appears. Minimally, there should be two lines. Improving the look of a page can often be achieved easily by rewording a sentence or two.

But we have left aside the birational nature we earlier attributed to natural systems: there will not be just one hierarchy, but *two* intercommunicating ones! Each of them will exhibit its own version of 'intelligence', and each its own version of 'sapience'. Correlation across a small number of scalar levels of the Newtonian hierarchy corresponds to 'logical' intelligence; its complement across a small number of complex scalar levels may best be described as 'emotional' intelligence (Matthews, Zeidner and Roberts 2004). There will similarly be two different forms of sapience, one 'logical', one 'emotional' in character. But we should not forget that the two nominally separate hierarchies are intimately entwined with each other: these dualities of intelligence and sapience are most certainly not mutually isolated, and they are all coupled into the fundamental character of their host's hyperscale as a final, high-level, now for the first time *singular* capacity, which we refer to as *wisdom*.

---

[1] The authors are well aware that a definition of intelligence in terms of the contextually-dependent 'successful' generates as many question-marks as it removes, but for the present we will leave this sentence as it stands.

4 Sapience and Life

So, where does all this leave us? Can we directly couple conclusions drawn from an abstract general model to the manner in which we think and act? Although we maintained earlier that life must be the most relevant paradigm for sapience, until now the picture we have drawn makes little reference to life itself. If we continue to accept that *living* and *non-living* entities are fundamentally different, this must naturally result in some degree of confusion!

We consider it unreasonable to presuppose that *alive* and *not alive* are categorically different without knowing what it is that makes life special. Consequently, in the absence of a scientific distinction, we will begin by supposing that the generally observable difference between *alive* and *not alive* results only from as-yet unevaluated features of an entity's constitution or its context. Robert Rosen (1991) has correspondingly suggested that life depends on the *relationships* between an entity's constituent parts, rather than on the parts themselves. This is an attractive distinction, as it also correlates well with differences we observe between *living* entities and *dead* ones. We have indicated elsewhere that hierarchy is a basic prerequisite for life (Cottam, Ranson and Vounckx 2005), and that a living entity *is* its hyperscalar representation (Cottam, Ranson and Vounckx 2006a). Close examination of Rosen's (1991) model of an organism reveals that it is the monoscalar contraction of a naturally hyperscalar entity (Cottam, Ranson, and Vounckx 2006b; Cottam, Ranson and Vounckx 2007a). Terrence Deacon (1997) has suggested that being alive is what it feels like to be evolution happening. In the light of Charles Peirce's (1998) self-consistent *semiotic* description of Nature, we believe that *life* is the dynamic interrelational maintenance of an evolving hyperscalar *semiosic* architecture (Cottam et al. 2000).

Intelligence may be said to be "the ability of a system to adapt its behavior to meet its goals in a range of environments" (Fogel 2002). *Sapience* goes much further than this, in its wide ranging considerations and cross-scale harmonizing and resolution of conflicting goals, causes and effects. We propose that sapience is a fundamental system property, but one which only manifests itself within systems whose hierarchical structure is sufficiently complex for hyperscalar interactions to be able to dominate the crude automatisms of inter-scalar slaving (Haken 1984), namely within *living* systems. Ultimately, we would associate *wisdom* with integrative access to the *complete* birational assembly illustrated in Fig. 5, but it is necessarily instantaneously inaccessible in its entirety with precision from *any* scale - a result of the relativistic limitation of communication speed (Langloh et al. 1993). The hyperscalar levels indicated in Fig. 4 are indeed 'integrations' of the entire scalar assembly, but they are also imprecise in the same way that reproductive definition of a small region of a complete hologram is limited.

Sapience is more dependent on the long-term integration of experience and its resulting multiscalar bias than on the immediacy of local algorithmic manipulation. There is a trade-off between descriptive precision and ease-of-description towards the higher *hyperscalar* levels (at the top of Fig. 4), as there is towards the higher *scalar* levels (at the right hand side of Fig. 1, for example). In the way that

Aristotelian final cause (Aristoteles 1857) in a hierarchy may be said to appear in a multiplicity of differently scaled and more or less self-consistent or definable forms, so it is for sapience. Integration of a wide range of different information or knowledge may well provide a generally applicable representation, but it will be one which is vague in its direct applicability. Integration across a narrow range of information or knowledge, on the other hand, may provide a relatively precise generalization, but it may catastrophically collapse following minor changes in application context.

There is some evidence that a major function of sleep is this integration of otherwise disparate informational elements into a 'bigger picture' (Ellenbogen, Hu, Payne, Titone and Walker 2007). Experimentation shows that electrical signals generated during the periods of deepest sleep evidence a degree of phase coherence across the complete neural assembly. Cottam et al. (1997) have pointed out that electrical phase coherence between different entities is evidence of a high degree of communication, and they suggest that the extended integration of information required for establishment of correlatory sapience takes place during the periods of deepest sleep. The conventional engineering approach to digital software module relocation or re-linking is to first take the machine off-line, perform the necessary maintenance, and then carry out simulations of normal operation in a 'close-to-real-conditions' but still-off-line environment. This makes it possible to safely evaluate the effects of reprogramming, to see if it successfully resolves known problems without creating new and possibly worse ones. Are dreams equivalent to computational re-correlation testing by simulation? It is difficult to be certain, but dreams *do* appear during the periods of lightest sleep as evidenced by experimentation into rapid eye-movement (REM) sleep, when the brain is close to "normal" localizing consciousness and the muscles are in a paralytic 'off-line' state. And between repeated dream periods the brain *does* apparently descend to a more phase-coherent and therefore more nonlocal state.

Sapience is a direct result of hierarchical structure, and it manifests itself as an aspect of life: true wisdom includes and can access all possible levels and degrees of integration, but only to the extent that this is feasible in a self-correlating model hierarchy.

5 Humble Unification and Neural Ecosystemics

The last few decades have witnessed great progress towards the establishment of a physical *unified field theory* through experimentation at smaller and smaller spatial scales and at higher and higher energies. The most well-known version of such a model is usually referred to as the Grand Unified Theory – or GUT. Unfortunately, as the reader will be aware from the pages of this chapter, any attempt at systemic unification must take account of the effects of scale, and most particularly the difficulties inherent in inter-correlating differently scaled models of the same system. GUT attempts to reductively simplify the structure of Nature to its smallest constituent elements and representative fields, and then integrate these into a single model, but the manner in which such a subdivided Nature may be reassembled into the complex variety of our surroundings is absent from its considerations.

The descriptions presented in this chapter are all based on what could be referred to as *Humble* Unified Theory (Cottam, Langloh, Ranson and Cottam 1995) – or HUT – where account is indeed taken of the problems associated with locally-rational inter-scalar transit. The resulting birational HUT representation is applicable 'from the bottom up' to the description of systemic-level 'emergence', and consequently it provides a valid modeling basis for multiscalar ecosystemic information-processing. It is worth noting that in principle HUT could be used to describe the formalized construction of GUT, but that its introduction would be worthless, as GUT is nominally formally complete, and scalar hierarchy collapses into a single level if inter-scalar transit becomes formalized (Cottam et al. 2003a).

The image we have now constructed effectively extends biological modeling in terms of 'organism' and 'ecosystem' to *all* of Nature – to elementary particles, to Newtonian physics, to Quantum Mechanics[2], to *every* differentiated entity – whose elementary isolations are *always* related to their surroundings. Biology and life now become sub-divisions of a more general description of Nature than either New-tonian physics or Quantum Mechanics on their own can offer. In this chapter we have concentrated on using HUT to describe information-processing *per se*, but the model is equally at home in representing the *material* nature of our environment. Our next task is to see how such a general model can represent an entity where complex in-formation-processing overlays complex material structure and the two are intimately coupled: the brain.

We pointed out in Section 2 that the interaction between the two hyperscalar sapiences of a birational information-processing system resembles the way we alter-nate between *explicate logic* and *implicate emotion* in extricating ourselves from a mental cul-de-sac. We do not maintain that these two sapiences *are* logic and emotion – to suggest that would be to ignore the scavenging meanderings and cannibalizations of evolutionary development (Cottam et al. 2000) – we propose that the general birational model provides a guiding template for the evolution of information-processing, much as the signpost at a road junction indicates which is probably the most useful way to go, rather than the precise compass direction of our desired destination. Similarly, we would expect to find *material* structures in the brain which relate, if distantly, to the duality of ecosystemic rationality.

Whilst being far from categorical, and far from conclusive, it is more than inter-esting to note that the two neural hemispheres apparently do indeed tend, in gen-eral, towards a bilateral ecosystemic distribution of information-processing which is reminiscent of the two sapiences. While there are exceptions, the left hemisphere in general processes information in a linear, sequential, logical, symbolic manner: it is specialized in "verbal skills, writing, complex mathematical calculations and abstract thought" (Rock 2004, p. 124) The right hemisphere in general processes

---

[2] In passing, we should point out that the best current model for inter-scalar transit appears to be a generic form of Quantum-Mechanical error correction (Cottam et al. 2003b).

information more holistically, randomly, intuitively, concretely and nonverbally: it specializes in "geometric-form and spatial-relationship processing, perceiving and enjoying music in all its complexity, recognizing human faces, and detecting emotions" (Rock 2004, p. 124). The two hemispheres are normally connected together by the *corpus callosum* – the cerebral commisure which is the largest nerve tract in the brain, containing more than 200,000,000 axons (Pearce 2007).

Studies in the 1940s following sectioning of the *corpus callosum* in human patients (Akelaitis 1941) – specifically as a treatment for intractable epilepsy (Akelaitis, Risteen, Herren and van Wagenen 1942) – amazingly showed *no* definite behavioral deficits. However, experiments later carried out by Sperry, Gazzaniga and Bogen (1969) provided even more amazing results: human 'split-brain' subjects apparently provided direct verbal confirmation that the left and right hemispheres provide *separate* domains of *consciousness*. Many of the experiments

1. presented the subject with information related to the right hemisphere, and
2. only elucidated related (or unrelated!) comment *a posteriori* from the subject.

Sperry et al. (1969) described their results as confirmation of separate consciousnesses associated with the two neural hemispheres, but concrete evidence appears to be lacking as to whether the two were experienced sequentially or simultaneously by the subjects. We are left to question whether states experienced by the subjects correspond to 'normal' high-level *consciousness*, or whether they are somewhat lower-level less abstract *awarenesses* which are more intimately coupled to the processing biases of the individual hemispheres. The latter conclusion would support a hypothesis that birational processing is indeed relevant in the brain. If, as we have suggested, information-processing in the two hemispheres is related to the two complementary sapiences of a birational system (Fig. 6(a)), then sectioning the *corpus callosum* would be expected to destroy the inter-sapient correlations which lead to the *singularity* of *wisdom* (Fig. 6(b)). Notably, opinion is undivided as to the singularity of 'normal' consciousness: Sperry et al.'s (1969) experiments appear to have confirmed the existence of the two different sapiences, corresponding to two independent *awarenesses*, which auto-correlate in the 'normal' cross-coupled brain to give a *singular* experience – that of consciousness (Fig. 6(c)).

Evolution is closely associated with the survival of a species through that of its individuals. What advantage do *Intelligence*, *Sapience* and *Wisdom* (*IS&W*) confer on an individual? Are *IS&W* of immediate use in responding rapidly to environmental threats? Well, not obviously. Do we really want to wait blindly until something untoward occurs, and then start trying to find a solution? If so, what is the evolutionary point of memory? Organisms survive by building up experience and assembling it into internal models of their necessary environmental relationships. This provides two main advantages. Firstly, it effectively 'pushes' a large part of information-processing 'into the past', by making 'ready-to-wear' threat-responses available 'off the shelf' for *IS&W* to use (Cottam, Ranson and Vounckx 2003d). Secondly, it supplies extensive ready-correlated information which can be used both in *anticipating* the results of its own actions and those of its opponents and in generating complicated plans of action. These prospective advantages to an organism

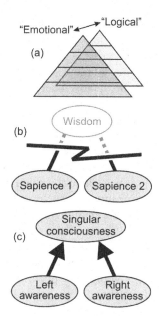

Fig. 6 (a) The two interacting sapiences in a birational system, (b) destruction of the singularity of wisdom when the *corpus callosum* is sectioned, and (c) integration of the two hemispheric awarenesses to the singularity of consciousness

depend not only on the availability of previously constructed internal models; they require *multiply-scaled* internal threat-response models to be mutually-correlated in a 'data-base' – or, rather, a '*model-base*' – whose internal structure *matches* that of the organism's environment (Cottam, Ranson and Vounckx 2001). This survival-related multiscalar structuring of a general ecosystemic model of Nature lies at the heart of HUT and of its optically-computational precursor AQuARIUM (Langloh et al. 1993).

Robert Rosen (1985) has described organisms as *anticipatory* systems. While we expect to find that the brain is anticipatory (Pribram 1999), we might presuppose that anticipation is restricted to intelligent organisms. There is, however, extensive current interest in anticipation as a fundamental physical property, for example as a feature of electromagnetism (Dubois 1999). In concert with Robert Rosen, we associate anticipative capability *at least* with life, and believe that anticipation is central in developing and maintaining environmental awareness.

6 Humble Unification and Neural Ecosystemics Asymptotic Anticipation, Awareness and Stasis Neglect

You are driving through town. Just before you arrive at a set of traffic lights the light turns to red. You stop and wait, looking ahead but still seeing the red light out of the corner of your eye. Mysteriously, the light slowly fades and disappears, until you move your head and there it is back again: you have experienced the necessity of change in maintaining visual attention. Now you are in a train, looking out of the window at the electric pylons going past, again, again, again... until you drift into a daydream unconnected with your journey. As Zeno effectively pointed out, any model of dynamics is static: repetitive movement is little different from stasis in its lack of impact on our attention.

It is instructive to model observation in terms of anticipation. If everything in a scene around us is static, or every change in the scene can be successfully predicted from a sequence of previous observations, then anticipation reduces to historically-based repetition, and *IS&W* are irrelevant. The possibly multiscalar structure of our observations effectively collapses to a single algorithmic or quasi-algorithmic recursive chronicle devoid of mystery or surprise. As Rosen (1991) has demonstrated, this situation is the very antithesis of life, entailing no *IS&W* and no incentive whatsoever for their evolution. Figure 7 illustrates the temporal progression of anticipation from initial exposure to a hypothetical static or repetitive scene.

As observations progress, information-processing reduces asymptotically to the realization of stasis – nothing is going to happen. Initially the 'processor' needs to track the 'stasis' carefully, as there is no previous observational chronicle to inform it, but after a while it will lose interest and replace attention by neglect. This process of 'stasis neglect' has important secondary effects, both for an individual and for a species. The banishment of quasi-stasis from awareness makes it possible for repeated actions to be transferred out of parts of the brain which consciousness 'keeps track of', and for them to become 'automatic' (Cottam, Ranson and Vounckx 2003e). Most people have at some time or other had the experience of driving back from work while thinking about something else, only to be amazed when arriving home because they cannot remember anything about the trip! Many of our bodily functions continue without our awareness or assistance: breathing, for example – which is easily controllable, however – or the heart's beating – which is less so – or bowel transit – which is not. The transfer of learned actions to the 'automatic' background leaves space in consciousness for events or actions whose immediacy is important.

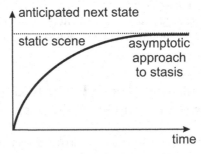

Fig. 7 The asymptotic progression of anticipation of a static or repetitive scene, from the introduction of the scene to establishment of stasis

While stasis can wipe out the attentive local application of intelligence, its effect on 'global' sapient processing can be even more profound. Boredom at one scale is incomparable with boredom at *every* scale! While anticipation is vital to survival, it is the *necessity* for anticipation which feeds the evolution of *IS&W*. Terrence Deacon (1997) has suggested that being alive is what it feels like to be evolution happening: being alive *is* anticipative *IS&W* evolving. Descartes concluded "I think therefore I am": maybe this could be updated to "I anticipate, therefore I am."[3]

7 Mirror Neurons, Autism and Empathy

It is no exaggeration to say that the current 'big thing' in neuroscience is the investigation of the properties and 'meanings' of *mirror neurons*. These were first described by Fadiga, Fogassi, Pavesi, and Rizzolati (1995) following the observation that a particular subset of macaque monkey motor-skill neurons fire, not only when a specific action is performed, but also when watching another monkey perform-ing the same action, and even on hearing the sound of the action's performance (Kohler, Keysers, Umiltà, Fogassi, Gallese and Rizzolati, 2002). Oberman, Pineda and Ramachandran (2007) have suggested that mirror neurons are vitally important to the development of social skills, by providing a means of learning from example, and their possible importance to *IS&W* cannot be exaggerated. Recent work (see Williams, Whiten, Suddendorf and Perrett 2001 for a review) has linked the occur-rence of *autism spectrum disorders* to defects in the Mirror Neuron System (*MRS*) which wipe out any ability to empathize with others.

Although the expression 'mirror neurons' provides an attractive pictorial metaphor, it does nothing to clarify what happens in the brain. Individual neurons do not 'mirror' anything, it must be an entire neural sub-system which is involved (usually referred to in the singular, as *the* Mirror Neuron System), and in any case we cannot poke into another person's head and 'see' their emotions. Empathetic 'mirroring' must be indirect, by way of observation of *actions*, and any emotional content is our own, and not another person's.

Figure 8 illustrates how empathetic 'mirroring' could work between first- (**A**) and second- (**B**) person social actors. (**A**) always experiences a particular *emotion* **J** on performing a specific *action* **J**. The mechanism proposed by Fadiga et al. (1995) permits (**A**)'s specially-located neural sub-system **X** to produce the same firing con-figuration corresponding to *emotion* **J** when (**A**) either performs *action* **J** or observes (**B**) performing *action* **J**. The supposition, of course, is that (**B**)'s sub-system **Y** *also* produces the firing configuration corresponding to *emotion* **J** when (**B**) performs *action* **J**, which is not necessarily correct: we have all experienced erroneous attri-bution of emotion based on recognized 'body-language' or gestures! In real terms

---

[3] . . . unless this seems too political in nature! Perhaps we should stick with the *real* mirroring of Tom Brocaw's post-modern version: "I appear on the video screen, therefore I am."

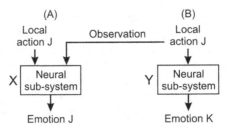

Fig. 8 Mirroring between first- (**A**) and second- (**B**) person social actors

the association must also be far more complex, as we are also *aware* that the emotion we feel is empathetic, and not simply internal.

If audio-visual imitation provides evidence for the existence of a Mirror Neuron System, then what are we to make of the way small children learn to speak? An ~18 month-old child will repeat bi-syllabic words which are spoken to it, even before it has learned to use language *per se*. There is no obvious connection to an action here, but it is difficult to imagine that this necessarily makes use of a different kind of neural structure, especially when we take account of the enhancement in linguistic understandability which is provided through a combination of audition and lip-reading. Molnar-Szakacs and Overy (2006) have proposed that "musical experience involves an intimate coupling between the perception and production of hierarchically organized sequential information, the structure of which has the ability to communicate meaning and emotion" and that "these aspects of musical experience may be mediated by the human mirror neuron system." Is there, then, a separate auditory *MNS*?; a separate visual *MNS*?; a combined audio-visual *MNS*? Or is 'neural mirroring' a mistakenly specific interpretation of a far more general neural technique? It would seem that visual imitative input must be 'injected' early on into the decision-to-action sequence of neural control: Fadiga et al. (1995) observed 'mirror' effects in area F5 of the monkey pre-motor cortex. This is reminiscent of an extensive group of the current mechanisms which are proposed for dreaming (Rock 2004). Random or structured input from different parts of the brain (Antrobus and Bertini 1992) is 'injected' early on into the visual processing chain, where it replaces the 'normal' retinal input to provide a dream's sense of reality, while being divorced from the subject's environment. In common with audio-visual 'mirroring', dream scenarios may be influenced by co-temporal input from other sensors, for example by sounds or smells.

There is a close resemblance between 'neural mirroring', 'dream mechanisms' and the techniques which are typically used to train an artificial neural network, where learning is stimulated by replacing the 'normal' environmental input to the network by pre-structured 'case studies' or 'templates'. Is this what is happening in 'neural mirroring'? All of these examples are similar to the 'slaving' of a hierarchical scale's constituent elements from a higher scalar level (Haken 1984). Is a *MNS* something very special, specific to audio-visually-based imitation, or are experimenters inadvertently interpreting as specific the first observations of a more general neural learning process? In the welter of publications about 'neural mirroring' a number of authors are focusing on the possibility that the usual philosophical position that concepts are necessarily abstract and symbolic may be quite wrong. Gallese and Lakoff (2005) argue that "a disembodied, symbolic account of the concept of *grasping* would have to duplicate elsewhere in the brain the complex neural machinery in three parietal-motor circuits, which is implausible to say the least.", and that "If all this is correct, then abstract reasoning in general exploits the sensory-motor system."

The idea of 'embodied concepts' is arguably foreign to neuropsychology and neurophysiology but not, however, to the bi-sapient rendering of the brain's information-processing structure we have presented in this chapter, where *every* property and phenomena is both derived from and embodied in the neural material. Bi-sapient inter-correlation also provides a satisfying description of empathy, and this leads us to question whether 'neural mirroring' occurs *only* between *different* social actors, or whether it characterizes *every* internal process in an individual brain.

8 Bi-Sapience and Auto-Empathy

We will briefly recapitulate. A birational information-processing system generates two cross-scalar correlations we have called *sapiences*: one is derived from the 'normal' set of Newtonian scalar levels, the other from their inter-scalar complex interfaces. These two sapiences interact to create a singular unification of the entire system, which we have referred to as *wisdom*. If we remember that each sapience provides an informational ecosystem for the other, we can see that the unification process itself resembles the 'neural mirroring' of imitation but with one vital difference: 'mirroring' apparently 'copies' the neural signature of an action, but each of the two sides of a birational correlation 'copies' the *complement* of the other. In Section 5 we pointed out that operation of the materially high-level neural hemispheres can be associated with a possibly birational evolutionary template, but this leaves us with an outstanding question: if the material nature of the brain corresponds to a birational information-processing system, then where are the *low-level*, or small-scale complements of its neural networks?

Karl Pribram (2001) has pointed out that there is a problem with the conventional image of a *real* neural network. Single neurons are commonly pictured with a myriad of dendritic inputs – maybe 50,000 – but only one output axon. In the brain this is far from reality, as the axon typically splits into a very large number of smaller axonites – maybe *also* 50,000 – which connect the primary neuron to secondary ones over comparatively long distances. This multiplicity of axonites from numberless neurons creates an untidy tangled mess between the neurons – the *axonite mesh*. Pribram notes that at their furthest extremities the axonites are very thin, and they do not appear capable of transmitting their localized electrical signals onward to the target axonites. He has proposed that quasi-waves form between the axonites in the mesh which ultimately transmit a positionally-dependent superposition of primary outputs to the secondary inputs, much as a quantum superposition of states collapses to a single final *real* state. The reader will remember that we described in Section 2 how a natural hierarchy may be decomposed into its two constituent parts, and that one part is related to Newtonian physics, the other to Quantum Mechanics. *Here*, finally, is the low-level complement of the brain's neural networks: the Newtonian assembly is represented by signal summation in the dendrites; the Quantum Mechanical assembly is *simulated* by quasi-wave superposition in the axonites.

We believe that the entire information-processing capabilities of the brain are embodied in the complementary structure of its interactions; between local scales and their local ecosystemic counterparts; between local scales and their intelligences; between multiple scales and their unifying sapiences; between the bi-sapiences and the singularity of wisdom. *Every part* of the brain's processing is similar to the pre-suppositions of imitation in 'neuron mirroring' – but the 'mirroring' or *correlation* is between an event, or artifact, and the image of it which can be generated from its rational ecosystem. In principle, it should be possible to observe correlatory activations in the brain which correspond to those of 'neuron mirror' experiments – but there is a problem. 'Neuron mirror' experiments reported in the literature distinguish between 'carrying out an action' and 'observing another carrying it out': the experimenters compare two measurement pairs – {action + neuron activation} and {ob-served action + neuron activation} – and draw their action/observed-action 'mirror neuron' conclusions because neuron activation is the same in both cases. If the 'mirroring' is entirely internal to the brain, then {one thought + neuron activation} and {another thought + neuron activation} are indistinguishable if the neuron activation is the same: there is nothing to measure, and indication of equivalence can only be obtained indirectly from a brain's owner's report.

If effective operation of the Mirror Neuron System is responsible for the development of social skills and empathy, then *autism* is not a condition which develops – it is the natural pre-developmental condition. The attribution of empathetic failure to *MNS* defects implies that 'neuron mirroring' is a major facilitator of intra-social communication: "The mirror neurons … dissolve the barrier between self and others."[4] This indirect recognition of another's emotional state depends, as we proposed in Section 7, on being able to correlate logic of action with its associated emotive potential, and it equips us with the ability to 'understand what others feel'. Empathy supports not only the social coupling between first-person logic and second-person emotion, but also the establishment of even wider social coherence through more indirect routes (e.g. between first-person logic and third-person emotion, through the news media).

If we now return to the purely internal information-processing of an individual brain we find a phenomenon similar to empathy – but here it is a *direct* process – literally an *embodied* process – an *auto-empathy*. Inter-sapient correlation is continuous, from logic, to emotion, to logic, to emotion,… which in addition to stabilizing the birational processing system arguably supports a sense of completeness, of logic

---

[4] An expression attributed to V. S. Ramachandran.

and emotion 'being in tune'. Auto-empathy is invaluable in steering our actions. It appears likely that the early evolution of a simple, extreme form of auto-empathy is at the root of 'fear-learning' (LeDoux 1992) – the amygdalic 'hard-wiring' which permits rapid reactions to threatening eventualities and which predates, and now bypasses, the comparatively slow processing of the cortex.

As we pointed out in Section 4, an entity *is* its hyperscale: hyperscale provides *identity*. A multicellular organism consists of a collection of cells, but it presents itself to the outside world as a unified entity. We are entitled to ask what the connection is, therefore, between our own *material* hyperscale – our 'structural' identity – and our internal 'mental' sense of identity – our sense of 'self'.

9 Self-Observation and Sapient Theories of Self and Mind

An important aspect of Intelligence, Sapience and Wisdom is the manner in which their application is moderated by our sense of 'self' and our relationships with others. But where and what is the 'self'? Metzinger (2004) has presented the hypothesis that we are unable to distinguish between the objects of our attention and the internal representations of them which we 'observe'. When we use a screwdriver, we are at the screw; when we drive a car, we become the car. The most astounding characteristic of this *transfer of presence* is the way in which we can effortlessly skip between different scales of an overall picture. Metzinger's (2004) hypothesis provides a credible model for the independence of 'mind'. As he states: "We are systems that are not able to recognize their subsymbolic self-model as a model. For this reason we are permanently operating under the conditions of a 'naïve-realistic misunderstanding': we experience ourselves as being in direct and immediate epistemic contact with ourselves. What we have in the past simply called 'self' is not a non-physical individual, but only the content of an ongoing, dynamical process – the process of transparent self-modeling." Metzinger provides no clue as to 'where' we can 'find' this 'self-model', or how it could be internally generated over the aeons of evolution. He concludes, however, that "the conscious self is an illusion which is no one's illusion." (Metzinger's 2004, p. 60).

While we would to concur with Metzinger that 'the self' is illusory – at least in objective terms – we would suggest that it is *its own* illusion. A critical aspect of first-person awareness is the capacity for introspection – the capacity of 'the self' to observe 'itself'. If we analyze concepts of identity within a traditional *monorational* system we are left with a myriad of uncomfortable conclusions which characterize the entire history of philosophical views of existence. *But not if we construct our analysis within a birational system!* Matsuno (2000) has generated a self-consistent view of 'reality' which is based on the interpretation of observation as a mutual measurement, and within which the Heisenberg impossibility of observing quantum particles without influencing them finds a natural home. Interactions between the two sapiences of a natural hierarchy are an example of mutual observation, and of indirect mutual self-measurement. As we indicated in Section 8, their correlation is continuously recursive, from logic, to emotion, to logic, to emotion,... and birational hierarchy provides evolutionary self-observation reminiscent of Deacon's (1997) 'life as evolution happening'.

Rosen (1991) has explained in great detail how both Newtonian physics and life depend on the 'truncation' of infinitely recursive chronicles. As he describes, New-ton's Second Law collapses the state of a particle, which is a nominally infinite series of variables, down to only two – position and velocity. So, in a birational information-processing brain, 'who' collapses the infinite mutual observations of inter-sapient 'introspection' down to the apparent, if illusory, stability of 'the self'? Well – no one! It is unnecessary. As we pointed out in Section 2, hyperscale is generated from the cross-scalar transmission of order, which dominates the trans-mission of novelty, and this maintains temporal stability in a natural hierarchy (as it does, also, in a crystal – Cottam et al. 2003a; Cottam and Saunders 1973). Each of the bi-sapiences is consequently approximately stable, but aware continuation of their mutual observation is subject to the necessity of change, as we described in Section.6. Consequently, approximate stasis in their interaction leads to asymptotic neglect, effective truncation of their otherwise infinite self-observations, and the stabilization of an introspective 'Theory of Self'', or 'Theory of the *Reality* of Self'.

'Neuron mirroring', whether interpersonal, neurologically internal or environ-mental, provides a useful pictorial vehicle for comparing different entity-environment correspondences, especially if, as Ramachandran suggests it 'dissolves the barrier between self and others.' An unknown external environment can be progressively described through diligent assembly by an organism of the stimuli to which it is subjected. Similarly, an unknown organism can be progressively described from outside, through assembly of the questions it poses of its envi-ronment and through its social relations. This constitutes the birational paradigm itself: a system of two mutually-evolvable inter-relating aware localizations, whose 'functions', as entity or ecosystem, are interchangeable. The creation of an internal transparent environmental model is automatically and intimately associated with the creation of an internal transparent *self*-model! The ecosystemic containment of a true natural hierarchy becomes internalized through the generation and main-tenance of its extant scalar levels, which creates hyperscalar self-constraint as an indistinguishable reproduction of relevant parts of its ecosystem.

We propose that long-term evolution of unification-maintaining hyperscalar sur-vivalist sapient behavior has resulted in development of the high-level transparent self-model Metzinger refers to. We believe that the 'spotlight of consciousness' in humans is momentarily focused at a single 'location' within a spatiotemporal hyper-scalar 'phase space' which we construct from the entire history of our individual and social existences, including the 'facts' of our believed 'reality', numerous apparently consistent but insufficiently investigated 'logical' suppositions, and as-yet untested or normally-abandoned hypothetical models which serve to fill in otherwise incon-venient or glaringly obvious omissions in its landscape.

We note equivalence, therefore, between 'Theory of Self' (belief in one's own independent reality), 'presence transfer' (the ability to functionally 'become' a tar-get object or person) and 'Theory of Mind' (the ability to understand that others have beliefs, desires and intentions that are different from one's own). We believe that all three are generated from the *bi-sapience* of neural information-processing, through 'neuron mirroring'. 'Theory of Self' is related to *true* sapient introspection: it results from the long-term stabilization of observations of an internal transparent model of an organism, by that internal model itself (c.f. "I think, therefore I am"). 'Presence transfer' is effected by viewing the internal model of an external targeted organism, artifact or situation, or the internal model of a fantasized organism, artifact or situation, through a transparent internal model of the 'self', so that the 'self' is indistinguishable from the target. 'Theory of Mind' is related to the indirect mirroring of logic and emotion between the 'self' and an *apparently* similar 'other', resulting, on the basis of a long experience of socially-coupled inter-personal quasi-introspection, in the conclusion of *real* similarity. Metzinger and Gallese (2003) have published the initial stages of a theory which is effectively aimed at attributing to the evolution of theories of Self and Mind a common action ontology through attention to 'neuron mirroring' in the motor system. As they state, "An elementary self-model in terms of body image and visceral feelings plus the existence of a low-level attentional mechanism is quite enough to establish the basic representation of a dynamic subject-object relation. The non-cognitive PMIR (Phenomenal Model of the Intentionality Relation) is thus what builds the bridge into the social dimension."

10 Bi-Sapient Structures for Intelligent Control

Our discussion throughout this chapter has been of sapience itself, and the manner in which it 'emerges' from its embodiment in the extant scales of an organism or entity. Right from the beginning, the thesis of this chapter has been that the evolution of *IS&W* has been driven by the *instinct* to survive. In Section 4 we noted David Fogel's (2002) description of intelligence as "the ability of a system to adapt its behavior to meet its *goals* in a range of environments". What, however, is the connection between instincts and goals, and how do they relate to sapience?

Newly-born animals have instincts which enable them to survive and learn. These are built up from conception to birth as a pre-structuring of neural connections. A high degree of plasticity remains, however, enabling the animal not only to build on these instincts, but to replace them in many cases with environmentally-derived variants. Animals clearly demonstrate inborn instincts: the instinct to select energy-giving sugary and fatty foods; the instinct to learn to walk; the instinct to seek company; the instinct to group together for safety; ultimately the instinct to survive. These are observations of instinct at a holistic animal level, but we can find their precursors at more primitive levels. If the biological cell is the most primitive living organism, then the most primitive organism instinct is cell *mitosis*, whereby a single fertilized cell divides into two identical daughter cells, providing the means for assembling billion-cell organisms which demonstrate holistic instincts. It is important to note that although these high-level holistic instincts may be associated with *abstract* logic, in that they can be inconsequential at a late stage of organism evolution (e.g. a human baby's immediately post-natal attempts at walking), cell mitosis is a primitive *natural* logic instinct (Cottam et al. 2003e).

During the first few months of its life, a human baby spends endless hours violently kicking with its legs. Why? - it does not need them to walk. At least, not yet, but later on when it finally gets to its feet it will need strong leg muscles to support it. *Instincts* finally give way to *goals*. Primitive *natural* logic instincts give way to unreasoned possibly *abstract* logic goals, which in turn give way to *reasoned* abstract logic goals, which are subject to intentionality.

Ultimately, in the most neurologically-complex organisms, goals may be subjugated to motives. A baby's kicking provides the basis for walking, which clears the way to succeed in gymnastics or dancing, which may become a gateway for social contact and valorization of the individual. A nice example of way a social "motive" may override a goal is given by "the cockroach experiment". If a very small thirsty child is shown a three beakers of water, one clean, a second into which the child has seen a dead cockroach dipped, and a third still containing the cockroach, it will drink from all three. A few months older, it will drink from the first two, but not from the beaker which contains the cockroach. Again a few months older, it will now avoid drinking from the beaker into which it saw the cockroach dipped: the child has learned about contamination – the basic instinct to drink has been overridden by a fundamental social concept destined to reduce disease and promote survival.

The clearest example of replacement of instincts by goals is the recent upsurge in computer combat games. Here there is a direct replacement of the *natural* logic (i.e. consequential) fight for survival required of primitive mammals by the *abstract* logic (i.e. inconsequential) "fight for survival" against computer-generated enemies (it is interesting to note that one such game is publicized as "brutal combat for the thinking man"!). Goals are created from evolving environmental information by the co-evolution of intelligence (Albus 2001; Fogel 2002), whether the information is from unintended uncontrolled occurrences or intentional social or instructive implantation. The major question of an entity which seeks to achieve or maintain states of its environment is "whose goals?"

So, instincts are genetically built in to an organism's nature 'from birth', as 'plastic'-wired (rather than 'hard'-wired) automated actions and reactions, while goals are later developments of phenotypical evolution and environmental influences. The relationship between the two is reminiscent of that between *genetics* and *epigenetics*. It is difficult to further categorize instincts and goals in any simple manner, other than to note that the progression from instincts, through unreasoned goals, to reasoned goals reflects a progressive development from local to global correlation in a multiscalar information-processing system. In that *instincts* are not subject to conscious manipulation we would tend to associate them with the second of the two sapiences – the 'complex' interface sapience, rather than that derived from the Newtonian scalar levels – and with the low-level processing of the brain stem. Conscious *goals*, on the other hand, could find association with any part of a multiscalar system, as they can be of any complexity, and can even be driven by unconscious influences. *Motives* are more far-reaching than either instincts or goals, and it would be tempting to associate them with the inter-sapient correlations which lead to wisdom – but only tempting!

The central issue is that of control. How can sapience be applied to the control of its possessor's physical actions and survival in a physical environment. The traditional view of reactive control is that of the sensori-motor loop: from perception of a threat, to planning a response, to validation and motor control, to reaction, to evaluative perception, to response modification... This, however, presupposes monoscalar information-processing, and we can expect to find far more complex relationships in a bi-sapient system. Simplistically, incoming sensory data must be integrated into the entire birational structure before it can have a valid effect on the next, planning stage of the loop. Cross-scalar integration may well provide a far more 'intelligent' response to external threat than monoscalar processing, but first of all the complex character of 'sapience' must apparently be 'reduced' to the mono-dimensional requirements of muscle activation. This is where *conscious hyperscalar sapience* plays a vital role. We suggested earlier that the 'spotlight of consciousness' in humans is momentarily focused at a single 'location' within a spatiotemporal hyperscalar 'phase space'. Operation 'from within' hyperscale makes it possible to 'visit' all scales of a system – and of its internal models of its environment – without taking account of the usual difficulties of inter-scalar transit (Cottam et al. 2006a), and muscle-activation can be directly initiated without performing complex data-reduction. LeDoux (1992) has described how the amygdalic cortex-bypass makes it possible to react quickly to incompletely-identified threats without making use of comparatively slow cortex processing. He suggests, for example, that a half-seen twisted brown stick on the forest floor *could* be a snake, and that the fast amygdalic path provides necessarily immediate reaction. But it is also important to note the close coupling this implies between perceived detail, high-level concept and low-level motor activity. Real-time operation 'from within' hyperscale is a *massive* advantage in promoting survival! We use this particularly sapient capacity *all the time* in everyday life, but it is notably *absent* from simplistic mono-intelligence. The conceptual 'visitation' of different scales from sapient hyperscale makes it possible to exert intelligent control *from whichever scalar representation shows the most promise, from a historical perspective*! The 'embodiment of concepts' which Metzinger and Gallese (2003) and Gallese and Lakoff (2005) refer to is closely related to this facet of birational hyperscalarity. As Gallese and Lakoff state: "According to our hypothesis, rational thought is an exploitation of the normal operation of our bodies. As such, it is also largely unconscious."

References

Akelaitis, A.J. (1941) Psychobiological Studies Following Section of the *corpus callosum*: a Preliminary Report. Amer. J. Psychiat. 97, 1147–1157.

Akelaitis, A.J., Risteen, W.A., Herren, R.Y. and van Wagenen, W.P. (1942) Studies on the corpus callosum. III. A contribution to the Study of Dyspraxia in Epileptics Following Partial and Complete Section of the corpus callosum. Arch. Neurol. Psychiat. (Chic.) 47, 971–1008.

Albus, J.S. (2001) Features of Intelligence Required by Unmanned Ground Vehicles. Available on the NIST publications list as
http://www.isd.cme.nist.gov/documents/albus/Features_of_Intelligence.pdf

Antoniou, I. (1995) Extension of the Conventional Quantum Theory and Logic for Large Systems. Presented at the International Conference "Einstein meets Magritte", Brussels, 29 May – 3 June.

Antrobus, J.S. and Bertini, M. (1992) The Neuropsychology of Sleep and Dreaming. Lawrence Erlbaum Associates, Hillsdale, NJ.

Aristoteles (1857) *The Metaphysics of Aristotle*. Translated from the Greek by J. H. Macmahon. H.G. Bohn, London.

Bateson, G. (1972) *Steps to an Ecology of Mind*. Ballantine, New York.

Cottam, R. and Saunders, G.A. (1973) The Elastic Constants of GaAs from 2K to 320K. J. Phys. C: Solid State Phys. 6, 2015–2118.

Cottam, R., Langloh, N., Ranson, W. and Cottam, E. (1995) Humble Unification Theory: Partial Comprehension in a Quasi-Particulate Universe. Presented at the International Conference "Einstein Meets Magritte", Brussels, Belgium, 29 May – 3 June.

Cottam, R., Ranson, W. and Vounckx, R. (1997) Localization and Nonlocality in Computation," In: M. Holcombe and R.C. Paton (Eds.), *Information Processing in Cells and Tissues*. Plenum Press, New York, pp. 197–202.

Cottam, R., Ranson, W. and Vounckx, R. (1998) Emergence: Half a Quantum Jump? Acta Polytechnica Scandinavica 91, 12–19.

Cottam, R., Ranson, W. and Vounckx, R. (1999a) A Biologically Consistent Hierarchical Framework for Self-Referencing Survivalist Computation. In: D.M. Dubois (Ed.), *Computing Anticipatory Systems: CASYS'98 - 2nd International Conference, AIP Conference Proceedings 465*. American Inst. of Physics, Woodbury NY, pp. 252–262.

Cottam, R., Ranson, W. and Vounckx, R. (1999b) A Biologically-Consistent Diffuse Semiotic Architecture for Survivalist Information Processing. Presented at the Seventh World Congress of the International Association for Semiotic Studies: Sign Processes in Complex Systems, Dresden, Germany, 6–11 October.

Cottam, R., Ranson, W. and Vounckx, R. (2000) A Diffuse Biosemiotic Model for Cell-to-Tissue Computational Closure. BioSystems 55, 159–171.

Cottam, R., Ranson, W. and Vounckx, R. (2001) Cross-scale, Richness, Cross-assembly, Logic 1, Logic 2, Pianos and Builders. Presented at the 2nd International SEE Conference: The Integration of Information Processing, Toronto, 6–8 October.

Cottam, R., Ranson, W. and Vounckx, R. (2003a) Autocreative Hierarchy I: Structure – Ecosystemic Dependence and Autonomy. SEED Journal 4, 24–41.

Cottam, R., Ranson, W. and Vounckx, R. (2003b) Autocreative Hierarchy II: Dynamics – Self-organization, Emergence and Level-changing. In: H. Hexmoor (Ed.), *International Conference on Integration of Knowledge Intensive Multi-Agent Systems*. IEEE: Piscataway, NJ, pp. 766–773.

Cottam, R., Ranson, W. and Vounckx, R. (2003c) Sapient Structures for Sapient Control. In: H. Hexmoor (Ed.), *International Conference on Integration of Knowledge Intensive Multi-Agent Systems*. IEEE: Piscataway, NJ, pp. 178–182.

Cottam, R., Ranson, W. and Vounckx, R. (2003d) Back to the Future: Anatomy of a System. In: D.M. Dubois (Ed.), *Computing Anticipatory Systems: CASYS'98 – 6th International Conference, AIP Conference Proceedings 718*. American Inst. of Physics, Woodbury NY, pp. 160–165.

Cottam, R., Ranson, W. and Vounckx, R. (2003e) Abstract or Die: Life, Artificial Life and (v)organisms. In: E.R. Messina and A.M. Meystel (Eds.), *Performance Metrics for Intelligent Systems: Proceedings of PerMIS '03 Workshop*, NIST Special Publication 1014, paper #WeAM1-4. NIST: Gaithersburg, MD, pp. 1–7.

Cottam, R., Ranson, W. and Vounckx, R. (2004) Diffuse Rationality in Complex Systems. In: Y. Bar-Yam and A.A. Minai (Eds.), *Unifying Themes in Complex Systems, vol. II*. Westview Press, Boulder, CO, pp. 355–362.

Cottam, R., Ranson, W. and Vounckx, R. (2005) Life and Simple Systems. Systems Research and Behavioral Science 22, 413–430.

Cottam, R., Ranson, W. and Vounckx, R. (2006a) Living in Hyperscale: Internalization as a Search for Reunification. In: J. Wilby, J.K. Allen and C. Loureiro-Koechlin (Eds.), *Proceedings of the 50th Annual Meeting of the International Society for the Systems Sciences*, paper #2006-362. ISSS: Asilomar, CA, pp. 1–22.

Cottam, R., Ranson, W. and Vounckx, R. (2006b) Replicating Robert Rosen's (M,R) Systems. In: J. Wilby, J.K. Allen and C. Loureiro-Koechlin (Eds.), *Proceedings of the 50th Annual Meeting of the International Society for the Systems Sciences*, paper #2006-378. ISSS: Asilomar, CA, pp. 1–10.

Cottam, R., Ranson, W. and Vounckx, R. (2007a) Re-Mapping Robert Rosen's (M,R) Systems. Chemistry and Biodiversity, in press.

Cottam, R., Ranson, W. and Vounckx, R. (2007b) Hyperscale Puts the *sapiens* in *homo*. New Mathematics and Natural Computation, in press.

Deacon, T.W. (1997) The Symbolic Species: The Co-Evolution of Language and the Brain. W.W. Norton & Co., New York.

Dubois, D.M. (1999) Review of Incursive, Hyperincursive and Anticipatory Systems – Foundation of Anticipation in Electromagnetism. In: D.M. Dubois (Ed.), *Computing Anticipatory Systems: CASYS'98 - 2nd International Conference, AIP Conference Proceedings 465*. American Inst. of Physics, Woodbury NY, pp. 3–30.

Ellenbogen, J., Hu, P.T., Payne, J.D., Titone, D. and Walker, M.P. (2007) Human Relational Memory Requires Time and Sleep. Proc. Nat. Acad. Sci. USA 104, published online 20 April, http://www.pnas.org/cgi/content/abstract/0700094104v1

Fadiga, L., Fogassi, L., Pavesi, G. and Rizzolati, G. (1995) Motor Facilitation During Action Observation: A Magnetic Stimulation Study. J. Neurophys. 73, 2608–2611.

Fogel, D.B. (2002) Evolving Solutions that are Competitive with Humans. In: In: E.R. Messina and A.M. Meystel (Eds.), *Performance Metrics for Intelligent Systems: Proceedings of PerMIS '02 Workshop, NIST Special Publication 990*, paper #PL1-1. NIST: Gaithersburg, MD, pp. 1–7.

Gallese, V. and Lakoff, G. (2005) The Brain's Concepts: The Role of the Sensory-Motor System in Conceptual Knowledge. Cog. Neuropsy. 22, 455–479.

Haken, H. (1984) *The Science of Structure: Synergetics*. Prentice Hall, New York.

Kohler, E., Keysers, C., Umiltà, M.A., Fogassi, L., Gallese, V. and Rizzolati, G. (2002) Hearing Sounds, Understanding Actions: Action Representation in Mirror Neurons. Science 297, 846–848.

Langloh, N., Cottam, R., Vounckx, R. and Cornelis, J. (1993) Towards Distributed Statistical Processing: A Query and Reflection Interaction Using Magic: Mathematical Algorithms Generating Interdependent Confidences. In: S.D. Smith and R.F. Neale (Eds.), *Optical Information Technology: a State of the Art Report*. Springer-Verlag, Berlin, pp. 303–319.

LeDoux, J.E. (1992) Brain Mechanisms of Emotion and Emotional Learning. Curr. Opin. Neurobiology 2, 191–197.

Matsuno, K. (2000) The Internalist Stance: A Linguistic Practice Enclosing Dynamics. Ann. New York Acad. Sci. 901, 322–349.

Matthews, G., Zeidner, M. and Roberts, R.D. (2004) *Emotional Intelligence: Science and Myth*. MIT Press, Cambridge, MA.

Metzinger, T. (2004) The Subjectivity of Subjective Experience: A Representationalist Analysis of the First-Person Perspective. Networks 3-4, 33–64.

Metzinger, T. and Gallese, V. (2003) The Emergence of a Shared Action Ontology: Building Blocks for a Theory. Consciousness and Cognition 12, 549–571.

Molnar-Szakacs, I. and Overy, K. (2006) Music and Mirror Neurons: from Motion to e'motion. Social Cog. Affect. Neurosci. 1, 235–241.

Oberman, L.M., Pineda, J.A. and Ramachandran, V.S. (2007) The Human Mirror Neuron System: A Link Between Action Observation and Social Skills. Social Cog. Affect. Neurosci. 2, 62–66.

Pearce, J.M.S. (2007) Corpus Callosum. Eur. Neurol. 57, 249–250.

Peirce, C.S. (1998) *Collected Papers of Charles Sanders Peirce*. C. Hartshorne, P. Weiss and A. Burks (Eds.), Thoemmes Continuum, New York.

Pribram, K.H. (1999) Free Will: The Brain as an Anticipatory System. In: D.M. Dubois (Ed.), *Computing Anticipatory Systems: CASYS'98 - 2nd International Conference, AIP Conference Proceedings 465*. American Inst. of Physics, Woodbury NY, pp. 53–72.

Pribram, K.H. (2001) Proposal for a Quantum Physical Basis for Selective Learning. Presented at the Fourth International Conference on Emergence, Complexity, Hierarchy and Order, Odense, Denmark, 31 July – 4 August.

Rock, A. (2004) The Mind at Night: the New Science of How and Why we Dream. Basic Books, New York.

Rosen, R. (1991) Life Itself: A Comprehensive Inquiry into the Nature, Origin and Fabrication of Life. Columbia U.P., New York.

Rosen, R. (1985) Anticipatory Systems: Philosophical, Mathematical and Methodological Foundations. Pergamon Press, Oxford.

Salthe, S.N. (1993) Development and Evolution: Complexity and Change in Biology. MIT Press, Cambridge, MA.

Sperry, R.W., Gazzaniga, M.S. and Bogen, J.E. (1969) Interhemispheric Relationships: the Neocortical Commisures: Syndromes of Hemisphere Disconnection. In: P.J. Vinken and G.W. Bruyn (Eds.), *Handbook of Clinical Neurology, vol 4*. North-Holland, Amsterdam, pp. 273–290.

Williams, J.H.G., Whiten, A., Suddendorf, T. and Perrett, D.I. (2001) Imitation, Mirror Neurons and Autism. Neurosci. Behav. Rev. 25, 287–295.

Paradigms behind a Discussion on Artificial Intelligent/Smart Systems

José Negrete-Martínez

Abstract What are we implying when we talk about smart artificial systems? I propose a list of implications pointing to paradigms of brain theories that cannot be disregarded in a discussion of this kind. The present contribution is to use the description of the paradigms for the benefit of an intelligent vs. a smart discourse. The "difference" between intelligent and smart discourses boils down to the fact that intelligent systems are those with the greatest degree of smartness. I postulate that the combining of paradigms leads to the implementation of artificial systems that are smarter than their components alone. I suspect that this is what the body-brain does dynamically.

1 Introduction

When we talk about smart artificial system or systems (AS) are we implying consciousness? Are we implying reasoning in symbolic logic? Are we talking about some expedient recognition of the outside world? Or are we implying self-organized responses of low-level modular systems? The previous list of implications point to paradigms of brain theories that cannot be disregarded in a discussion of this kind. The contribution of this chapter is to use the description of the foregoing paradigms for the benefit of an intelligent vs. a smart discourse:

- AS with conscious intelligence would be the result of the development of quantum computers.
- AS with logical modules are implemented in our present computers.
- AS expedient recognizers of the outside world are implemented with artificial neural networks.
- AS supportive of smartness are implemented with low-level behavior generating modules.

J.Negrete-Martínez
Departamento de Biología Celular y Fisiología, Unidad Periférica Xalapa,
UNAM, Xalapa, Veracruz, México
e-mail: jnegrete@uv.mx

R.V. Mayorga, L.I. Perlovsky (eds.), *Toward Artificial Sapience,*   201
© Springer 2008

The "difference" between intelligent and smart discourses boils down to the fact that intelligent systems are those with the greatest degree of smartness. The AS proposed here always imply restricted resources for problem solving. Typically, systems or machines are dubbed "smart" when they solve special problems with fewer resources than the brain. Each AS is smart and self-organized. The combining of paradigms leads to the implementation of artificial systems that are smarter than their components alone. This is what the body-brain does dynamically. The mechanism of the body-brain makes its smartness superior to that of any other mechanism because it is supported by a large menu of resources combined by the brain on demand.

2 Paradigms and Smartness

Typically, systems or machines (artificial systems) are sometimes dubbed smart when they solve specific problems with fewer resources than the brain (body-brain). Body-brain resources are considered suppliers of intelligence. Resources are mechanisms bound by their originating paradigms. An example: the mechanisms bound by classic physics paradigms vs. those bound by quantum physics paradigms. In this sense, we have chosen four paradigms to designate the resource domains for a discussion of smartness.

2.1 Quantum Physics

In a remote future, artificial systems with consciousness would be the consequence of the development of quantum computers (Hameroff and Watt 1982). The range of resources of these machines would be potentially broader than those of the present computers and the present ad hoc electronics, and thus they will be potentially smarter.

2.2 Classical AI Systems

These systems, as implemented in today's computers, are mostly bound by symbolic logic (Nilsson 1998). Their potential resources, therefore, are more restricted than those expected to become available with quantum physics computers. The quantum physics computers are potentially, at least, smarter than those we have now.

2.3 Recurrent Networks

This kind of paradigm belongs to the nonclassical AI called "connectionist." Here, we would like to individualize recurrent networks (Hertz et al. 1991), specifically those that solve through chaotic behavior. The resources of these networks share, along with the formal neural networks, a limited capacity to handle symbols. Thus, in this respect, they are less smart than the classical AI systems, although they do have a greater capacity to recognize patterns. In regard to pattern recognition, the recurrent networks are smarter; in addition, recurrent networks with chaotic behavior seem to potentially offer the resources to create symbols (King 1991). They are also potentially smarter than their class relatives. This paradigm exemplifies the case in which the evaluation of the resources depends on the nature of the problem to be solved.

2.4 Behavior-Oriented Multimodular Systems

I consider that the paradigms in this class have fewer resources than the recurrent networks with chaotic behavior. Most of them are modular nets with a certain connectional finitude: they are "small world" networks (Smith-Bassett and Bullmore 2006). Paraphrasing a Brook's 1999 book title, they produce "Cambrian smartness." Four paradigms of this class based on their self-organization are to be considered:

1. Self-organization through self-inhibiting modules.
2. Self-organization through motivating modules.
3. Self-organization through subsuming modules.
4. Self-organization through reciprocally inhibiting modules.

1. Self-organization through self-inhibited modules (Negrete-Martinez and Cruz 2002). The sequential calling of self-inhibiting modules is the mechanism in question. We found that the sequential calling of a simple set of self-inhibiting modules with no interconnections can self-organize them to produce complex behaviors. In this regard, they are potentially smarter than the rest of the behavior-oriented paradigms.

2. Self-organization through motivating modules (Maes 1990). Some nonbehavioral motivating modules promote behavioral modules. An activation-state variable is incremented in each module when it receives the "impact" of the world. Next, part of the activation state of some modules is channeled into some others. A threshold for this variable in each module determines whether or not the module triggers its open behavior. Part of the process just mentioned involves the modification of the activation-state variable in some selected modules by the motivating modules as well. The plasticity in this paradigm is a resource that makes it smarter than the one that follows.

3. Self-organization through subsuming modules (Brooks 1986). Some behavioral modules are subsumed by others. Modules in lower hierarchic layers are interfered with in their outputs or inputs by their higher modules.

4. Self-organization through reciprocal inhibition (Beer 1990). This mechanism relies on biasing some reciprocally oscillating modules. There is a population of

spontaneously activated modules called pacemakers. Each of these modules commands a set of nonspontaneously activated modules. Pacemakers can be modulated by other pacemakers. If there is a population of these pacemakers modulated through reciprocal inhibition, an oscillation in this population can be generated. This oscillation can be controlled through biasing some of the pacemaking modules of the set, thus producing a given behavior. As such the paradigm is potentially less smart than the previous two. However, synaptic plasticity can be added to this paradigm, thus making it potentially smarter than the previous two.

3 Smartness Discourse

The "difference" between intelligent and smart discourses boils down to the fact that intelligent systems are those with the greatest degree of smartness. The paradigms proposed here always imply restricted resources for problem solving. Typically, systems or machines are dubbed smart when they solve special problems using fewer resources than the body-brain does. Each paradigm discussed here is a self-organized one. As previously mentioned, some paradigms can lead to others, as in the case where chaotic recurrent networks lead to symbol formation. I suggest that when dealing with self-organizing paradigms, the transition from one paradigm to another is feasible.

4 Conclusions

It is postulated that combining paradigms leads to the implementation of artificial systems smarter than their individual components. This is what the body-brain does dynamically. The mechanism of the body brain makes its smartness superior to that of any other mechanism because it is supported by a large menu of resources combined by the brain on demand.

References

Beer, R. D. (1990). *Intelligence as Adaptive Behavior: An Experiment in Computational Neuroethology*. Academic Press. Boston.

Brooks, R.A. (1986). A robust layered control system for a mobile robot. *IEEE Journal of Robotics and Selfmation* Ra-2: 1, pp. 14–23.

Brooks, R. A. (1999). *Cambrian Intelligence: The Early History of the New AI*. MIT Press, Cambridge.

Hameroff, S.R. and Watt, R.C. (1982). Information processing in microtubules. *Journal of Theoretical Biology*, 98, 549–561.

Hertz, J., Krog, A., and Palmer, R. (1991). *Introduction to the Theory of Neural Computation*. Addison-Wesley, Reddwood City.

King, C. (1991). Fractal and chaotic dynamics in nervous systems. *Progress in Neurobiology*, 36, 1279–1308.

Maes, P. (1990). A bottom-up mechanism for action selection in an artificial creature. *In From Animals to Animats: Proceedings of the First International Conference on the Simulation of Adaptive Behavior*, Wilson S, and Meyer J-A (eds.). MIT Press, Cambridge pp. 238–246.

Negrete-Martinez J., and Cruz R. (2002). Self-organized multi-modular robotic control. In Proceedings of the *Third International Symposium on Robotics and Selfmation*, Mayorga A, and Segovia D (eds), ISRAU2002. pp. 421–425.

Nilsson, Nils J. (1998). *Artificial Intelligence: A New Synthesis*. Morgan Kaufmann, San Francisco.

Smith-Bassett, D., and Bullmore, E. (2006). Small-world brain networks. *The Neuroscientist*, 12 (6), 512–523

Part IV
On the Development of Sapient systems

Kinetics, Evolution, and Sapient Systems

**V. Angélica García-Vega, Carlos Rubén de la Mora-Basáñez,
and Ana María Acosta-Roa**

Abstract The anticipatory task is a compulsory issue for a sapient system, Neuroscience research has found that locomotion and anticipatory tasks are related (Llinás 2003). In this work, we show some results about how intermittent behavior described by a kinetic model can be used to explore some aspects of the modulation of the activity by perception. Our aim is to highlight how perception can be taken as an evolutionary pressure by modeling intermittent locomotion behavior.

1 Introduction

Thinking is just internalized movement (Llinás 2003), Llinás defines mental state as one of the biggest functional states produced by the brain: brain and mind are inseparable. The mental state has evolved as a tool implementing anticipative and/or intentional interactions between the living organism and its environment. We wish to have sapient systems, so this anticipative and intentional interaction with the environment must be developed. Kinetics is a concept widely used through chemistry and mechanics with different meanings. In this work we take the kinetic concept to describe movement models, in particular locomotion models. In neuroscience intentional movement is known as voluntary movement, also as active movement, unlikely as reflex movement. Active movement is produced by the organisms themselves not by environmental influences. We are looking for relationships between perception and movement or behavior laws describing active movements. The chapter is organized as follows: in Section 2 some models of motor organization related to locomotion foundation are reviewed, and the study of these models is proposed as a way to understand the mechanisms underlying motion and related to intermittent behavior. Section 3 introduces the kinetic model of intermittent behavior. Results are presented in Section 4. In Section 3 we discuss the results and suggest some future work.

V.A. García-Vega
Dept. de Inteligencia Artificial, Universidad Veracruzana, Xalapa, Veracruz, México
e-mail: angegarcia@uv.mx

R.V. Mayorga, L.I. Perlovsky (eds.), *Toward Artificial Sapience,*
© Springer 2008

2 Models of the Motor Organization of the Brain

There are two views about the execution of the movement, one rooted in William James' (1950) work: according to which the functional organization of the central nervous system (CNS) is based on reflexes. The brain is just a complex input/output system reacting to instant requests of the environment. The sensation must lead the movement, so movement is a reponse to a sensed external signal. These ideas have led to the study of synaptic transmission and neuronal integration, fundamental concepts in modern neuroscience. The other view is due to Brown (1914), who studied deafferented animals and found that they could walk in an organized fashion. Brown proposed that the spinal cord has a self-reference organization based on neuronal circuits through impelling electric pattern generation for organized movement. He proposed that organized movement is generated intrinsically without any sensorial input. The sensorial input only modulates the activity of the neural network of the spinal cord and enables the adaptation of locomotion to the irregularities of the ground. His proposal explains, among other things, how respiration works. The senses are needed to modulate the content of the induction of perception, but not for the perception deduction. Llinás proposes that the brain is a semiclosed self-reference system, a closed system because it is beyond direct experience. The skull separates the brain from the world, and the brain knows the external world only by means of specialized sensorial organs. The evidence in neurological science supports this thesis (Llinás 2003).

The brain is a mechanism that has evolved to organize anticipating tasks. It emerges when the active translational movement appears, skewing the probability of success in the environment. In the next section we review some strategies of movement control, in particular intermittent behavior.

3 The Kinetic Model of Intermittent Behavior

Intermittent behavior is observed in various invertebrate and vertebrate species and is associated with a large number of tasks such as feeding, exploring, mating, and running away, among others (Kramer and McLaughlin 2001). The earliest studies of intermittent exercise physiology noted that moving intermittently (i.e., alternating brief movements with brief pauses) could transform a heavy workload into a submaximal one that can be tolerated and sustained (Weinstein 2001).

Our goal here is to show some results about how intermittent behavior can be described by a kinetic model. We have selected a kinetic model of locomotion in order to explore some aspects of the modulation of activity by perception, trying to highlight how perception can be taken as an evolutionary pressure. Our work is based on simulation of an agent in a closed world, which performs two basic activities: ballistic displacement without perception (pure action) and perceptually guided exploration (simulated as a diffusion process), both as alternating behaviors (Bénichou et al. 2005). The model is a two-state stochastic one, which provides

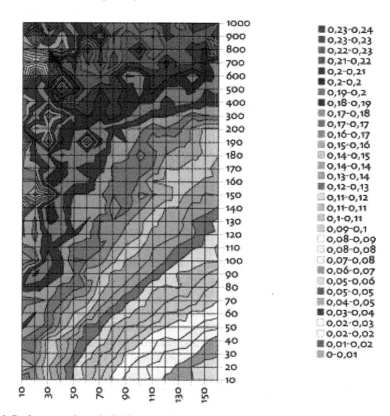

Fig. 1 Performance through displacement time vs perception time

a power law relationship between the characteristic times spent in each state. The performance of the agent is the result of the ordered pair (T_s, T_d), where T_s is the time used to sense and T_d is the time used for displacement.

4 Results

The sensory search phase involves very complex biological mechanisms and the model describes the main features of this activity that are relevant from a kinetic point of view. Figure 1 depicts the performance of the agent through graphing the times for the displacement phase in the x axis and the perception phase in the y axis.

5 Discussion

The performance of the agent is analyzed from a general energetic point of view and the comparison of the many combinations of those activities shows that the same overall behavior can be obtained from many different combinations. The best 'energetic' performance that occurs when a shorter time is dedicated to pure actions than to perception.

We have reviewed some literature in artificial intelligence, but have not found references of this kind of kinetic model use. From a practical perspective the model could be used to optimize searching tasks as an appropriate issue of a control strategy for a cleaning robot. From a theoretical point of view, our results show that survival is favored when the time used to sense the world, T_s, is longer than the time used for displacement T_d, this suggests that we adopt the control strategy that promotes the success of the individual in its environment. We can observe an inexpensive solution from an energetic point of view with an acceptable performance when there is a small quantity of energy and time dedicated to for displacement and sensing, although sensing is greater than displacement.

In line with the Llinás proposal, the brain evolves from active translational movements. Our results shows that an evolutive pressure can promote the survival of the individual by favoring the sensing task over the displacement task, but that both are required. By this means the probability of survival is skewed, meaning that this is a path to an anticipated task based only on kinetics considerations. Sensors, actuators, and control coevolve as a whole.

The kinetics model is incomplete; it gives a general description of the global evolving pressure, but the essentials of the individual and the relationships with its environment require another description, and according to (Collier 2000) a closure semantic is needed. This work is another exploration of the subject of modeling representation development and behavior with complex networks (Mora-Basáñez et al. 2004) and plasticity in sapient systems (de la Mora et al. in this volume).

References

Bénichou, O., Coppey, M., Moreau, M., Suet, P-H., and Voituriez, R. (2005). Optimal search strategies for hidden targets. *Physical Review Letters* 94, 198101.
Brown, G. (1914). On the nature if the fundamental activity of nervous centers, *Journal of Physiology* 48, 18–46.
Collier, J., (2000) Autonomy and process closure as the basis for functionality, *Annals of the New York Academy of Sciences*, J.L.R. Chandler and G. Van der Vijver (eds.), 901 pp. 280–290, New York.
de la Mora-Basáñez, C.R., Gersherson, C., and García-Vega, V.A. (2004). Representation development and behavior modifiers, *Advances in Artificial Intelligence*: Iberamia 2004, *Lecture Notes in Artificial Intelligence*, 3315: pp. 504–513, Berlin.
James, W. (1950). *Principles of Psychology*. Dover.
Kramer, L. D., and McLaughlin, R. L. (2001). The behavioral ecology of intermittent locomotion. *American Zoologist*. 41, 137.
Llinás, R. R. (2003). *El cerebro y el mito del yo*. Norma, Colombia.
Weinstein, R. B. (2001). Terrestrial intermittent exercise: Common issues for human athletics and comparative animal locomotion. *American Zoologist*. 41, 219–228.

Emotions and Sapient Robots

V. Angélica García-Vega, and Carlos Rubén de la Mora-Basáñez

Abstract In this chapter we review some issues related to emotions and their role in reasoning and behavior. We propose complex systems methods to design control architectures for sapient robots with an embedded emotion model.

1 Introduction

Emotions are very complex processes produced by motives, beliefs, and perceptions among others. The task to make the knowledge related to emotions explicit has been associated with näive or folkloric psychology. This idea has led to the separation of emotions from other issues of intellect and a dramatic dissociation concerning the definition of emotion among biology, neurobiology, and psychology researchers. However, emotions play an important role in reasoning; they are related to basic mechanisms such as memory and remembering. Emotions have been considered necessary to acquire knowledge. (Minsky 1986): argues "The question is not whether intelligent machines can have any emotions, but whether machines can be intelligent without any emotions". However, although there continues to be new information about how emotional processes take place (Dolan 2002), there is no accepted general model about what emotions are or how they work (Picard 1998), which is the reason that different computer models have been used to incorporate emotions in artificial systems. Why are emotions important for intelligent and particularly sapient robots? How can robot control architectures be integrated to use a model of emotion? Are emotions essential to obtain sapient robots? Can we have the mathematical formalisms for these aspirations? Human reasoning models based on pure logical reasoning have shown serious faults, so we are interested in the use of complex system formalisms to explore and exploit a new approach for designing robot control architectures that embed emotion models. (Sloman 1981) and (Arkin 2003) have argued that motivations (and emotions) affect the underlying control of a cybernetic system by altering the underlying behavioral parameters of the agent,

V.A. García-Vega
Dept. de Inteligencia Artificial, Universidad Veracruzana, Xalapa, Veracruz, México
e-mail: angegarcia@uv.mx

R.V. Mayorga, L.I. Perlovsky (eds.), *Toward Artificial Sapience,*
© Springer 2008

whether biological or artifactual (i.e., a robot). Certain internal states, that are used to represent various motivation/emotional qualities are maintained by processes that reflect an agent's time course through the environment as well as its perception of the immediate situation.

2 What Are Emotions?

The answer to this question is not unique; from an artificial perspective we have two definitions:

- Emotions are complex processes produced by motives and beliefs interacting in an agent (Sloman 1981).
- Emotions are emergent phenomena and there is no need for a specific component to produce them (Pfeifer 1982).

These opposing definitions lead us to think that emotions can be something different for different animals and cultures.

From the neurophysiology perspective, there are some common biological aspects of emotion definition (Pfeifer 1982, Llinás 2003)

- Emotions are a complex collection of chemical and neuronal reponses forming patterns.
- Emotions are biological processes, determinated by philogenetic, ontogenetic, and epigenetic mechanisms.
- Emotions are bioregulator devices used for surviving.

2.1 Biological Function of Emotion

Emotions are embedded in specific reactions produced to face inductive situations. Regulating the internal state they help prepare an organism to face the specific reaction. Neurophysiology research has shown that emotions are an essential component for regulating life and part of the basic requirements for surviving and reasoning. Learning mechanisms allow emotions to help self-regulating processes in agents through relating homeostatic values to events and objects during daily experiences.

Damasio (1994) has proposed the somatic marker hypothesis to explain how emotions help our bodies feelings play an important role in reasoning. All emotions generate feelings but only some feelings generate emotions.

Emotions can be produced or can be recognized. These two tasks lead to a discussion about intelligence and sapience: if a machine can show some kind of emotion can we say that it is intelligent? Or if a machine can recognize emotional states can it be considered both as Arkin (2003) proposed that motivations and emotions provide two potential crucial roles for robotics:

1. Survivability: Emotions serve as one of the mechanisms to complete autonomy and that help natural systems cope with the world. Darwin (1965) postulated that

emotions serve to increase the survivability of a system. Often a critical situation does not allow time for deliberation, and emotions modulate the behavioral response of the agent directly.

2. Interaction: Many robots that are created to function in close proximity to people need to be able to relate to them in predictable and natural ways. This is primarily a limitation of the human, whom we do not have the luxury of reprogramming. In order to make robots interact effectively and efficiently with people it is useful for them to react in ways that that are familiar and comfortable for humans.

3 Our Proposal: A Bottom-Up Approach

We do not consider emotions as basic emotions implemented as innate "modules" as in Velazquez (1999), or as kismet as in Breazeal (2002), etc. Rather, we prefer the functional definition of emotion: a reaction of an agent, be it man, animal, or an artificial system, to two aspects of its relation to reality, namely:

- Entropy or uncertainty of the environment
- Competence

The first aspect refers to the degree of predictability or anticipative behavior an agent can have and the second is the capability to cope with situations. This means that emotions are based on the 'knowledge' a system has about a situation.

To define and measure entropy and competence is not easy. In Dörner's (2003) experiments, these concepts are given ad hoc and always related to 'survival.' In a previous paper, Dörner used the idea that *emotions should be considered as modulations of cognitive processes. This means emotions are not processes on their own, but distinct forms cognitive processes adapt under certain conditions.* The difference is that in this definition they do not use the entropy or competence terms. They use the idea of behavior modulators being parameters that modify aspects of behavior. What makes emotions differentiable is the ulterior categorization humans make of the behaviors resulting from the configuration state of the behavior modifiers.

We found it necessary to view semantics as a fundamental issue of knowledge creation, and exploitation. In Mora-Basáñez et al. (2004, 2007) we have proposed a methodology and carry out experiments to explore the minimal autonomy an agent must have to explore and exploit knowledge successfully.

4 Discussion

Mayorga (2005) has proposed a new paradigm to characterize sapient systems; this mathematical formulation is in its initial stages and lacks biological foundations to model natural sapient systems. Scholicki and Arciszewski (2003) proposed seven approaches to distinguish sapient agents (SA) from the entire class of inteligent agents (IA). From their preliminary results they proposed a definition for an SA as distinguished from an IA as *an autonomous system situated within an environment, which senses its environment, maintains some knowledge and learns upon obtaining new data, and, finally, acts in pusuit of its own agenda to achieve its goals, possibly influencing the environment*; for every proposed approach they postulated some capabilities for an SA. They acknowledge that the concept of SA is still incompletely understood and more research is needed. In our proposal, we use complex network formalisms (scale-free and small-world networks) to model an agent that shows similar behavior patterns from biological evidence. We have found some alternative means to evaluate the complexity that an agent must have.

5 Conclusion

We believe that new paradigms for sapient agents require a new course different from mixing formalisms, they must provide tools and means to understand what makes agents (including robots) sapient. They have to be near to biological evidence provided by neurobiological and neurophysiological research.

References

Arkin, R. (2003). Moving Up the Food Chain: Motivation and Emotion in Behavior-Based Robots. In *Who Needs Emotions: The Brain Meets the Robot*, J. Fellous and M. Arbib (eds.), Oxford University Press, 2005.

Breazeal, C. (2002). *Designing Sociable Robots*, MIT Press, Cambridge.

Damasio, A. (1994). Descartes' Error -Emotion, reason and human brain

Darwin, C. (1965). *The Expression of the Emotions in Man and Animals*. University of Chicago Press.

Dolan, R. J.(2002). Emotion, Cognition, and Behavior Science 298: pp. 1191–1194.

Dörner, D. (2003). *The Mathematics of Emotions. Fifth International Conference on Cognitive Modeling*, ICCM Bamberg, Germany, April 10–12,

Llinás, R. R. (2003). *El cerebro y el mito del yo: El papel de las neuronas en el pensamiento y el comportamiento humanos*. Grupo Editorial Norma.

Minsky, M. (1986). *The Society of Mind*. Simon & Schuster, New York 339 pp.

Mora-Basáñez, C.R. de la, Gershenson, C., García-Vega, V.A. (2004). Representation development and behavior modifiers, In *9th Iberoamerican Conference on Artificial Intelligence. Lemaitre*, C., Reyes, C.A., Gonzalez, J.A. (eds.), Iberamia 2004. LNAI series Vol. 3315, p. 504, Springer-Verlag. Berlin, Heidelberg.

Mora C.R. de la, Guerra A., García V.A., Steels, L. (2007). On Plasticity and Complexity in Sapient Systems. this volume.

Mayorga, R., (2005) Towards computational Sapience (Wisdom). A Paradigm for Sapient (Wise) Systems. In *Rough Sets, Fuzzy Sets, Data Mining, and Granular Computing, 10th International Conference*, D. Slezak et al (eds.): RSFDGrC 2005, LNAI 3642, pp. 726–732. Springer-Verlag. Berlin, Heidelberg..

Pfeifer, R. (1982). Cognition and emotion. An information process approach. CIP Working paper 436. Department of Psychology. Carniege-Mellon University.

Picard, R. (1998). *Affective Computing*. MIT Press, Cambridge.

Sloman, A. (1981). Why robots will have emotions? Cognitive Science Research Paper 176, Sussex University.

Velasquez, J. (1999). *Building Affective Robots. Proceedings of HURO99*. Tokyo.

Scholicki, Z., and Arciszewski, T. (2003). Sapient agents: seven approaches. *Proceedings of the IEEE International Conference on Integration of Knowledge Intensive Multi-Agent Systems*. KIMAS-2003. Sept 30 - October 4, 2003. Boston.

Scheme of an Abducing Brain-Based Robot

José Negrete-Martínez

Abstract Robot implementations suggest robot brain schemes with local incremental inverse motor functions feeding their direct motor functions. Reported living brain experiments on planning large movements suggest that global inverse motor function schemes can be feeding the same direct motor functions. Perception direct function and inverse perception, global and local incremental, complete the scheme. Global inverse perception is abductive.

1 Introduction

The work described in this chapter is designed to determine brain schemes that would guide the directed evolution of a robot to acquire the ability to abduce. Abduction can be understood as inference for the best explanation (Josephson et al. 2003). I have proposed elsewhere that a robot reaching this stage is ready to be developed into a sapient system (Negrete-Martínez 2005). Brainlike systems have been implemented in robots with unsupervised computational formal neural nets (Kirchmar and Edelman 2002). Instead of following this last approach a more living-brain morphofunctional net should be the starting point of brain-based robots: modules in the shape of black-box schemes: boxes with input-output vectors (function of time) representing direct or inverse functions of the dynamics.

2 Schemes

Consider as a starting point a direct motor function dynamics. Examples are the body mechanic dynamics of a robot and the spine-skeleton-muscular dynamics (see Fig. 1). The inverse motor function dynamics is presented in Fig. 2. The examples of the figure are suggested by (Kawato et al. 1988).

J. Negrete-Martínez
Departmento de Biología Celular, y Fisiología, Unidad Periférica Xalapa, UNAM, Xalapa,
Veracruz, México
jnegrete@uv.mx

R.V. Mayorga, L.I. Perlovsky (eds.), *Toward Artificial Sapience,*   217
© Springer 2008

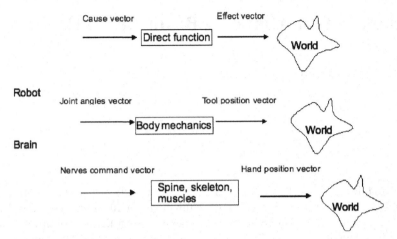

Fig. 1 Representation and examples of direct motor functions (DMF)

2.1 Motor Schemes

Two models of direct-plus-inverse motor dynamics are considered: one in which there is a global inverse dynamics response to an initial perceived error (Fig. 3, Scheme 1) and the other in which there is a local, incremental, inverse dynamics that reacts to the estimation of a value of significant perceived error (Fig. 3, Scheme 2).

Figure 4 shows the motor scheme adopted in the present paper (Scheme 3). The global inverse function reacts ballistically to the initial sensed error difference and the incremental inverse function takes the remaining sensed error left by the ballistic correction and then proceeds by incremental successive corrections.

Scheme 2 has been implemented in a robot (Negrete-Martínez 2007) (see Fig. 5). The names inside the boxes in this figure are those of the microcontroller modules

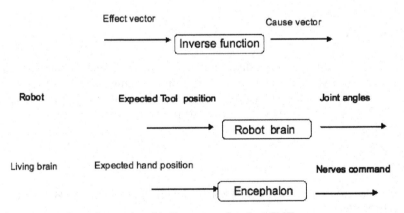

Fig. 2 Representation and examples of indirect motor functions (IMF)

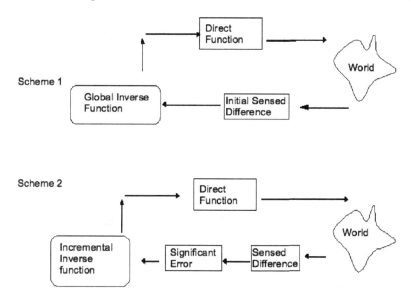

Fig. 3 Two motor schemes

that perform the brain functions. They include a coarse motor representation of the arm: a robotunculus (Negrete-Martínez 2007). Sensed difference is an analog-digital module that samples the world and outputs the difference with the previous sample. Significant difference is a microcontroller that estimates whether the difference is significant for the robot. The payoff module provides a value to the difference. The bandit module decides on the incremental value of the inverse function given the previous incremental movement executed. The scheduler is a microcontroller that designates which of robotunculus modules is going to produce the incremental movement.

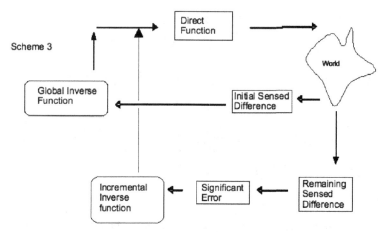

Fig. 4 Scheme combining the direct with the two inverse motor dynamics

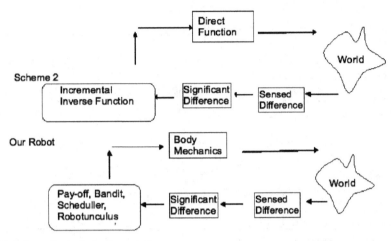

Fig. 5 Scheme 2 robotic implementation

Figure 6 depicts a postulated living-brain version of the modules of the robotic brain (Negrete-Martínez 2007). The BD4 (Brodmann #4) is the brain cortex area for the motor homunculus (Penfield and Erickson 1941).

Figure 7 is the living-brain version of Scheme 3. In this figure, the global inverse function is represented by the basal ganglia function (Desmurget et al. 2003).

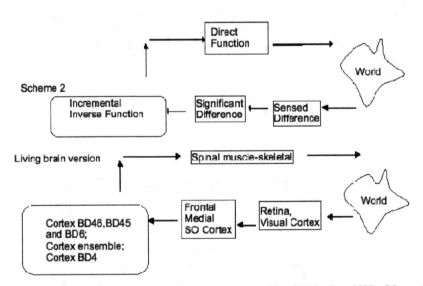

Fig. 6 Living-brain modules corresponding to a robot brain (Negrete-Martínez 2007): SO stands for supraorbital, BD# stands for several Brodmann cortex areas. Ensemble (several areas). BD#4 is equivalent to the cortex area of the motor homunculus

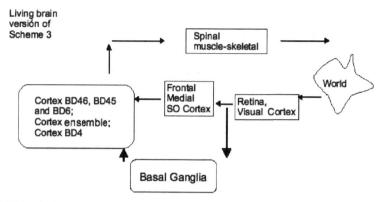

Fig. 7 Living-brain version of Scheme 3. This figure includes basal ganglia as a candidate to support a scheme with a global inverse motor function

2.2 Perception Schemes

A sensorial scheme similar to the one shown previously for the motor scheme is presented. In this domain, there is a perception direct function and a perception inverse function connected in parallel. The net result of these two functions is to transform (the "real world") in a represented world: a version of the perceived world. The inverse perception function cannot faithfully reconstruct the input: the real world; it produces only its representation (Fig. 8). As in the case of the motor inverse functions, a global inverse perception is proposed as well as a local incremental inverse perception. The former generates an initial world representation ballistically, "at first glance," and the latter will refine the perception incrementally.

The perception scheme in Fig. 8 is supported by several living-brain computational models and experiments (Riesenhuber and Poggio 2000; Filimon et al. 2005).

2.3 Final Scheme

A final scheme is shown in Fig. 9. Errors are no longer labeled as such, but as *perception + representation* errors, and would be the result of perceptual abductions (Shanahan 2005) modified by the represented world produced.

3 Important Schemes Missing

Other sensorial modality schemes are missing. Introducing these schemes would demand schemes for parallel processing, which would demand consideration of arbiter modules (Negrete-Martínez 2007). A more complete scheme requires the addition of memory enriching the represented world and the postulation of the dynamic enrichment of the memory by abductive reasoning.

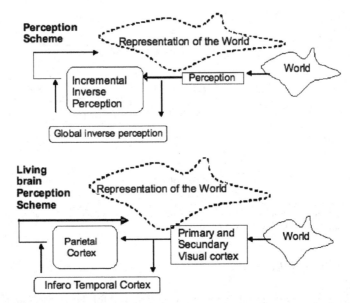

Fig. 8 Upper part: the basic perceptual scheme: here perception plays the role of a direct function and the inverse perceptions are inverse functions. The corresponding living-brain scheme is presented in the lower part the figure

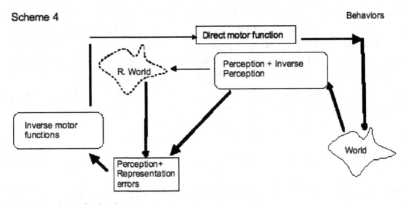

Fig. 9 Scheme 4 is a final scheme

4 Conclusions

Robot implementations suggest robot brain schemes with local incremental inverse motor functions feeding their direct motor functions. Reported living brain experiments on planning large movements suggest global inverse motor function schemes feeding the same direct motor functions.

- Total perception is considered to be composed of a direct sensorial function and an inverse perception function.

- The role of the inverse perception function is to provide a representation of the "real world" (by abduction).
- The inverse perception components are supported by living-brain models and experiments.

The represented world is the result of the two inverse perceptions modulated by the memory. The memory itself is modified by abducing reasoning. The action of an incremental inverse motor function mediated by the direct motor function and supported by the two inverse-perception functions (these preceded by direct 'sensing') suggests that actions are required to accurately represent the world.

References

Desmurget, M., Grafton, S.T., Vindras, P., Gréa, H., and Turner, R.S. (2003). The basal ganglia network mediates the planning of movement amplitude. *European Journal of Neuroscience* 19 (10), 2871–2880.

Filimon, F., Nelson, J. D., and Sereno, M.I. (2005). Parietal cortex involvement in visually guided, non-visually guided, observed, and imagined reaching, compared to saccades. *Journal of Vision*, 5, 8.

Josephson, J. R., Chandrasekaran, B., and Carroll M. T. B. (2003) Toward a generic architecture for information fusion. In *Proceedings of the Collaborative Technology Alliances Conference on Advanced Decision Architectures* pp. 111–116.

Kawato, M., Uno, Y., Isobe, M., and Suzuki, R. (1988). Hierarchical neural network model for voluntary movement with application to robotics. *Control Systems Magazine, IEEE* Apr. Vol. Issue: 2, pp. 8–15

Kirchmar, J.L., and Edelman, G.M. (2002). Machine psychology: Autonomous behavior, perceptual categorization and conditioning in a brain-based device. *Cerebral Cortex* 12(8), 818–830.

Negrete-Martínez, J. (2005). Three Steps to Robo Sapiens. In Slezak D. et al. (eds.) Part II. *Rough Sets, Fuzzy Sets, Data Mining, and Granular Computing*, 3642. Regina, Canada, LNAI, Springer-Verlag, Berlin.

Negrete-Martínez, J. (2007). The search for a robotic brain scheme, *Journal of Applied Bionics and Biomechanics*. In press

Penfield, W., and Erickson, T.C. (1941). Epilepsy and Cerebral Localization: A Study of the Mechanism, Treatment and Prevention of Epileptic Seizures. Charles C Thomas, Springfield, IL.

Riesenhuber, M., and Poggio T. (2000). Computational Models of object recognition in cortex: A review. MIT. A.I. Memo No. 1695 August 7,. C.B.C.L. Paper No. 190

Shanahan, M., (2005) Perception as abduction: turning sensor data into meaningful representation. *Cognitive Science* 29, 103–134

From Robots with Self-Inhibiting Modules to Habile Robots

José Negrete-Martínez

Abstract I describe a new robot control architecture based on self-organization of self-inhibiting modules. This architecture can generate a complex behavior repertoire. The repertoire can be performance-enhanced or increased by modular poly-functionality and/or by the simple addition of new modules. I postulate that this architecture can evolve, in the hands of the designer, to a Habile robot, a version of Nilsson's habile system. Each program module controls a joint motor or a motor for a pair of wheels. Every module estimates also the distance from a sensor (placed in the hand of the arm) to a beacon. If the distance is shorter or longer than a previously estimated distance, the module drives its motor in the corrective direction; if the movement produces no significant change in distance, the module self-inhibits. A self-organization emerges: once a module self-inhibits, any module can be the next to take control of the motor activity. The overall behavior of the robot corresponds to a reaching attention behavior. This is easily switched to an 'adverse' attention behavior by changing the sign of the same parameter in each module. The addition of a "sensor-gain attenuation reflex" module and a "light orientation reflex" module provides an increase in the behavioral attention repertoire and performance enhancement. The 'brain' is actually providing action induction rather than action selection.

1 Introduction

I postulate here that combining AI paradigms leads to artificial systems' implementation smarter than their individual components alone. I suspect that this is what the brain does dynamically. The mechanism of the brain makes its smartness superior to that of other mechanisms because it is supported by a large menu of resources used/combined by the brain on demand: the body-brain would be a habile robot as described by Nilsson (1995). I discuss an architecture with self-organized modules able to produce a complex attention repertoire that can be performance enhanced or increased by modular multifunctionality and/or by the addition of new

J. Negrete-Martínez
Departmento de Biología Celular, y Fisiología, Instituto de Investigaciones Biomédicas, Unidad Periférica Xalapa, UNAM, Xalapa, Veracruz, México
e-mail: jnegrete@uv.mx

R.V. Mayorga, L.I. Perlovsky (eds.), *Toward Artificial Sapience,*
© Springer 2008

modules. Behavior oriented systems (BOS) and recurrent modular systems (RMS) are two self-organizations that could generate habile robots. In some BOS, self-organization emerges: in BOS1 by the interference of higher-hierarchy modules with the inputs or outputs of subsumed modules (Brooks 1986) and in BOS2 by spreading activation among behavior-generating modules (Maes 1990). In some RMS self-organization emerges: in RMS1 by the modulation of some recipro-cally oscillating modules (Beer 1990) and in RMS2 by scheduling recurrent self-inhibiting modules, as we have proposed elsewhere (Negrete-Martinez and Cruz 2002).

In order to test the possibility of a brainlike system with a self-organized control based on self-inhibiting modules, we built a simple RMS2 robot.

2 Implementation of an RMS2 Robot

2.1 Mechatronics

We built a hybrid RMS2 robot that is both ad hoc hardware and computer software. The main mechanical part is a three-wheeled car that carries, on its deck, an artic-ulated arm (consisting of a hand, elbow, and shoulder) plus a mount for a sensor in the hand segment. Other functional parts of the robot include: five servomotors that move the three joints of the arm and the sensor and two modified servomotors, each of which drives a front wheel of the car (Fig. 1).

Another piece of hardware is composed of an infrared sensor (IRS) that receives the light signal from a beacon B; an amplifier-filter-detector circuit (A-F-D) that gets the IRS output signal; an analog-to-digital transducer (AD) to the computer; and a digital-to-servomotor position transducer (DS) as the interface from the computer. The software includes a payoff function, a decision function, and an action function.

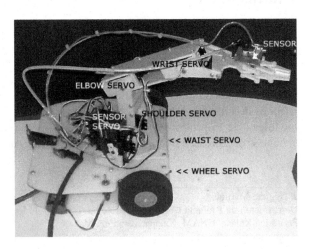

Fig. 1 Body and motors.
Denotation of servos and
parts

There is a beacon in the robot's environment that produces a flickering IR light. This light generates a corresponding square-wave voltage in the IRS. This voltage wave is amplified and then filtered (in order to eliminate the high-frequency noise); the resulting wave is filtered once again (detection) leaving only its DC envelope as the output of the A-F-D.

2.2 Software

Implementing the Basic Self-Inhibiting Module (SIM). Figure 2 shows the basic software organization scheme of the SIM. The process is implemented with a 'while' function of a C language in a PC. Each module, during its activation, reads the light intensity coming from the IR beacon. A payoff function calculates the difference in IR intensity before and after the module's motor action and maps the difference into a payoff value $(-1, +1 \ or \ 0)$. Zero is within a predefined range near zero. There is also a decision function that uses the payoff value to determine the direction of the next movement. The module repeats the movement or its opposing motion until the payoff is in zero range, at which point the module self-inactivates. The movement generated by this module is actually a step movement added to the joint's present position in one direction or the other or, for the wheel motors, a clockwise step rotation of the car.

In every module, the decision function uses an algorithm related to the 'two-arm bandit' algorithm (Kaelbling 1993) inputting the payoff value and its own previous output value. The decision function output has the same value as the last output when the payoff is positive, switching to the opposite last output if the payoff value changes to negative. The output value of the function $(+1, -1)$ calculated by the aforementioned algorithm is multiplied by a step value and then added to the last action value stored in the function (Fig. 3). However, if the payoff value of the movement is in the zero range, the function self-inactivates before proceeding to calculate anything more. Every SIM is labeled with the name of the joint that it moves: SHOULDER, ELBOW, WRIST. Joints labels are shown on the previous picture of the robot (Fig. 1). The name WHEELS stands for the SIM that produces rotation of the car.

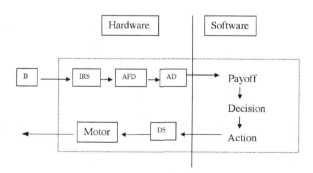

Fig. 2 Implementation of a generic self-inhibiting module (SIM). The module has an ad hoc hardware part and a software part

Fig. 3 Detail of the payoff, decision, and action functions of a SIM module

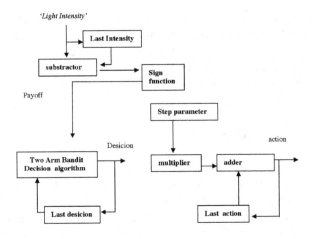

The Organization among the Modules. The modules are called in an endless cycle by the computer's main program. Their rotation was changed in the various experiments.

Changing Parameters. For performance-enhancement purposes, we changed several parameters of each module. A qualitative change in performance occurred when the sign of the step parameter was changed.

2.3 Adding a Searching-Light Module

To avoid the stopping of movement due to the lack of light stimulation, a new module was added to those previously described. This module produces a rotation of the sensor mount in the absence of light and self-inhibits when a significant light signal is encountered. Dubbed SENSOR-JOINT, this module acts on the ad hoc mount of the IR sensor (Fig. 4). The mount rotates the IR in a plane parallel to the hand. The SENSOR-JOINT differs from the rest of the modules in that it self-inhibits when the payoff passes from positive to negative and it changes the sign of the step every time the sensor-joint servo reaches its extreme position. Before the SENSOR-JOINT self-inhibits, it calls another module, WHEELS, that rotates the car by acting on the modified servos of each wheel. The module 'reads' the last angle taken by the sensor-joint and rotates the car in an angle similar to that angle

Fig. 4 Detail of the sensor mount on top of the hand. It is a pull-to-rotate gear box that rotates the infrared sensor parallel to the hand

and then unconditionally self-inhibits. The SENSOR-JOINT is called by the main program after every joint module is called.

2.4 Adding Hardware and a New Module

The A-F-D was modified so that the gain of the A stage could be attenuated by the action of an added gain attenuating module (GAM). The module samples the output voltage of the A-F-D and its activation moves a relay that attenuates the gain in the hardware of the A stage. The activation is produced only when the output voltage of the A-F-D reaches the saturation level of the AD. The module is not self-inhibiting. GAM is scheduled by the main program after the call of each joint module.

2.5 Performance of the Robot

Scheduling the modules in different order in the first implementation of the RMS2-ROB produced different approach movements of the arm and car toward the beacon. In each of several trials, providing that the sensor picked up light from the beacon, the grasping tool and its sensor eventually reached the beacon from all the initial positions and attitudes of the robot. Irrespective of scheduling and long before the robot nears the beacon, the arm is already in a grasping attitude. In its final position the sensor's tip frequently touches the beacon (Fig. 5). The addition of the searching-light module allowed us to experiment with the robot in any initial attitude or position, even facing away from the beacon. We could momentarily interrupt the light or move the position of the beacon, and the robot would eventually turn to face it. Before adding the searching-light module, when we changed the sign of the step parameter in the decision function, we could reverse the reaching behavior to an opposite 'adversive', behavior. However, without the SENSING JOINT, an incomplete adversative behavior was produced. When the searching-light module was included in the endless calling cycle, a very interesting behavior of turning toward the beacon alternated with the adversive behavior. Without the GAM, the robot searches for the nonsaturated regions of the emitted light when near the beacon, producing a sidearm approach. When the GAM is incorporated the robot reaches the beacon in a more direct way. The relative autonomy of the modules suggests that the reaching action could not be completely suppressed even with the

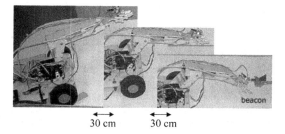

Fig. 5 Position and attitude of the robot at the beacon. The sensor is nearly touching the beacon

30 cm   30 cm

external hindering of part of the robot's movement. Thus, when we hindered the robot's movement with an obstacle, the arm still stretched out toward the beacon. A similar arm behavior was observed when the beacon was placed too high for the arm to reach.

3 Discussion

If we assign the term "burst" to the sequence of movements produced in a given joint without interruption, the robot produces a series of movement bursts. The order of the joint bursts as well as the duration changed during the observed behaviors (see Table 1). This is a clear manifestation of an implemented self-organization.

The self-organization explains why there was an unexpected pregrasping attitude of the arm long before it reached the beacon as well as why, when the car movements were hindered or the beacon was out of reach, the arm-reaching behavior was still found. In the RMS2-ROB, self-organization generates a behavior that is more than a simple light-reaching behavior. It should be classified as an open-reaching neurological attention; see previous simulations of a similar robot (Negrete-Martínez et al. 2002). The SENSOR-JOINT is an attentive module per se. Its addition and implementation is the solution of the problem implicit in the need to find the general location of the object of attention—in this case, the beacon. The result is equivalent to having implemented the orienting-reaction component of attention (Parasuraman 2000). The module SENSOR-JOINT is a modified copy of the self-inhibiting modules. As mentioned above, the module inverts the sign of the parameter step every time the servo reaches its extreme position, which makes the servo oscillate in the absence of light. The addition of this module can be seen as a case of the RMS.2-ROB's growth and evolution through a copy-modify-add policy. The implementation of a module that attenuates the amplification gain in the A-F-D is conceptually the addition of a reflex 'on top' of the whole attention behavior. This mechanism has a role similar to the gain attenuation found in the retina circuits (Smith 2004). The IR sensor, the A-F-D and the AD are nonintentional hardware implementations

Table 1 Bursts of Movements in the RMS2-ROB with the Orienting-Reaction Module[a]

CALL/CYCLE	1	2	3	4	5	6	7	8
SENSOR-JOINT	94	3	3					
WHEELS	1	1	1					
SHOULDER		3		4	5	2	2	1
ELBOW				4		2	2	1
WRIST				4	3	6	5	

[a] The rows of the table are the calling order of the endless program and the columns indicate the program cycle turn. The numbers in the body of the table are the number of successive participations of the corresponding module in its turn. SENSOR-JOINT and WHEELS are the modules that produce the orienting reaction and the rest of the modules are responsible for the reaching behavior. WHEELS produces the rotating movement of the car. Note that in each cycle some modules did not contribute to the movement of the robot. This qualifies the module as self-organized.

of an equivalent single pathway cone-bipolar-ganglion cell chain of the vertebrate retina—the sensor being a cone; the A-F-D, the bipolar cell and associated retina circuit. The D stage in the A-F-D and the AD are performing some of the ganglion-cell coding. A functional correspondence with a ganglion-cell field can also be considered to be in the payoff function, which performs an evaluation of light intensity contrast in the time domain, instead of contrast in space as the ganglion-cell does. The unsolved conflict between the orienting-reaction and adversive-attention behaviors shown in our experiments is similar to the commonly reported behavioral conflicts in general ethology (Lorenz 1985). This conflict persistence has for the robot, as well as for animals, a potentially adaptive value (the robot is turning away but keeps sight of the beacon). The elicitation of an adversative behavior through a change of sign in the step parameter in the joint modules can be seen as an instance of multifunctionality (at least bifunctionality).

4 Conclusions

Since the calling of a module in RMS2 does not guarantee its sustained intervention, the main program of this function is actually carrying out an action induction rather than an action selection. We postulate that combining organizations should lead to the implementation of more realistic brains for robots, i.e., the calling by program of the self-inhibiting modules can subsume the SENSOR-JOINT and thus the GAM module; the sensor-joint scanning can be implemented by a reciprocally inhibiting organization; and the switching between reaching and adversive behaviors can be accomplished by spreading activation among the modules. In our attempt to implement an RMS2 made primarily out of self-inhibiting modules, we have built a structure that must be conceptualized as the beginning of a robotic habile brain because it is modular, self-organized, openly attending, multifunctional, and potentially evolving. This evolution has been detailed in one of my recent papers (Negrete-Martínez 2005). A more brainlike mechanism for a robot should be built out of ad hoc hardware modules. Robots so built would provide the opportunity to explore the behavioral restrictions imposed by the hardware harnessed to their electromechanics. More important, however, is the fact that these robots would enable us to discover unsuspected emergent behaviors that would lead us to the implementation of desirable unplanned reflexes and behaviors. The orienting-reaction conflict with the adversive behavior in the experiments reported here is just such a case of the emergence of a desirable variant appearing after the implementation of an unplanned new behavior.

5 Future Work

Combining AI paradigms leads to the implementation of more versatile artificial systems (habile systems). The desirable final prerequisites for the activity for a future sapient system in the laboratory would combine AI resources, among them abduction performed on an explicit knowledge-memory structure. However, the system must perform combined actions in the physical world that would result in abductive modifications in its memory structure. This sapient performance is akin to the human activity known as "meaningful learning." I suggest that some evolutionary steps have to be be taken before a laboratory robot can reach an initial state of sapience. Each step is a directed coevolution process of skills that begins with an improved mechatronics, continues with improved pattern recognition, and ends with a symbol manipulation that adapts the previous improvements. Presently, we are committed to a simplified implementation of the first step of such a directed evolution.

References

Beer, R.D. (1990). *Intelligence as Adaptive Behavior: An experiment in Computational* Neuroethology. Academic Press. Boston.

Brooks, R. A. (1986). Robust layered control system for a mobile robot. *IEEE Journal of Robotics and Automation*. Ra-2:1, 14–23.

Kaelbling L.P. (1993). *Reinforcement Learning*. MIT Press, Cambridge.

Lorenz K. (1985). *Foundations of Ethology*. Springer-Verlag. Heidelberg.

Maes, P., (1990) A bottom-up mechanism for action selection in an artificial creature. In *From Animals to Animats. Proceedings of the First International Conference on the Simulation of Adaptive Behavior*. S. Wilson and J-A Meyer (eds.). MIT Press, Cambridge pp. 238–246.

Negrete-Martinez J., and Cruz R. (2002). Self-organized multi-modular robotic control. In A Mayorga, D, Segovia, (eds.) *Proceedings of the Third International Symposium on Robotics and Automation*, ISRAU2002. pp. 421–425.

Negrete-Martínez, J. (2005). Three steps to *Robo Sapiens*. In *Rough Sets, Fuzzy Sets, Data Mining, and Granular Computing Tenth International Conference*, D. Slezak et al (Eds.): RSFDGrC 2005, LNAI 3642, Heidelbergpringer-Verlag. Berlin, pp. 726–732.

Nilsson N. J. (1995). Eye on the Prize. *AI Magazine*. 16(2), 9–17.

Parasuraman R. (2000). The attentive brain: Issues and prospects. In Parasuraman R, (ed.) *The Attentive Brain*. MIT Press. Cambridge, pp. 3–15.

Smith R.G., (2004) Retina. In *The Handbook of Brain Theory and Neural Networks*. M. A. Arbib (ed). The MIT Press, Cambridge.

Index